541349

D1761127

 Southampton

Cinema and Community

Cinema and Community

D. W. McKiernan

First published 2008 by
PALGRAVE MACMILLAN
Houndmills, Basingstoke, Hampshire RG21 6XS and
175 Fifth Avenue, New York, N.Y. 10010
Companies and representatives throughout the world

PALGRAVE MACMILLAN is the global academic imprint of the Palgrave Macmillan division of St. Martin's Press, LLC and of Palgrave Macmillan Ltd. Macmillan® is a registered trademark in the United States, United Kingdom and other countries. Palgrave is a registered trademark in the European Union and other countries.

ISBN-13: 978–0–230–51761–5 hardback
ISBN-10: 0–230–51761–7 hardback

This book is printed on paper suitable for recycling and made from fully managed and sustained forest sources. Logging, pulping and manufacturing processes are expected to conform to the environmental regulations of the country of origin.

A catalogue record for this book is available from the British Library.

Library of Congress Cataloging-in-Publication Data
McKiernan, D. W., 1945–
 Cinema and community / D.W. McKiernan.
  p. cm.
 Includes index.
 ISBN 0–230–51761–7 (alk. paper)
 1. Motion pictures—Social aspects. I. Title.
PN1995.9.S6M37 2008
 302.23′43—dc22   2008011401

10 9 8 7 6 5 4 3 2 1
17 16 15 14 13 12 11 10 09 08

Printed and bound in Great Britain by
CPI Antony Rowe, Chippenham and Eastbourne

Dedicated with love to my wife, Barbara McKiernan

Contents

Acknowledgements

I would like to thank:

The publisher's anonymous reviewers of the initial proposal and of the first draft for encouraging and detailed criticisms.

Jill Lake and Christabel Scaife at Palgrave Macmillan for knowing when to help and when to leave me alone.

Ed Brush for his willingness to say yes to every unreasonable request for technical assistance.

Liz Murphy and Gillian Leach for professional library advice.

Fiona Thompson for smoothing over logistical problems associated with being a semi-detached scholar.

All those students and colleagues who had to listen to me trying out my ideas on them over too many years. If they read this book they will know who they are.

Ramindar Singh and Qadrat Shah for helping me gain some understanding of the complexities of ethnic relations in and around Bradford.

Michael Higgins and Amy Kenyon for encouragement during the early stages of the book.

Yousaf Ibrahim for comments on Chapters 6 and 7.

Merle Tönnies for commenting on an earlier draft of Chapter 4.

Joanne Hollows for her valuable suggestions for improvements to Chapter 5 and her warm encouragement.

Zygmunt Bauman for his quiet but not always diplomatic encouragement since 1972. I hope I have not bowdlerized his ideas too badly.

Mike Pickering for critical advice sensitively expressed throughout the whole process – from proposal to completion.

Stefan Herbrechter for his hospitality, enthusiastic encouragement and unfailingly rigorous criticisms of my ideas.

Jim McGuigan for his friendship and inspiration in what now seems like another life on another planet, far, far away.

Dan, Dave and Trevor; under-performing golfers but great companions.

Siobhan McKiernan for her incisive critique of an earlier draft of Chapter 3 and helpful advice.

Beth McKiernan for her help with Chapter 6.

Catherine McKiernan for her expert editing skills and her willingness to listen to my ideas whilst taking otherwise enjoyable walks in the Yorkshire Dales.

Barbara McKiernan for her patience in waiting for our retirement years to begin.

Beatrice and William Frederick McKiernan, my Mom and Dad, who took me to the pictures on Friday nights.

1
Reading Community in the Cinema

Introduction

In an attempt to attract the teenage audience to the cinema, US film studios over the past 15 years have revived and developed the teen movie genre. A significant sub-genre is the female-oriented High School or College based film, of which *Clueless* (dir. Amy Heckerling, 1995) is probably the best known and most influential example.[1] A minor film of this sub-genre, *Slap Her... She's French* (dir. Melanie Mayron, 2002), focuses on the experience of a high school student participating in a foreign student exchange programme and the consequent misunderstandings and deceits that ensue.

The film begins by following the progress of student Starla O'Grady (Jane McGregor) as she attempts to win the 'Splendona Beef Pageant', her College's annual beauty competition. Typical of such pageants there is a moment of gravitas when participants are required to say something of moral significance to sum up their personal philosophy. Aghast to discover that another participant, a supposed friend, has stolen her thunder by 'playing the God card', Starla has to think of an alternative idea on the spur of the moment. On being asked by the pageant's host to sum up her personal philosophy in just one word Starla hesitates for a few seconds before declaring,

Community!

This world would be better off if we didn't spend so much time on our knees worshipping at the altar of self. Now, I admit I have enjoyed enormous success as an individual. Yes, I was a junior intern for the Texas State Legislature two summers in a row. Of course, my peers voted me person most likely to wind up in *People* magazine. But all of these accolades mean nothing if I am not servicing my community.

[Leaving the podium she senses that her earnest statement has been received badly by the audience. She returns and retakes the microphone.]

And gosh, I'm just so darn proud of Splendona that I want the world to know what a very special community we live in. And so, in the spirit of global warming, my family, the Arnold O'Gradys of Mockingbird Lane, has decided to host Splendona's first ever, all the way from Paris, France, foreign exchange student.

[Rapturous applause follows.]

The good people of Splendona might have been taken by surprise at Starla's endorsement of the virtues of community. However, they should be seen as a special case for hardly a day goes by without the idea and practice of community finding a place in the headlines of local and national newspapers and major broadcast news bulletins in the United Kingdom and throughout much of the world. Politicians, publicists and social workers fight with each other over their support for one particular community or another, and over the significance of community in general.

As a political concept, community is attractive to both the right, in the form of 'golden ageism' and ardent nationalism, and the left, in the form of the self-defining counter cultural politics of the alternative society of the sixties and seventies and in feminist, gay, lesbian and ethnic minority community activism. Mainstream political parties and governments have seized on the significance of community and the British government has been no exception. In response to voiced concerns by citizens over increasingly troublesome behaviour of neighbours and the perceived threat posed by groups of youths roaming the streets, the New Labour government has implemented a policy of issuing anti-social behaviour orders against miscreant citizens. One poster announcing this policy reads, 'Your community knows who UR: Together'.[2] The slogan captures perfectly the ambivalence of community since it is difficult to tell whether the expression is intended as a Big Brother-style threat or as a friendly arm-around-the-shoulder gesture to a vulnerable youngster.

Community is high value currency for publicists too. For example, Cornhill Insurance, a significant presence in the UK insurance market, believed it was financially beneficial to be seen to sponsor the Leeds Fire Service. Cornhill advertised the fact by paying to post the slogan,

'Cornhill Insurance: Serving the Community' on the sides of fire service tenders.[3]

Social interest in community is more than matched by academic interest. Academics, particularly social scientists, have discussed the idea, practice and, as we shall see, the representation of community for many years.[4] For example, early sociological arguments concerning community were often defined in terms of an alleged loss of 'traditional' bonds, usually in the context of the growth of industrialization and urbanization.[5]

Academics continue to present distinct and compelling contributions to our understanding of the idea and practice of community. In broad terms, contributions tend to come from one of two sources, the first of which comprises critical theorists and social philosophers, such as Jean-Luc Nancy (1991) and Zygmunt Bauman (2001), who question the theoretical foundations of the idea of community. The other source comprises academics, for example Bhikhu Parekh (2000a,b) in the UK and Robert D. Putnam (2000) in the US, who have grounded their work on research into the experience and practice of community. They have also expressed concern over the difficulties involved in living the communal life. The work of these authors and many more has become increasingly pertinent in attempting to make sense of the implications of major social and political developments most people are experiencing at the beginning of the new century. Globalization, the resettling of international relations following the end of the Cold War, neo-liberal economic practice, urban restructuring and new town planning, communitarian politics, inter- and intra-national migration and the changing dynamics of multicultural and multi-faith societies have all contributed to altering established patterns of human sociability. In addition, the attacks in the USA on 11 September 2001, subsequent attacks in Madrid, the Philippines and London and the war of regime change in Iraq and against the Taliban in Afghanistan have served to awaken many people to the complexities of the emerging world order.

Each development, either taken separately or together, has impacted on communal life throughout the world. The forces behind them often pull populations apart but almost as often throw them together. This can be a bewildering experience and it is frequently risky not only for the people immediately concerned but also for those who think, perhaps wrongly, that they are innocent bystanders. Sometimes, too, the risk is exacerbated by the assurances and demands formulated by those who speak, or claim to speak, with such certainty on behalf of, or in the name of, religious, political and economic interests. Evoking the significance of community, they speak in terms, frequently violent terms, of exclusion and inclusion, of identity and difference and of unity and separation.

The risky world I describe presents each of us with a familiar ethical challenge that can be expressed, quite simply, as a question: How am I going to live with my neighbours; neighbours who I might not physically meet, neighbours who might be drawing their first breath or their last, neighbours who have no reason either to like me or dislike me, neighbours who see the world quite differently from the way I see it but who are my neighbours nevertheless? As I hope to demonstrate, simple questions often elicit complicated answers.

Cinema

How, then, does this concern for community, or its absence, relate to the cinema? Of course, the cinema neither stands outside community nor our understanding of it. Indeed, it is the argument of *Cinema and Community* that commercial, mainstream cinema provides a site on which dramas concerning the idea, practice and representation of community have been, and continue to be, played out and witnessed. Niki Caro's international success, *Whale Rider* (2002), provides an excellent recent example. The film works on two levels. On one level it provides a specific account of how a particular Maori community copes with social change. The film focuses on a single clan and its requirement that it must have a male leader. Hope for the clan's future is invested in Pourourangi (Cliff Curtis), son of Koro (Rawiri Paratene) who is the present chief. However, hope is dashed when Pourourangi's wife and male twin baby die in childbirth. Grief-stricken Pourourangi wants to leave the clan and New Zealand to begin a new life. To make matters worse, Paikea (called 'Pai', Keisha Castle-Hughes) the surviving twin is female and thus, according to Koro, cannot lead the clan. The film follows Pai's determined attempt to change Koro's mind.

On a second level the film works to universalize the particular story and it does this in two ways. First, it confronts the sociological challenge of globalization, here represented by the son's departure. Cinema audiences in many places might immediately recognize this situation. At one point Pourourangi returns to the clan to meet Pai and to show pictures of his new life as an artist and his girlfriend in Germany. Pai is attracted by the possibility of leaving with him but ultimately she decides to stay. Secondly, and perhaps paradoxically, it uses the narrative device of a traditional Maori ancestral, foundational myth. In one sense myths are local to the society that generates them – the place, the characters and so on. However, they can also be read outside of a particular environment on a structural level. This particular myth concerns the story of Paikea, in which a Maori ancestor is able to avoid death in Haiwiki by escaping on the back of a whale to Aotearoa or New Zealand. At the film's climax, Pai is able to demonstrate her destined 'right' to be considered as a suitable clan chief by saving some whales that have been beached on the clan's seashore. She rides one of the becalmed whales out into deep waters. The film concludes with the whole clan, including Pourourangi and his now pregnant girlfriend, gathered to celebrate Pai's accession to clan chiefdom. *Whale Rider* is beautifully, if somewhat didactically, affecting. Its underlying story is that for a community to survive in a global world it has to change.[6]

The cinema does more than 'represent' community. The cinema itself has been and continues to be a significant part of communal life, as Giuseppe Tornatore's *Cinema Paradiso* (1988) beautifully suggests, in this case in Italy. Terence Davies's deeply moving *The Long Day Closes* (1992) performs a similar function, although perhaps less romantically expressed, in British cinema. The integral relationship between cinema and community has recently been made clear by the recent discovery of films made between 1900 and 1907 by Sagar Mitchell and James Kenyon, mostly in northern Britain and Lancashire in particular. Despite their age the films are in excellent material condition.[7] Mitchell and Kenyon, adopting the practice pioneered by the Lumière brothers in France, filmed people going about their everyday lives, for example, going to and leaving work, attending sports events and political meetings and so on. Mitchell and Kenyon subsequently processed their films very quickly, advertised them extensively and showed them at local public venues such as drill halls and Mechanics Institutes to the very people they had filmed.

There is, however, a surprising dearth of sustained academic discussion about community in film studies. Of course, 'community' does appear as an important term in some film books, for example, in Charles Barr's *Ealing* Studios (1998) and Hamid Naficy and T.H. Gabriel's *Home, Exile, Homeland* (1989), but few of them take more than a passing glance at the complexity of the word.[8] The particular interest of Barr's work, for example, lies in his account of the history of the Ealing studios whose films frequently extolled the importance of the intimacy and sensitivity of community in opposition to state bureaucracy and business heartlessness. Barr writes, 'Ealing makes films about community and co-operation – the central themes of the cinema of the 'forties, and not just the cinema – from the inside' (1998, p. 10). Although Barr is not enamoured by some of Ealing's portrayals of community, he does not question the idea of community itself (p. 162). The legacy of Ealing cinema can be found in Christopher Monger's *The Man Who Went Up a Hill, But Came Down a Mountain* (1995) and more ambivalently in Bill Forsyth's *Local Hero* (1982).

The idea of community is sometimes signalled in accounts of national cinema, particularly when Benedict Anderson's notion of the nation as an imagined community is invoked. For example, in his important study, *Waving the Flag: Constructing a National Cinema in Britain* (1995), Andrew Higson uses Anderson's notion, perhaps rather uncritically, to introduce the idea of a national cinema and to illuminate his discussion of 'the documentary idea and the melodrama of everyday life' (1995, pp. 176–272).

In other studies where one might expect to find a discussion of community, it is surprisingly absent. This is the case in two recent major studies of cinema audience members who, in both cases, are understood not as discrete individuals but clearly grounded as socio-cultural subjects who share collective experiences. Annette Kuhn's *An Everyday Magic: Cinema and Cultural Memory* (2002) offers a fascinating ethnohistorical study, largely undertaken in the 1990s, of people's memories of visiting UK cinemas in the 1930s. Kuhn also draws on cultural theory to explore how the informants' accounts can be used to explore the ideas of cinema memory and collective memory. However, the term 'community' does not appear in the book's index and is not addressed directly in the text.

Marc Jancovich et al's study, *The Place of the Audience: Cultural Geographies of Film Consumption* (2003), is based on the changing patterns of the modes of film consumption in Nottingham over the past century and provides a cultural history of 'film consumption as an activity' (2003, p. 3). The authors focus on the way in which audiences do not just consume films but consume them at specific sites, from local cinemas to fireside VCRs. They suggest that the meanings that audiences take from films bear some sort of relationship to the site of consumption. It is a detailed and compelling account. However, aside from a single reference to Benedict Anderson and a further reference to the role of the local press in forming a local imagined community in a chapter sub-section entitled 'Communities, culture and spatial relations', there is barely a mention of community. Perhaps one should not necessarily complain; the authors might be wise to avoid the use of such a term, which, as we will see repeatedly throughout *Cinema and Community*, is a seriously contested one.

Margaret Butler's *Film and Community in Britain and France: 'From La Règle du Jeu' to 'Room at the Top'* (2004) provides an exception to this general neglect.[9] Her study is an illuminating and path-breaking discussion of the idea and practice of community as represented in British and French cinema during the Second World War and the years immediately after. Commenting that defining community is not a 'straightforward task' (2004, p. 5), Butler characterizes it through reflecting on the significance of shared locations, shared ties, shared functions and, following Benedict Anderson, shared national imaginings, all of which has been made possible through modern media. Rather than providing either a single or compound definition of community, Butler prefers to note that the idea, practice and representation of community varies with circumstance. For example, she examines how the UK and France valued community quite differently between 1939 and 1945 and how evidence of this could be found in the respective national cinemas. The idea of community was positively supported by British intellectuals from across the political spectrum whilst in France the 'notion of community was more problematic' (2004, p. 7). Butler suggests that given the differing views of France held by the Resistance, the Communist Party and the Vichy government this was, perhaps, inevitable.[10]

Although Butler's analysis goes beyond other work in acknowledging the complexities surrounding community it does not go much further than this. *Cinema and Community* seeks to address this lacuna in the literature. It has three main aims. The first is to provide an original and substantial analysis of largely mainstream, commercial and contemporary films, nearly all of which have been made for the cinema and which take community – or its absence – as a significant theme.

Secondly, the films under analysis have been selected so that they might cast some light on the social and cultural changes to which I referred earlier. The analysis, therefore, locates the films, sometimes clustered together, in the context of the historical conditions of their production and reception. Focusing on films in this way, I am thus able to explore, where appropriate, any congruence that might exist between the films' subject matter and the experiences of cinema audiences who might share or have witnessed or have an interest in aspects of community. With this in mind, the films have been selected from a variety of film cultures including those of Denmark, India, Ireland, Sweden and particularly the UK and the US.

However, what I hope distinguishes *Cinema and Community* is its third aim which is to explore the idea of community itself, as represented in the cinema. This will be done, in part, by drawing on the work of authors who work across a range of disciplines including contemporary history, cultural studies, film studies, philosophy, political science and sociology:

1. who have theorized community, such as Zygmunt Bauman (2001), Jean-Luc Nancy (1991), Victor Turner (1969) and Iris Marion Young (1990); or
2. whose work impacts on the idea or practice of community, such as Emmanuel Levinas (1989) and Alberto Melucci (1995, 1996); or
3. who have expressed concern about particular communities or communal practices, such as Robert D. Putnam (2000) and Bhikhu Parekh (2000a,b); or
4. who have explored aspects of cinema that relate directly to community, such as Hamid Naficy (2001).

By engaging with these writers and others, *Cinema and Community* does not take community for granted but seeks to explore its ambivalences, contradictions, attractions and risks as presented to us on cinema screens.

Perhaps at this point I should say something about my preference for using the word 'cinema' rather than 'film'. 'Cinema' and 'film' are words locked together by confused cultural histories to such an extent they are used almost interchangeably, at least in Britain. Take, for example, *An Introduction to Film Studies*, 3rd ed. (2003). Edited by Jill Nelmes, this is one of the very best introductions to the study of film and cinema available in English. It is lucid, current and wide-ranging. However, it fails to make a clear distinction between film and cinema. The book has a useful glossary but neither term is in it. There appears to be no editorial policy that provides a uniform approach to the distinction and, indeed, in Nelmes' introduction the terms tend to slip and slide around.[11]

The confusion here is not unusual, and probably not damaging, as the meanings of the terms are usually obvious from their context. I do favour, nevertheless, the use of the term 'cinema'. In the United Kingdom, the cinema – in my youth, the Tivoli at the Swan, South Yardley, a working class district of Birmingham – constituted the site where the film industry, about which I knew absolutely nothing, and my pleasure met. It is in the cinema that audiences, having made their preference for this film, star or genre over other films, stars or genres, sit down to view a film that has been produced for their consumption by a complex, multi-layered and multi-faceted industry. This is the use of the word 'cinema' that guides the audience studies undertaken by Kuhn (2002) and Jancovich et al. (2003) to which I referred above.

The grounds for a more sophisticated explanation are those explored by Hamid Naficy in his important study, *An Accented Cinema* (2001), in which he examines the place of social and cultural migration in film production and consumption. As we shall see in Chapter 7, Naficy is particularly concerned with exilic and diasporic experiences that connect with all aspects of an accented cinema. His analysis of films produced by exiles, sometimes for exiles and sometimes for those populations from which they have been exiled shows they bear the mark – the accent – of their home culture but also, occasionally, their host culture too. Of accented cinema Naficy writes,

> This is by no means an established or cohesive cinema, since it has been in a state of preformation and emergence in disparate and dispersed pockets across the globe. It is, nevertheless, an increasingly significant cinematic formation in terms of its output, which reaches into its thousands, its variety of forms and diversity of cultures, which are staggering, and its social impact, which extends far beyond exilic and diasporic communities to include the general public as well.
>
> (2001, p. 4)

I take Naficy's particular articulation of an accented cinema that comprises a set of cultural and material practices as a useful guide for my study and will use the term 'cinema' accordingly. I reserve the term 'film' to refer strictly to texts and text-related matters.

Approach

Although the analysis is informed by the work of the authors identified above, its main inspiration is taken from the writings of Raymond Williams and Zygmunt Bauman. Williams is important in two respects. First, the general theoretical and methodological framework I have adopted for *Cinema and Community* is cultural materialism, an approach to the study of culture developed by him and employed by, amongst others, Jonathan Dollimore and Alan Sinfield (1994), Hamid Naficy (2001), Michael Pickering (1997) and Edward Said (1985). Secondly, throughout his career Williams wrote about the idea of community and he was one of the first authors to identify its problematic status. Zygmunt Bauman, although coming from a very different academic point of departure, is the contemporary writer who has done most to expose and explore this status.

Andrew Milner (2002), in a thorough account of William's work, describes cultural materialism as Williams' major contribution to cultural theory and cultural analysis.[12] Unfortunately, when it comes to complex matters Williams is famously cautious and not given to providing simple, unqualified commentary, and clear definitions of cultural materialism are not to be found in his work. Jonathan Dollimore and Alan Sinfield are more helpful. In their foreword to the first edition of *Political Shakespeare: Essays in Cultural Materialism* (1985), they claim that cultural materialism comprises four elements in combination: historical context, theoretical method, political commitment and textual analysis. Each of these elements is found in harness in Williams's work, although the emphasis on one or another of them varies from study to study.

I have translated these elements into my approach by triangulating historical, sociological and cultural factors in the following manner:

1. I have sought to establish what people – academics, citizens and journalists – understand by the term 'community'. I say something of a general nature about this in the present chapter but much of the detailed discussion takes place in the subsequent chapters as appropriate.
2. In discussing how cinema represents the idea and practice of community, I have identified a diverse range of topics that are of particular importance including communitarianism, multicultural society and globalization. These topics reveal common themes, particularly concerning community boundary management and social exclusivity and inclusivity.
3. In most chapters I make some preliminary remarks about the topic so as to place the film analyses in their historical and sociological contexts. Thus, for example, in Chapter 6, 'Honour and community in multicultural Britain', I not only discuss the representation of Muslim fathers in recent British films but also the history of immigration to Britain since 1945, surveys of social values expressed by sections of Britain's new immigrant population and recent trends in non-Muslim media representations of Muslims.
4. I have worked with films through which each of the topics can be addressed. I make no claims for the aesthetic quality of some of these films, indeed some of them, such as *School for Seduction* (dir. Sue Heel, 2004), are distinctly mediocre. Nevertheless, many of the films have won international prizes and/or have been very successful at

the box office and subsequently on TV and through video and DVD distribution.
5. Most of the films have a political dimension, but generally with a small 'p'. In some cases politics is a less significant feature than ethics.

Williams was a complex and original scholar who coined a number of terms in developing his approach to cultural analysis. I make a limited use of one of these, 'structure of feeling', in Chapters 4 and 6 in this study. Although Williams was never entirely happy with the somewhat contradictory phrase, he deployed it throughout almost all his career from *Preface to Film* (1954, co-written with Michael Orrom) to *Marxism and Literature* (1977).[13]

Williams argued that although a novel or film – both form and content, to use somewhat old-fashioned terminology – might represent particular aspects or elements of social life, it could not represent the felt experience of living the life itself. He wrote,

> In the study of a period, we may be able to reconstruct, with more or less accuracy, the material life, the social organization, and, to a large extent, the dominant ideas [...] To relate a work of art to any part of that observed totality may, in varying degrees, be useful, but it is a common experience, in analysis, to realize that when one has measured the work against the separable parts, there remains some element for which there is no external counterpart.
>
> (1954, pp. 21–2)

'Structure of feeling' is the term Williams used for describing the 'element for which there is no external counterpart'. As he noted in *The Long Revolution* (1961), it is used to capture the sense of those aspects of lived felt experience that are both 'firm and definite' but yet are 'the most delicate and least tangible' (p. 48). His use of the word 'feeling' indicates that Williams is not just discussing ideologies, which do indeed have external counterparts, but something more variable and indeterminate. Thus he writes in *Marxism and Literature*,

> We are talking about characteristic elements of impulse, restraint, and tone: specifically affective elements of consciousness and relation-ships: not feeling against thought, but thought as feeling and feeling as thought: practical consciousness of a present kind, in a living and inter-relating continuity.
>
> (1977, p. 132)

Williams suggests that structures of feeling are not evident in a single work alone, but amongst a body of works that includes not only novels and dramas but also films, buildings, dress fashions and, in the context of Williams' view that 'culture is ordinary', in everyday social relations including communities. Structures of feeling emerge against a backdrop of established cultural patterns, ideological frameworks and institutional practices. Initially the relationship between specific works is inchoate, but as more works are created that express 'thought as feeling and feeling as thought' a perceptible structure emerges. In effect, Williams argues that the emergent contemporaneous and complementary works that often represent similar feelings in similar ways and against the grain of the dominant culture are a sign, to put it crudely, that 'something is happening'. It is true that there is a degree of vagueness attached to the concept; how long does a structure of feeling last, how extensive is it? It is, nevertheless, at least heuristically useful.

For example, I suggest in Chapter 4 that what is 'happening' is that a series of very successful British films presented the cinema audience with a significant number of fictional characters, in recognizable situations, who were feeling personal helplessness in the face of macro social changes in industrial Britain in the 1990s. I also suggest that the representation of fictional felt experiences is related to the changing political landscape that included the rise to power of New Labour. Taken together, and viewed in hindsight, the films, the changes in political consciousness and the felt experiences to which they connect represent an emergent structure of feeling.

The second respect in which Williams' work is important for this study concerns his discussion of the idea of community which, as I have already noted, is hotly disputed, particularly within cultural studies from even its earliest days.[14] Throughout his career, Williams was a keen promoter and defender of the idea and practice of community. He always valued its reference to immediacy, the associated ideas of 'the local' and of shared experiences and responsibilities. In the celebrated concluding chapter of *Culture and Society 1780–1950* (1959), Williams incisively criticized the way in which the communal aspects of working class culture, popular culture or 'ordinary' culture had either been ignored, dismissed or explained away as mass culture by elite cultural critics, such as F.R. Leavis and T.S. Eliot, or had been exploited for political or economic purposes (1959, p. 289). He demonstrated how it suited academic critics, politicians and capitalists to reduce the idea of the vitality of working class culture to the state of a mass as in mass culture, mass communication and the masses. Famously, Williams countered, 'There are in fact no masses; there are only ways of seeing people as masses' (ibid.).

Williams's critique here is a part of his argument for the need to develop a clearer understanding of the idea of communication which, he argued, is not just about transmission but also about reception and response – that is, interactivity. ' [...] any theory of communication,' he wrote, 'is also a theory of community' (ibid., p. 301). Williams continued,

> Active reception, and living response, depend in their turn on an effective community of experience, and their quality, as certainly, depends on a recognition of practical equality. The inequalities of many kinds which still divide our community make effective communication difficult or impossible.
>
> (ibid., p. 304)

Williams developed this and related ideas in *The Long Revolution* (1961) where he argued that the idea of human activity cannot be reduced to abstractions such as the state and the market because men and women are not just voters or consumers. Thus, he concluded in a powerful critique of consumerism that 'Unless we achieve some realistic sense of community, our true standard of living will continue to be distorted' (1961, p. 219).

Williams has been criticized for having a rose-tinted view of community. Some commentators, for example Francis Mulhern (1989), have argued that Williams ignored the fact that the idea of community obscures the reality of difference and that it can be oppressive (1989, p. 85). Mulhern's critique is a local example of a more general one that has been powerfully expressed by Iris Marion Young (1990). Young argued, that 'The ideal of community [...] privileges unity over difference, immediacy over mediation, sympathy over recognition of the limits of one's understanding of others from their point of view' (1990, p. 300). She suggested, further, that whilst dreaming of community is understandable, it is, nevertheless, politically problematic as it '[...] totalizes and detemporalizes its conception of social life' (ibid., p. 302).[15] Writing specifically about women and feminism, Young argued that in principle the concept of community can obscure the 'reality of difference' and, as I demonstrate in Chapter 4, her point is borne out by this study.

However, it is worth noting that even as early as *Culture and Society*, Williams acknowledged that formations of solidarity have to address difference and, indeed, he suggested that community is not a social formation that demands identity but one in which difference can be confidently found. He argued that a community must be capable of '[...] achieving diversity without creating separation [...] It is necessary to make room for, not only variation, but even dissidence, within the common loyalty' (ibid., p. 319).[16]

Despite Williams' use of some unfamiliar terms it is clear, even from these brief extracts, that he was aware of the problematic status of community. He confirmed this in a lecture, 'The importance of community', he delivered to the Plaid Cymru Summer School in 1977.[17] Although Williams was discussing Wales, his comments were, and indeed remain, more generally applicable. He warned his audience:

> For there is, of course, a habit of mutual obligation which easily becomes the ground on which exploitation is possible. If you have the sense that you have this kind of native duty to others it can expose you very cruelly within a system of the conscious exploitation of labour. And it is for a long time a very powerful appeal, one that is still repeatedly used in politics, that you have this kind of almost absolute obligation to 'the community', that the assertion of interest against it is merely selfish.
>
> (1988, p. 114)

Williams is gently reminding his audience that the concept of a nationalist politics based on the rhetoric of community is fraught with potentially fascistic implications. He later acknowledged that after the 1960s the term became difficult to use for certain purposes. In an extended interview with the *New Left Review* he said, 'It was when I suddenly realized that no one ever used "community" in a hostile sense that I saw how dangerous it was' (1981, p. 119).

Williams' misgivings about community are more conditional than those expressed by Iris Marion Young. Nevertheless they were powerfully expressed. The dark shadow of community identified by Williams was beautifully realized in Terence Davies's film *Distant Voices, Still Lives* (1988), released in the year Williams died.[18] Davies's work has a distinct place in British filmmaking in that he combines an interest in the experiences of everyday life with a poetic cinematographic style. This is apparent in *Distant Voices, Still Lives* in which Davies characteristically moves his camera very slowly and even films deliberate, still, quasi-photographic shots, particularly of domestic spaces. He also occasionally dislocates sound from vision and deploys non-sequential narrative editing techniques. Through a combination of these means, Davies provides opportunities for the audience to reflect on the projected images particularly with regard to the dynamics of close, personal relations both in chronological time and in memory.

In addition, there are two other elements that would have particularly interested Williams. First, the film presents memories of a Liverpool working class childhood, adolescence and early adulthood from the 1940s through to the early 1960s that is, in turn, frequently physically and discursively violent and almost always achingly touching. The memories are not arranged in a neat and tidy fashion to tell a single story but to convey a sense of the changing pattern of the working class community to which the characters cleave. The second element involves the diegetic use made by Davies of popular culture, particularly romantic popular song, which acts as a countercheck to the film's remembered past.[19] The cinematic power of these two elements is particularly telling in the representation of Tom (Pete Postlethwaite), the husband/father of the four other main characters of the film. The film explains neither Tom's frequent acts of violence nor his displays of tenderness. This openness makes it difficult to judge him, not least because, on her wedding day, daughter Eileen (Angela Walsh) sobbingly declares, 'I want me dad.'

As the children grow up, the film introduces the audience to a cast of characters who form the community. The women's relationships with their 'men folk' are, in many respects, presented as being shaped in Tom's shadow. Some of the men are kind, thoughtful and loving but others are hectoring and bullying. The women develop strategies for coping with them and with the unhappiness they cause. And throughout there is popular song. Women take the lead in unaccompanied singing at home and at house parties and pubs; sometimes the men join in too but they never lead. Davies allows the camera to dwell on such scenes so that the audience can witness the sentiment and savour the atmosphere – 'feeling as thought and thought as feeling' (Williams, 1977, p. 132).

On occasion, too, Davies brings together the two worlds of patriarchal domination and popular song to withering effect. In *Distant Voices, Still Lives* Mum/Ellen tells her daughter that she had been attracted to Tom because 'he was nice and a good dancer'. Davies cuts to the family house where Tom is beating Ellen/Mum (Freda Dowie), knocking her to the floor whilst we hear Ella Fitzgerald singing in her gently swinging, mellifluous voice, 'Taking a chance on love'. This is not an example of tragic-irony. These working class women knew that in pre-feminist times they have little option but to take a chance on love and perhaps this is why Eileen is crying. The community is frequently there to mop up the tears but it also knowingly allows pain to be inflicted and, indeed, part of the community is responsible for inflicting it. Although the women threaten to counter the men's violence perpetrated against family and friends they never do so.

Williams' intermittent discussion of the potential danger of community can be understood as a precursor of the work of Zygmunt Bauman, who has written extensively about ambivalence and particularly the ambivalence of community.

Bauman's ideas form an extension of a theme he had worked on since the publication in 1973 of *Culture as Praxis*, his first book written in English following his emigration from pre-1989 Communist Poland. The general problem Bauman sought to address concerned the relationship between structure and culture that in mainstream sociology and anthropology had largely been understood to be antithetical terms (1999, p. 116).

Bauman has persistently argued that culture and structure are locked into a reflexive relationship; culture creates structures but structures, in turn, place limits on culture. Culture always involves choice and choice requires a 'structured' menu from which to select. The menu is not arbitrary but a product of classification, a form of cultural praxis. Twenty years after the publication of *Culture as Praxis* he expressed the relationship between culture, specifically classification, and structure thus:

> To classify, in other words, is to give the world a *structure*: to manipulate its probabilities; to make some events more likely than some others; to behave as if events were not random, or to limit or eliminate randomness.
>
> (1993a, p. 1, Bauman's emphasis)

Classification is an activity of language, in both its narrowest and broadest senses, but it is also an organizational and a technical/managing activity and an ethical one too. Such activities, which always involve making choices, cannot be undertaken lightly for the duties can be onerous and the implications serious; which person can I marry, where should I live, what architectural style best suits my life requirements and reflects my personality?[20] To choose one means to reject another. To opt for one class or one category is to opt out of another. To include one thing means excluding another. So, how do we choose? What are the appropriate criteria? What codes do we follow? And what happens after the choices have been made? The boundary between those included and excluded has to be respected and managed. Everything is fine, so long as 'we' all agree what the boundaries are and that they are set 'fair' or 'just' or 'reasonable' and that they apply to everyone. And there should be no doubt, no ambivalence. Oh, that life could be so simple! Mum/Ellen in *Distant Voices, Still Lives* decided to 'take a chance on love' and marry the nice man who liked dancing. Eileen, Mum/Ellen's daughter, took her chance too.

Very often, of course, choices seem to have been made for us. In natural terms our sex is fixed and our ethnicity too. Culturally, we are born into languages/discourse, social class, nationality and so on although the lucky ones amongst us can make alterations, if we choose to do so and others let us. More often, we have to come to terms with the fact that to live in one community might mean being excluded from another. Sometimes this does not matter much; we can apply for admittance or for transfer or for co-habitation rights. Sometimes it does matter, as millions of Muslims, Sikhs and Hindus discovered so tragically when the British partitioned India and Pakistan in 1947.

Many of us appear to have little choice in making our future and even those of us who do sometimes find the whole thing baffling. Luckily, help is at hand. We can engage the assistance of scientists, technologists, finance advisors, officials, educators, lifestyle gurus, doctors, lawyers, accountants and so on, all of whose task it is to help us make sense of the menu of choice alternatives; to remove any possibility of misunderstanding or mistaking one thing for another. Bauman writes,

> The typically modern practice, the substance of modern politics, of modern intellect, of modern life, is the effort to exterminate ambivalence: an effort to define precisely – and to suppress or eliminate everything that could not or would not be precisely defined.
>
> (1993a, pp. 7–8)

This is a vain effort but it continues and it will continue, and it will continue to fail. All attempts at ordering, even in modern times, create new possibilities of and for disorder, this is the beauty of culture. But, of course, each possibility produces its own waste product and this is culture's tragedy. Bauman argues that 'If modernity is about the production of order then ambivalence is the waste of modernity' (1993a, p. 15).[21]

Bauman made the implications of this painfully clear in his award-winning study *Modernity and the Holocaust* (1989), in which he describes the Nazi's ruthless drive to exterminate ambivalence. Jews, homosexuals, gypsies were humans out of place in the modern, rationally calculating, Aryan Third Reich and 'matter out of place', as Mary Douglas famously wrote in *Purity and Danger* (1966), is dirt. And that is how the Nazi's treated its 'outsiders'; as dirt, pollutants or waste that must be disposed of. This was the fate of all Jews who lived under Nazi regimes, even, perhaps especially, 'assimilated' Jews; those Jews who, against the logic of the undeniability of ambivalence, dared to think of themselves also as Germans.[22] Bauman goes on to argue that the Nazis' methods of 'waste disposal' laid bare the fact that the Holocaust, despite the recourse to mythic symbolism, was not simply a return to pre-modern barbarism but a rational calculation consistent with a modern society. It was made possible by the wilful and meticulous application of the iron rules of modernity itself by which everything is measurable: detailed plans, flow charts and records can be kept, the amount of gas required to exterminate six million people finely assessed, gold teeth valued, extracted and recycled, the trains made to run on time and to terminate at the death camps.[23]

In *Community: Seeking Security in an Insecure World*, Bauman draws on his previous work on order and classification, structure and culture to discuss community. In the context of community then, Bauman identifies a choice that has to be made. This is not a local choice simply between material and local alternatives; which colour, which house, which university? It is, rather, a choice made at a deep level of human activity or consciousness; it is a choice between security and freedom. He writes,

> There is a price to be paid for the privilege of 'being in a community' – and it is inoffensive or even invisible only as long as the community stays in the dream. The price is paid in the currency of freedom, variously called 'autonomy', 'right to self-assertion', 'right to be yourself'. Whatever you choose, you gain some and lose some. Missing community means missing security; gaining community, if it happens, would soon mean missing freedom.
>
> (2001, p. 4)

Bauman's account echoes Williams' fear for community, but Williams only sketches out a concern; Bauman provides a full working drawing in which the details of community's ambivalence are fully realized. Thus he explores the appeal to and rejection of community found in a variety of different social forms and bounded spaces; in business and work, in urban spaces and suburban gated communities and so on.

Whatever the particular context, in thinking about communities there are always two related boundaries to consider. The first is the boundary between the individual and the community and, of course, individuals can belong to or be outside more than one community. The second is the boundary between communities. As a free person in this free world,

I want to know the boundary lines that both separate me from and connect me with my community(ies), and what the limits of my freedom are. And I want to know the boundaries between the community to which I feel or think I belong and the others to which I feel or think I do not belong.

Bauman argues that freedom comes at a cost; a cost that can be measured in terms of anxiety created through the removal of the availability of guaranteed securities. He writes,

> Insecurity affects us all, immersed as we all are in a fluid and unpredictable world of deregulation, flexibility, competitiveness and endemic uncertainty [. . .] It is precisely this falling back on our individual wits and resources that injects the world with the insecurity we wish to escape.
>
> (ibid., p. 144)

Notes on method

The three interrelated aims of *Cinema and Community* identified above can be reiterated briefly. They are to

1. provide an analysis of largely mainstream, commercial and contemporary films which take community – or its absence – as a significant theme;
2. explore, through these films, major social and cultural changes of the period in which the films have been produced and received;
3. explore the idea of community itself, as represented in the cinema.

Most of the chapters address more than one aim, indeed, Chapters 3 and 4 address all of them. However, Chapters 2 and 8 are concerned largely with the third aim.

In seeking to achieve the aims, my approach draws on the two resources offered by the work of Williams and Bauman. Williams' cultural materialism provides the basic framework on which I build my analysis of the films, with particular reference to addressing the first and second of the book's aims. I make specific use of Williams' concept of 'structure of feeling' in Chapters 4 and 6.

The second resource is, as I have shown, less historically specific. The ambivalence regarding community to which Williams and Bauman refer in their different ways is a more structural, universalizing notion. Communities always have boundaries, there are always exclusions and some people are always to be found at their margins. The secure possibility offered by community is counterchecked by the possibility of a loss of freedom. My analysis is frequently drawn to such boundaries and margins and to the relationship between freedom and security.

In the following chapters, then, I draw on both resources as appropriate. It is important to stress, however, that they do not provide a single unifying interpretative matrix through which every film, topic or issue can be read or each aim pursued. Whilst the identified aims are connected together they each have their distinctive characteristic or emphasis. For this reason, I have adopted what might loosely be described as a case study approach. Importantly, this has provided some freedom with regard to the process of identifying the selection criteria governing the suitability of my choice of film for analysis. I discuss film selection in each chapter but there is an important general methodological issue that arises from my pragmatic approach which should be addressed here. This concerns the thorny question of how representative are the films that I have chosen to analyse.

I regard representativeness as an important criterion but not in itself the defining one. In selecting films for analysis, I have sought representative films wherever possible but not at the extent of either conceptual naivety or appropriateness. The substantive chapters of *Cinema and Community*, Chapters 3 through 8, operate in different ways that reflect the relationship between the three aims of the book. In the more historically grounded chapters, for example Chapters 4 and 6, I pay particular attention to the extent to which the films selected are representative of the class of films that deal with the issues at stake: communitarianism and multicultural society respectively. In each case I state my selection criteria and must accept the criticism that might follow.

However, representativeness has its limits. Chapter 3, which is also historically grounded, examines films about American suburban society. Although, there is a huge choice of films from which to select, I have been guided in my selection by my concern to explore a particular notion of community associated with the work of Jean-Luc Nancy – that is the inoperative community. The two films I have selected are, I think, representative of their type but they are also sufficiently contrasting, at least superficially, to allow me to draw on Nancy's work. The outer limits of the significance of representativeness are indicated by Chapters 2 and 8 which have been designed to examine specifically conceptual issues. Chapter 8, for example, explores the importance of Victor Turner's concept of 'communitas'. However, even here I have

sought to ground the discussion by selecting films from within the admit-
tedly broad parameters of Scandinavian counter culture and the specific
context of Dogme films.

There are other general methodological matters that require comment.
I have adopted a thematically substantial and narrative-based method
with all of its attendant strengths and weaknesses. On the whole, this
suits the cultural materialist approach I have used to consider the very
diverse range of films and topics discussed. My major concern has been,
in the context of mainstream cinema's engagement with macro social
issues, to open up the idea of community to a greater degree of scrutiny
than has been attempted before. This has, therefore, required sufficient
plot and character exposition to enable readers unfamiliar with the films
to see often complex connections – similarities and differences – with
other films and, also, with wider issues.

Finally, with regards to method, the reader should be alerted against
assuming that mainstream, commercial cinema implies 'popular'
cinema. Clearly some films are, in absolute terms, more popular than
others; for example *American Beauty* (dir. Sam Mendes, 1999) and *The
Full Monty* (dir. Peter Cataneo, 1997) were major international box office
successes whereas *My Son the Fanatic* (dir. Udayan Prasad, 1997) was not.
However, international box office success is not the only criterion for
judging popularity. Some films are locally, sometimes nationally, popular. Thus, for example, whilst *Italian for Beginners* (dir. Lone Scherfig,
2000), a Danish Dogme film, proved to be only modestly successful in
Europe it was hugely popular in Denmark.[24]

Chapter summary

In Chapter 2, I develop the idea of the ambivalence of community, particularly concerning community boundaries and associated inclusionary
and exclusionary practices. This I do through a close analysis of *Babette's
Feast* (dir. Gabriel Axel, 1987) and *The Magdalene Sisters* (dir. Peter Mullan,
2002). I draw on aspects of Emmanuel Levinas' philosophy to discuss the
ethical issues raised by each film. Chapter 2 is one of the two chapters
in which I discuss general conceptual issues. Accordingly, I make no
attempt to provide a single overarching historical framework in which
to explore the two films.

A concern with community, and its absence or decline, has found
recent expression in the work of American sociologist, Robert D. Putnam.
It has also been represented in a raft of contemporary American films, for
example *The Virgin Suicides* (dir. Sofia Coppola, 1999) and *About Schmidt*

(dir. Alexander Payne, 2002). I begin Chapter 3 with a brief discussion of the development of the American suburb since 1945 before turning to an analysis of Frank Capra's *It's a Wonderful Life* (1946), in which George Bailey's great achievement is to provide suburban homes for the citizens of Bedford Falls in Bailey Park. I use this as a backdrop against which to discuss two more recent representations of the suburbs, *American Beauty* (dir. Sam Mendes, 1999) and *Pleasantville* (dir. Gary Ross, 1998). I begin by arguing that the former suggests that American suburban life might be threatened by 'too little' community and the latter by 'too much'. However, following reflections on the work of Jean-Luc Nancy, I speculate on whether or not this distinction is really appropriate.

In the following three chapters, I turn my attention to British society and cinema. In Chapter 4 I address the emergence of a new structure of feeling in the 1990s. Between the late 1980s and the late 1990s many Britons began to fall out of love with Thatcherism and its emphasis on individualism and the purity of the market. The political expression of this was the rise of New Labour and its espousal of a 'third way' political economy and the adoption of the moral/political philosophy usually called communitarianism. Tony Blair's embrace of communitarianism had its discursive counterpart in a series of films set in the North of England – *Brassed Off* (dir. Mark Herman, 1996), *The Full Monty* (dir. Peter Cataneo, 1997) and *Billy Elliot* (dir. Stephen Daldry, 2000). I explore possible connections between New Labour ideology and these films and pay particular attention to the marginalization of women found in each of the films.

The issue of women and community that emerges in Chapter 4 is examined directly in Chapter 5 where I focus on the highly popular *Calendar Girls* (dir. Nigel Cole, 2003) and the less commercially and critically successful *School for Seduction* (dir. Sue Heel, 2004). I discuss the films in the context of debates around feminism, post-feminism and femininity. Drawing on Beverley Skegg's ethnographic study *Formations of Class and Gender* (1997) and Alberto Melucci's work on collective action (1995, 1996), I conclude that communal marginalization is not the inevitable fate for women in mainstream films concerning community.

In Chapter 6, I examine how mainstream British cinema has at last begun to take a serious interest in the fact that Britain is a multicultural society. I begin the chapter with a brief historical overview of patterns of post-1945 immigration to Britain and an examination of recent debates concerning cultural diversity and community. I then turn to some reflections on the cinema's representation of Britain's ethnic minorities. In an attempt to make this manageable, and to reflect the fact that the general discourse of racism and ethnic relations currently centres on Islam, I focus attention on Muslims and what is frequently called the Muslim community. With that in mind, I have chosen to look at four films made and distributed either side of the 11 September attacks on the New York Twin Towers and the Pentagon in 2001. The films are *My Son the Fanatic, East is East* (dir. Daniel O'Donnell, 1999), *Ae Fond Kiss* (dir. Ken Loach, 2004) and *Yasmin* (dir. Kevin Glenaan, 2004). In each case the dramatic pressure falls most heavily on the shoulders of Muslim fathers who, fearing a loss of honour, feel responsible to their communities for the actions of their children.

The shifting dynamics of Britain's increasingly multicultural society constitute a national variation on a more universal theme. Indeed, it is only one feature of the rapidly globalizing developments taking place at the turn of the twenty-first century. Thus, in Chapter 7, I turn to consider how contemporary cinema is contributing to an understanding of the impact of globalization on the idea or practice of community represented on a wider scale. Specifically, I compare *Lost in Translation* (dir. Sofia Coppola, 2003) with *Monsoon Wedding* (dir. Mira Nair, 2001) to consider two forms of cosmopolitanism. I then turn to the different experiences associated with migrancy, human trafficking and refuge and asylum represented in *Last Resort* (dir. Pawel Pawlikowski, 2000), *Lilya 4-Ever* (dir. Lukas Moodysson, 2002) and *In This World* (dir. Michael Winterbottom, 2003) respectively.

In Chapter 3 I explored, in the context of the post-1945 suburbanization of the USA, what might be regarded as community's other, that is alienation. However, in so far as community structures not only those whom it includes and excludes but also those whom it marginalizes, then alienation is also a structural function of community. There is a different way of thinking of community's other and that is through the concepts of communitas and anti-structure. In Chapter 8, I reflect on the work of British anthropologist, Victor Turner, who was particularly interested in the significance of those moments when social structures dissolve, collapse or slip away only to be reconstituted in sometimes different but sometimes similar form. I explore the implications of this for understanding community through an analysis of *Together* (dir. Lukas Moodysson, 2001), *The Idiots* (dir. Lars von Trier, 1998) and *Italian for Beginners*.

2
Representing the Ambivalence of Community

Cinema and Community explores the way in which the highly ambivalent idea and practice of community has been represented in a number of different contexts in mainstream cinema. One aspect of this merits particular attention as it will crop up frequently throughout the book, albeit in different guises. I refer to the way in which many mainstream films focus on community boundaries and how these films reveal practices of inclusion and exclusion, of unification and separation and of identity and difference. Crossing and guarding community boundaries and managing inclusive and exclusive practices raise some important ethical issues.

I began discussing these issues in Chapter 1 through my account of Bauman's work on the ambivalence of community. In order to build on this conceptual discussion here, I have chosen to analyse two films that are very different from each other in many respects but nevertheless share a common concern with community and ethics. *Babette's Feast* (dir. Gabriel Axel, 1987) presents a discourse on communal hospitality whilst *The Magdalene Sisters* (dir. Peter Mullan, 2002) explores communal violence.

Babette's Feast

The setting of *Babette's Feast*, Gabriel Axel's adaptation of Isak Dinesen's short story of the same title, is a coastal fishing community in Jutland, in northern Denmark in the late 1800s.[1] The focal point of the community is the house of a Lutheran Pastor and his two daughters, Martine and Filippa. Under the Pastor's guidance, the community, despite one or two personal differences, finds shelter in God's embrace. Two outsiders court Martine (Vibeke Hastrup/Birgitte Federspiel) and Filippa (Hanne Stensgaard/Bodil Kjer).

Martine's suitor, Laurens Löwenhielm (Gudman Wivesson/Jarl Kulle), is an army officer. He likes to smoke, drink alcohol and enjoys gambling but he is in debt and in danger of losing his way in life. His father is aware of this and decides to send him to stay with his Aunt who lives on Jutland, near the Pastor's village, so that he can reflect on his life. His Aunt (Ebba With) is elderly and pious and life with her is much quieter. Löwenhielm has time to ride his horse around the country and one day he visits the Pastor's village where he meets Martine. He asks his Aunt to provide an introduction to the Pastor (Pouel Kern) and he begins to court Martine. However, whilst he is welcomed by the community and Martine seems attentive he realizes that the more time he spends there the less significant he feels he becomes. He decides to leave. He kisses Martine's hand and says, 'I am going away forever, never to see you again. For I have learned here that life is hard and relentless and there are things that are impossible.' He dedicates his life to his career, marries one of Queen Sophie's ladies-in-waiting and subsequently becomes a general. Martine retains her memories of the young officer and does not marry.

Filippa's suitor is a resting French opera singer, Achille Papin (Jean-Phillipe Lafont), who, on hearing her sing, declares that she could charm the angels with her voice. The Lutheran Pastor gives approval to the Papist Papin's request to teach Filippa to sing. She progresses well. He trains her voice and begins to teach her some operatic arias. However, when they sing together the seduction duet from Mozart's opera *Don Giovanni* she becomes uneasy. Axel's direction of this duet is beautifully choreographed. Although the emotions are tautly drawn the fluidity of the camera catches the lilt of the melody's rhythm. The lyrics speak of love and Axel's direction convinces the audience that, in the same way that Giovanni is seducing Zerlina, Papin is enticing Filippa from her home. It is very affecting; too affecting for Filippa. Although she is flattered by Papin's attention and enjoys singing she resists the call of opera so that she might continue to sing for her family and community. Papin returns to Paris where he resumes his career. Neither Papin nor Filippa marry.

Time passes, the Pastor dies and as the sister's grow old they try to lead the community in the way in which their father had taught. However, little differences within the community become more sharply defined. One dark and stormy night the sisters' quiet world is awoken by the sudden arrival of Babette (Stéphane Audran) who, we learn later, had been the celebrated chef at the Café Anglais in Paris but had been forced to flee Paris following the establishment of the Commune in 1871. On

Papin's recommendation she travels to Jutland with only a few belong-
ings and to seek shelter at Martine and Filippa's home. Revealing nothing
of her past Babette offers to work for them for subsistence only. The sisters
take her in without question.

Slowly but surely Babette becomes a valued member of the now fractious community without sharing its religious beliefs. Out of the blue
she hears that a lottery ticket that she had forgotten she possessed has
won a prize of ten thousand francs. On receipt of the news of her prize,
she asks the sisters if they would permit her to cook the special meal
they have been planning in celebration of the hundredth anniversary of
their father's birth for them and for the community. The sisters reluctantly agree, not because they think they will enjoy the meal but because
they recognize that it will give Babette pleasure. All the community
members are invited including the once soldier suitor, now General
Löwenhielm, and his Aunt. The meal is a great success. The General
recognizes the quality of the food, appreciates its preparation and cooking and reflects that he has eaten its like only at the Café Anglais. Taking
his example, the Lutheran community elders, who had vowed not to
comment on the food, now feel free to express their pleasure. The sisters are reconciled to losing Babette. She tells them of her true identity
but also declares that she has spent all her lottery winnings on the fine
wine and food and would like to continue to stay with them, if they will
have her.

Babette's Feast is a gentle but complex example of a film that demonstrates both the hospitality of a community to a stranger and the
reconstituting power of the same stranger in the service of the community. Babette repays her hosts' hospitality in a distinctive fashion and
in doing so helps rebuild, without intending to do so, the strength of
an ailing community that had grown stale and even fractious since the
death of its spiritual leader. At the meal's conclusion community members are talking to each other again with respect, old antagonisms are
resolved and unrequited love is acknowledged. The General tells Martine that he had been wrong before. 'I have learned this evening that in
our lovely world everything is possible.' The stars shine brightly over the
community and gentleness returns to the earth.

Gabriel Axel's film tells its story with a subtlety, humour and grace
that is present in Dinesen's text and that is, indeed, a hallmark of her
writing. It also shares with Dinesen's short story a perceptible calmness
and a clear, quiet insistence on the relationship between love, in its many
forms, aesthetics and an ethics, here dressed in a Christian cloak. The
climax of the film, and indeed Dinesen's short story, lies in the depiction

of Babette's gift of a dinner to the community that in turn forms the basis for the revival of the community. Set in a religious community, this is not a film specifically about religion although the tale is partly told through Christian ritual and discourse. The religious symbolism of the gift of food is clear and Axel films the dinner and its preparation with a chef's attention to detail and a priest's commitment to her/his vocation.[2]

As an allegorical tale *Babette's Feast* is untrammelled by politics, social unrest and economic forces and thus it is an excellent lens through which to focus on ethics. Although the depicted community, but not Babette, is Lutheran, the film represents ethics that are equally consistent with Catholicism, Judaism, Islam or secular humanism. Indeed, I suggest the film articulates a pre-social ethics such as that proposed by Emmanuel Levinas.

> Responsibility for my neighbour dates from before my freedom in an immemorial past, an unrepresentable past that was never present and is more ancient than consciousness of [...] a responsibility for my neighbour, for the other man, for the stranger or sojourner, to which nothing in the rigorously ontological order binds me – nothing in the order of the thing, of the something, of number or causality.
>
> (Levinas in Hand (ed.) 1989, p. 84)

When Martine and Filippa first see Babette they see only her face; they know nothing of her. They invite Babette in, sit her down, dry her face and remove her cloak's hood. As they read a letter of introduction from Achille Papin, they stitch together their hospitality and their memories. They ask no questions.

Levinas's ethics is a 'first philosophy' in that morality comes before knowing or being. Morality is not conditional on whether you know someone or like someone but on acknowledging that there is someone not defined as a personality but, as Levinas expresses it, by a face. His philosophy draws directly on the Talmud from which he frequently recites.

> Our masters have said: those that are offended without giving offence, those that are defamed without defaming, those that obey in love and rejoice in suffering, are like the sun that rises in its glory.
>
> (ibid., p. 296)

Being ethical means that on being offended, you do not have to offend and on being defamed you do not have to defame. The assumption of an unconditional responsibility for the other is precisely the ethics of the sisters as expressed in both Dinesen's story and in Axel's film. Martine and Filippa exist for Babette even before they have met her. As guardians of their community they welcome Babette, as their Lutheran father had welcomed the Papist Papin and the General and as he had allowed his daughters to decide their own future. Babette's attitude towards the community is also open. She offers herself and her future to the sisters and the community unreservedly.

Ethics, of course, are relatively easy to present in an allegory and *Babette's Feast* is an allegorical film about the ethics of communal hospitality, openness and absolute responsibility to the other whether or not the other is a stranger, a potential friend or enemy. In stark contrast, Peter Mullan's *The Magdalene Sisters* is a historically specific film about the absence of ethics and particularly of the denial of the right to be ethical. And if *Babette's Feast* is defined by the presumption of peaceful inclusion then *The Magdalene Sisters* can be defined by the presence of the violence of communal exclusion.

The Magdalene Sisters

At the top end of Dublin's Grafton Street, just a stone's throw from Trinity College, is St. Stephen's Green, a landscaped Victorian park. It is a restful place in which, on one of those occasional hot days of an Irish summer, tourists and locals can take their ease by sitting on one of the many benches dotted around. A plaque on one bench bears an inscription that reads,

> To the women who worked in the Magdalene laundry institutions and to the children born to some members of those communities – reflect here on their lives.
>
> (Tanner, 2003, p. 410)

Many strangers and even some locals, particularly younger ones, are unlikely to know the chilling history behind the inscription. Some might be intrigued by the use of the term 'communities' – what were they, what were they like, who lived in them? Others will know, however, that the inscription relates to a legal and condoned practice that brought shame and obloquy on Ireland in general and to the Catholic Church and the Order of the Sisters of Mercy in particular.

The Irish Magdalene laundries were set up by Catholic nuns of the Order of the Sisters of Mercy in the 1880s to provide places where prostitutes might redeem themselves through work and penitence.[3] However, their use was extended to redeem young women and girls who had become pregnant out of marriage or had reported being raped or been deemed to be too pretty or behaved in any way thought to be offensive to the sensibilities of right-thinking, God-fearing Irish men and women. Here, behind the locked doors and in the care of the Sisters, the penitents would be 'out of sight and out of mind'. Here, also, they would be required to endure hard physical labour in the laundries for the profits of the institutions but usually for no personal pay. And here, finally, they might be subjected to ritual humiliation, corporal and mental punishment and a brutal regime of discipline bordering on terror.

The last laundry was closed in 1996; incredibly 2 years after apartheid was formally dismantled in South Africa. Between their opening and closing, some 30 000 women were given over by parents and other family members to be excluded from their communities and taken into care.[4] When the bench in St. Stephen's Green was inaugurated neither the Order of the Sisters of Mercy nor any representative of the Catholic Church attended although they were invited. The Order, however, has subsequently made an unconditional apology to all inmates, alive or deceased.

The Magdalene's Sisters' subject matter is drawn from written documents and, more importantly, the oral testimony of laundry inmates, some of which had been used in British TV Channel 4's documentary *Sex in a Cold Climate* (dir. Steve Humphries, 1998). Further research revealed more evidence. There is little room to doubt that the incidents and attitudes depicted in the film are factually accurate and, indeed, might even underrepresent the cruelties suffered by the inmates.

The plot of *The Magdalene Sisters* is easy to relate. Three young women have been identified by their families and communities as, in one way or another, sexually loose or irresponsible. Margaret (Anne-Marie Duff) reveals she has been raped by her cousin, Rose (Dorothy Duffy) bears a child out of wedlock and Bernadette (Nora-Jane Noone), an orphaned schoolgirl, is thought to be too fond of flirting with the boys who encourage her from outside the school railings. They each are sent to be incarcerated at Magdalene's under the supervision of Sr Bridget (Geraldine McEwan) who, we quickly learn, relishes the application of firm discipline for the good of the inmates. The three women join the community of nuns and penitents and particularly Crispina (Eileen Walsh), who has been at Magdalene's for a while and who, like Rose – renamed by Sr Bridget as Patricia, because they already had a Rose – has had an illegitimate child. Crispina, who is mentally unstable, occasionally sees her son when her sister brings him to one of the laundry's gates, but she never speaks to him nor does she even know his name. Through following the lives of the four women the film exposes the violence, venality and hypocrisy of all those responsible for the laundry. By the end of the film, Margaret, through the intervention of her younger brother, has been released and Bernadette and Rose have escaped. However, Crispina, who has been preyed upon for sexual pleasure by Fr Fitzroy, has been locked up in the local mental asylum and reduced to a semi-vegetative, anorexic state before dying at the age of 24.

Historically and sociologically accurate and uncompromisingly shot, *The Magdalene Sisters* proved on its release to be highly controversial, particularly for the Catholic Church. There are many disturbing scenes. In some Sr Bridget appears to relish verbally and physically assaulting her charges. In another, nuns ritually abuse the inmates as they are paraded naked in a 'game' of physical comparisons; who has the biggest breasts, biggest bottom and hairiest privates? Further scenes show how a 'senior' inmate, Katy (Britta Smith), takes on the role of 'guard' over the young girl and behaves in the manner she thinks will please the nuns. In yet another discreetly shot scene, Fr Fitzroy is shown taking oral sex from Crispina.

These and many other disturbing moments provided ammunition for critics and defenders of the Church, particularly when the film won the Golden Lion Award at the 2002 Venice Film Festival. A film review for the Vatican's *L'Osservatore Romano* describes the film as an 'angry and rancorous provocation'.[5] Steven D. Greydanus provides a more considered response, accepting fully that the Magdalene system required 'critical scrutiny'. He concludes, however, that Mullan, '[...] betrays his subject with smug Catholic-bashing. It's a tragedy that the enormity of what went wrong at the Magdalene asylums has been trivialized by cheap manipulation.'[6] Taking a distinctly opposite position, Crispin Jackson, the cinema critic of the British-based Catholic weekly magazine, *The Tablet*, opens his highly positive review of the film by insisting that everyone, particularly Catholics, should see it. He is disappointed, however, that Mullan gives no insight into one major aspect of organizations such as the laundries. 'The question why so many people given charge of the young and vulnerable end up by abusing them is a vexing one, and I rather feel that the film dodges it in its very understandable desire to expose the levels of abuse in the Magdalene laundries.' Nevertheless, he concludes that in so far as the film arouses compassion and indignation '[...] it is a highly moral; even Christian, piece of work.'[7]

I would argue that *The Magdalene Sisters* is not so much anti-Catholic as anti-institutional abuse. The laundries are examples of what Erving Goffman (1961) calls 'total institutions' that are run by the Catholic Church and condoned by Catholic citizens in a State with strong Catholic connections.[8] In many respects, as Jackson suggests, the film is a Christian 'piece of work'. Three of the four inmates whose lives we follow seem to have faith and act with appropriately Christian charity and humility. Even Bernadette, the least 'Christian' of the four, displays a curious form of charity towards Crispina and Katy.

Many of the critical reviews of the *The Magdalene Sisters* focus on Sr Bridget, the dominant and domineering character of the film. The Mother Superior rules Magdalene with a rod of iron, or rather a belt of leather, and a whiplash tongue. The inmates follow her orders and her Sisters enforce them when they do not. However, power is rarely exercised in simple ways and the film is all the more successful because it displays this.[9] Although, Sr Bridget is the highlighted figure, her authority is given through the power structure of the Roman Catholic Church populated by men – priests, bishops, archbishops, cardinals and the Pope – and this authority is embraced by the wider society. Diarmaid Ferriter argues that the Magdalene laundries '[...] could not have operated without co-operation from society at large, particularly the many parents who consented to their daughters being sent there, and co-operated with the Church to force them to give up their babies' (2005, p. 538).

That so many families and communities gave up their own children is in many respects the most chilling issue raised by the film. The manner in which this is done is brilliantly realized in the film's prologue in which we see each of the new inmates, Margaret, Rose and Bernadette, given up and taken away. The betrayal of Margaret is particularly affecting. Somewhere in rural County Dublin in 1964 a wedding reception in a village hall is in full swing. The young local priest, Fr Doyle (Sean Mackin), is singing a traditional song, 'The well below the valley', which prophetically tells of a maiden, her lost children, her suffering and her salvation.[10] He accompanies himself on the bodhrán. As he sings his playing becomes more passionate and Mullan zooms closely onto his face, cutting back and forwards to the rapt attention of the community. This lively scene is the image of Ireland's community ideal beloved of the marketing staff of Tourism Ireland. *Your Very Own Ireland* explains, 'Festivals in Ireland operate in an entirely different dimension from anywhere else. Jazz, opera, comedy or horseracing become entwined with the community and involves everybody – including you!' (2007, p. 3).[11]

As Fr Doyle reaches his musical climax, Mullan shows us that there is some playfulness between the young people and his camera directs our attention towards a young man and woman. We do not hear what is being said but we see the pair go upstairs. Kevin (Sean McDonagh), we learn, has persuaded his cousin Margaret to 'see something'. Having tricked her into going upstairs with him he rapes her. Meanwhile the ceilidh is underway and amidst a whooping and a hollering everyone appears to be enjoying themselves. Mullan, however, discreetly shows us Margaret who has returned downstairs and is looking distressed. Other women begin to notice her too and one young woman goes to her side and they talk. Once again Mullan does not let the audience hear what is being said, the music is too loud. The young woman gets up and talks to Kevin and then to a man who, in turn, talks to the Priest. Without speech, eye contact is being made across the room. A number of men leave and some women look anxious. This is highly disturbing because the audience is being made aware that it, like Margaret herself, is being excluded from something important. The audience and Margaret soon find out exactly what this is. The scene cuts to Margaret's house where at dawn her father brusquely calls her from her bed and pushes her into Fr Doyle's car. She is driven away from her home community without courtesy of explanation to the Magdalene community. Margaret is about to pay the price for 'the privilege of "being in a community"' (Bauman, 2001, p. 4). Bauman adds the rider that this is fine as long as the community 'stays in the dream'. Unforgivably, Magdalene's is a 'community' that offers Margaret, Rose, Bernadette and Crispina only nightmares.

Although Sr Bridget, as the Mother Superior, is the focal figure, the truly powerful figures, that is those who legitimate her authority, are men. It is a man who rapes Margaret, it is another man, her father, who gives her up and it is yet another man, Fr Doyle, who takes her to the laundry. In Rose's case it is men, including her father and another priest, who take away her new-born baby and likewise, in Bernadette's case, it is men who affirm the need for her incarceration. At the laundry it is a tradesman who offers Bernadette money for sex and betrays her in an escape attempt. It is a father who returns his escaped penitent daughter. It is a priest who takes sexual advantage of Crispina. It is a man, a doctor, who confirms that Crispina should be placed in an asylum. It is a man, the Archbishop, who confirms Sr Bridget's authority. Sr Bridget is the operational director of the laundry but it is the Priests and the male members of the 'community' who provide her with the 'moral authority' to undertake her duties. Nor are the other Irish women innocent; at best they are represented as quietly compliant.

As an allegory *Babette's Feast's* simple ethical tale is not required to address the kind of grounded social issues found in *The Magdalene Sisters*. Indeed, one of the points of the latter is to challenge the common elision of ethics and law found widely but here, specifically, in the Catholic Church. Sr Bridget's laundry's treatment of the women is an example of an apparently legally sanctioned institutional intolerance of the women's right to be ethical. Margaret is denied the right to forgive or condemn Kevin, her rapist. Rose and Crispina are denied the right to take responsibility for their children. Bernadette is denied the right to manage her youthful sexuality and vitality. They are each denied these rights by a religious institution and its 'community' that reduces individual responsibility to simply obeying or disobeying its law.

The denial of the right to be ethical is clear throughout the film but it is startlingly challenged towards its conclusion in a sequence that is reminiscent of Ivan Karamazov's dream of the Grand Inquisitor in Dostoyevsky's *The Brothers Karamazov* (1958). In Dostoyevsky's novel, Christ returns to Seville during the period of the Spanish Inquisition. When the Grand Inquisitor hears that Christ is performing miracles he has him arrested. The Inquisitor visits Christ in his cell on the evening before he is due to be burnt to death at the following day's auto-da-fé. In a complicated theological discussion, the Inquisitor criticizes Christ for undoing the hard work the Church has undertaken in building the Faith. He tells him that although Christ was strong enough to resist Satan's temptations the people are not. It is the duty of the Church to stop people from making the wrong choice and if that means restricting their freedom to choose then so be it. The Church must carry the burden of freedom for the people. Ultimately, the Inquisitor tells Christ to leave Seville.

Looked at charitably, Sr Bridget has shouldered the Grand Inquisitor's burden and authority to withdraw the right of the laundry's inmates to choose to be ethical. However, Margaret challenges her power. Margaret's brother (Eamonn Owens) has arrived during Christmas celebrations at Magdalene's to take her away. As she leaves she sees Sr Bridget, the Archbishop and distinguished visitors walking down a corridor towards them. Initially, Margaret and her brother stand close against the wall so that Sr Bridget and the others may pass. But at the last moment she steps in front of the party and asks Sr Bridget to allow her to go past. Representing the law, Sr Bridget replies,

Sr Bridget: You'd better be joking girl. (She laughs) Because if I thought
for a second you would seriously expect one of the person's here to
step aside for the likes of you then, brother or no brother, I would
punish this insolence most severely, most severely.
Margaret: I'm not moving Sister.
Sr Bridget: Fine. Then you'll be staying with us then.

Margaret drops to her knees but instead of begging Sr Bridget's forgiveness, as she might previously have done, she begins to recite the Lord's
Prayer. Before she finishes it the Archbishop says to Sr Bridget, 'I think
we should be moving on.' They do. Against the established power of the
Mother Superior, Margaret offers the Lord's Prayer and, in effect, a higher
authority.

In concluding his study of postmodern ethics, Zygmunt Bauman,
taking up Levinas's 'first philosophy', writes,

Moral responsibility is the most personal and inalienable of human
possessions, and the most precious of human rights. It cannot be taken
away, shared, ceded, pawned, or deposited for safekeeping. Moral
responsibility is unconditional and infinite, and it manifests itself in
the constant anguish of not manifesting itself enough.

(1993b, p. 250)

Margaret has asserted, against Sr Bridget and the men who have given her
authority and for whom Sr Bridget has done her work, her right to take
moral responsibility for herself and her actions. Margaret still believes in
God, but it is the God as expressed by Christ in the Lord's Prayer and not
the one annexed by Sr Bridget.

Babette's Feast and *The Magdalene Sisters* provide contrasting snapshots
of two faces of community, demonstrating its potential either to nur-
ture or to destroy human lives. Communities, it seems, can be cold,
violent and unforgiving social forms for those outside of them or at
odds with them from within. But they can be warm, peaceful and generous social formations too. The potential for exclusion and inclusion, for
peace and violence is, as I hope to show, rarely far away in communities
and representations of them.[12]

There is, of course, much more to be said about the idea and practice
of community. The simple distinction I have proposed between 'good'
community and 'bad' community will not hold. There is another way of
thinking, for example, about the distinction between the communities represented by *Babette's Feast* and *The Magdalene Sisters*. The idea

of community in *The Magdalene Sisters* is of a community that is once and for ever, already fully formed; one that people are allowed or are forced to join or from which they are permanently excluded. Joining the community means accepting its rules. This can be distinguished from a community that is always in the process of becoming, in which the community forms without intention and without expectation; the community of *Babette's Feast*. I address the dynamics of this distinction in the following chapter, particularly when I turn to the work of Jean-Luc Nancy.

3
Realizing Community in Suburban America

Introduction

Writing in 1977 in his influential study, *The Fall of Public Man*, the distinguished sociologist and cultural historian Richard Sennett observed,

> A long and essentially fruitless debate among American urbanists has gone on in the last two decades about whether the suburbs are 'real' communities or not; the important thing is that the issue is raised at all, that community has become a problem on people's minds.
>
> (1986, p. 298)

Twenty-three years on, the American political sociologist Robert D. Putnam was able to state quite definitely that even if the suburbs had been 'real' communities in the 1950s, they were certainly not in 2000. He was also able to confirm that community remained 'a problem on people's minds'. This chapter is concerned not only with the sociological evidence on which Putnam drew his conclusions but also with the representation of suburban community, or its absence, in American mainstream cinema. Through their cinemas, American audiences and others have been able to see for themselves how much community might be a problem.

The publication of Putnam's *Bowling Alone: The Collapse and Revival of American Community* (2000) was a major academic event. His analysis of data, largely derived from already published material, was accompanied by his suggestions for a range of appropriate social policy options. He was invited to discuss his book with politicians on both sides of the Atlantic, including the British Prime Minister Tony Blair. There were a number of reasons for the success of *Bowling Alone*. First, Putnam digested and analysed a huge amount of data found in diverse forms, synthesised his findings in a satisfyingly comprehensive fashion and presented it all in an accessible form for the expert and the lay reader alike. Second, Putnam placed all of this data in a clear historical framework. Finally, the subject itself was, as Sennett's observations made clear, close to the heart of many sociologists, political scientists and social policy makers.[1]

Putnam argues that despite the fact of the presence, in the 1950s and 1960s, of serious and extensive social discrimination of all kinds including those of race, gender, class and sexuality, 'Engagement in community affairs and the sense of shared identity and reciprocity had never been greater in modern America' (2000, pp. 17–18). From that time, however, such engagement has waned. Putnam sets out to demonstrate what has happened and how it might be addressed.

Given Putnam's reference to community in the book's title it is disappointing that he fails to define what he means by it, except to say that it means different things to different people (2000, p. 273). It is, he claims, different for gay and lesbian communities, virtual communities and ethnic communities and so on although he does not go on to explain what the differences are. It is clear that for Putnam 'community' is, in effect, a tag by which to label what happens, expressed in terms of statements of identity and behaviour, when people engage in civic social life.

The key to engagement for Putnam lies in the idea of social capital; a concept that he shows has a significant history not only in sociology but also in social action and policy studies. He suggests that social capital is the manifestation or accumulation of 'social networks [that] have value' (2000, p. 19). It is both a 'private good' and a 'public good' that involves '[...] mutual obligations and not just contacts' (ibid., p. 20). Social capital can take many forms. It can be, for example, multi-stranded or single-stranded, formally organized or loose, publicly oriented or private and involve bridging or bonding activities. The expenditure of social capital may have pro-social, but also possibly anti-social, consequences and he cites the example of the Ku Klux Klan whose members are not short of social capital (ibid., pp. 21–2).

Recognizing the dangers of romanticizing the idea of community, Putnam's approach is much more down to earth. He argues that the long-term decline in community, measured in terms of the diminution of civic engagement, social action and social capital found in many walks of life, is anathema to the good health of American politics, society and culture. Specifically, he writes,

> We shall review hard evidence that our schools and neighborhoods don't work so well when community bonds slacken, that our economy, our democracy, and even our health and happiness depend on adequate stocks of social capital.
>
> (ibid., pp. 27–8)

Much of *Bowling Alone*, then, is taken up with an examination of the symptoms of disengagement in most areas of social life, for example, the workplace. Putnam's review of the sociological data reveals that over the past 50 years trades union membership amongst blue-collar workers declined by 50 percent (ibid., p. 81), and that amongst white-collar workers membership of professional associations has declined absolutely (ibid., pp. 84–5). In addition, despite popular notions of water-cooler friendships at work, there is no evidence to suggest that connectedness at work has increased (ibid., p. 87). There is evidence, however, to suggest that workplace ties have become casualized (ibid., p. 87). Thanks to globalization, downsizing and 'business re-engineering', jobs are held much more contingently (p. 88) and part-time, on-call and short-term contracts are held by 30 percent of US workers at the end of the twentieth century (ibid., p. 90). Putnam concludes his chapter on the workplace by declaring that all the evidence points to the fact that 'The workplace is not the salvation for our fraying civil society' (ibid., p. 92).

Putnam's analysis is graphically represented in Alexander Payne's satirical and touching road movie, *About Schmidt* (2002). Warren Schmidt (Jack Nicholson), a vice-presidential actuary for a large insurance company in a provincial city, lives with his wife, Helen, in a standard detached house in a standard suburb. The film opens with him sitting at his cleared office desk on his retirement day. The dull and formulaic retirement dinner passes without pleasure or sincerity and Schmidt is launched out into the world for which he is ill-prepared. He appears to have no friends at work or in his suburb, thus when his wife dies suddenly from an aneurysm he is alone. He subsequently discovers that his wife has had an affair. Schmidt does have a daughter but she lives out of state and, worse, is engaged to a salesman he does not like. He is a burnt out, lonely man who has no social capital and is not engaged in any civic activity. He sets off in a mobile home across the States to visit his daughter for her wedding but never really connects with the people he meets en route or with the wedding guests.

A second example taken from Putnam concerns suburbanization, a key feature of post-1945 American social life and the central theme of this chapter. Some of the conditions for suburbanization were set in place in the 1920s when real estate developers, taking advantage of local road programmes, subdivided land into low-density projects. In the 1930s, restructured mortgage provision made finance easier to obtain, particularly for ethnically white, blue- and white-collar workers.[2] The unprecedented expansion of the suburbs began in the immediate post–Second World War years. The proportion of the American population living in the suburbs rose from 23 percent to 48 percent between 1950 and 1996 whilst, over the same period, the proportion living in small towns and other non-metropolitan households, for example farms, dropped from 44 percent to 20 percent (2000, fig. 52, p. 208).[3]

In the immediate post-war years, the public and private sectors across the States combined to invest in the creation of suburbs and the appropriate infrastructure to house the growing lower and middle classes of its economy. The government, through the GI Act (1944), set up the Veterans Administration that kick-started the initial economic growth that, in turn, stimulated the construction industry and encouraged new forms of financing. Amy Kenyon (2004) argues that '[...] mass suburbanization would have been impossible without the staggering increase in credit financing that encouraged the post-war recovery' (p. 34).

Any hope that melting pot America might find a new home in the suburbs was quickly dispelled. Putnam notes,

> As suburbanization continued, however, the suburbs themselves fragmented into a sociological mosaic – collectively heterogeneous but individually homogeneous, as people fleeing the city sorted themselves into more finely distinguished 'lifestyle enclaves,' segregated by race, class, education, life-stage, and so on. So-called white flight was only the most visible form of this movement toward metropolitan differentiation.
>
> (2000, p. 209)

Putnam shows that segregatory zoning policies and practices, that, for example, often excluded local shops and cafés from suburbs and whose apotheosis is the 'gated community', produce a contradictory finding in terms of civil engagement.[4] Despite one's expectations that housing people like-by-like might produce 'a certain social connectedness', the opposite turned out to be the case (ibid., p. 210).

However, even with easier finance credit availability the suburbs would not have expanded as they did without the American love affair with the motor car. Widespread car ownership allowed and continues to allow people to live in the suburbs, work in the towns or industrial estates and shop at the out-of-town malls.[5] Given the significance of the automobile in American life, one might imagine that the amount of time Americans spend between home, work and the mall might provide the opportunity for some social connectedness. But again, the expectation is dashed. Americans spend more and more time in their cars, travelling greater distances, more frequently and more often in single occupancy. When they get home from work, they spend increasingly more time watching entertainment television.[6] The direct effect of this, Putnam argues, is a diminution of involvement in community affairs that spills out beyond the individual driver into wider society (ibid., p. 213). The privatization of the culture of the car only emphasises the loneliness of the zoned suburb.

In addition to drawing together the empirical evidence of the decline of civic engagement and social capital in the suburbs, Robert Putnam also tellingly quotes American architects, Andres Duany and Elizabeth Plater-Zyberk, who write, 'The suburb is the last word in privatization, perhaps even its lethal consummation and it spells the end of the authentic life' (ibid., p. 210). He also quotes historian Kenneth T. Jackson on the same theme, 'There are few places as desolate and lonely as a suburban street on a hot afternoon' (ibid., p. 211).

Putnam's account of the diminishing presence of communal life in American suburbs is disturbing, especially given suburbia's ideological status in American society.[7] When, during the 1940s, 1950s and 1960s, the virtues of small-town America – neighbourliness and the pursuit of the common good – seemed irredeemably lost in the urban centres of Chicago, Detroit and New York, there seemed to be some hope that they would resettle in the suburbs. This was the dream created in Bailey Park, the fictional suburban development built by George Bailey (James Stewart) in Frank Capra's *It's a Wonderful Life* (1946). It is also the image used in selling suburbia in the 1950s.[8] Putnam quotes the famous marketing appeal observed by William Whyte in researching his influential study *The Organization Man*:

> You Belong to PARK FOREST!
> The moment you come to our town you know:
> You're welcome.
> You're a part of the big group
> You can live in a small town

Instead of a lonely big city
You can have friends who want you –
And you can enjoy being with them.
Come out. Find out about the spirit of Park Forest.

(2000, p. 209)

The kind of mystification, represented here, has been explored at length by Amy Kenyon (2004). She presents a highly original and stimulating account of the structural changes of the spaces through which US capital reconstructs itself and in which people try to live their lives, often in quiet, but sometimes noisy, desperation. Kenyon argues,

> [...] that the success of postwar suburbanization depended on a kind of cultural dreaming [...] We might have dreamed ourselves to be American; now we dreamed ourselves to be suburban.
>
> (2004, p. 2)

Kenyon suggests that the way in which suburbanization was sold to Americans, not only directly through marketing campaigns and government sponsorship but also indirectly through popular literature and the cinema, has had a troubling effect. On the one hand it seemed to sell the dream of the suburbs in terms of 'attachment, consensus and inclusion' but on the other it actually produced 'social detachment, separation, and exclusion' (ibid., p. 44). This is exactly the segregation by race, class, education and life stage described by Putnam. It seems it is possible for suburbanites to dream the world as homogeneous, provided the rest of the world can be excluded or kept at a distance whilst they sleep. Sometimes, however, the arts, in this case the cinema, step across the suburban threshold to disturb the sleep of the righteous.

Dreams turning to nightmares

Robert Beuka (2000) argues that by the late 1960s, the suburbs that had nurtured a new post-war suburban generation became the object of criticism bordering on contempt by that same generation. Although writing specifically about *The Graduate* (dir. Mike Nichols, 1967), Beuka makes the more general claim that hopes for the continuation of the suburban dream were being dashed. He argues, for example, that the new generation American popular culture found in music, the cinema and in the new subcultures was beginning to attack '[...] the materialistic

and anaesthetized sensibilities of the adult generation in suburbia [...]'
(2000, p. 16). In terms that might have been taken directly from Putnam
or Kenyon, Beuka writes that the very evidence of the material success
of the suburban life was now being interpreted as '[...] evidence of the
failure of the suburban dream'. He continues,

> That is, capitalism's victory was seen as spelling the death of a sense
> of community in the suburbs, as the utopian vision of inclusion
> and togetherness that informed the postwar suburban migration had
> given way – at least in the popular imagination – to disjointed devel-
> opment neighborhoods characterized by a form of crass materialism
> readily observable on the very landscape.
>
> (ibid., p. 16)

Suburbia, that is largely white suburbia, has continued to be a major
theme of American cinema since the 1960s. The suburban dream has
formed the focus of important movies, some of which have achieved
iconic status, for example, *The Stepford Wives* (dir. Bryan Forbes, 1974),
Blue Velvet (dir. David Lynch, 1986), *SubUrbia* (dir. Richard Linklater,
1996), *Happiness* (dir. Todd Solondz, 1997), *The Truman Show* (dir. Peter
Weir, 1998) and *Far from Heaven* (dir. Todd Haynes, 2002).

In selecting films through which I can discuss the relationship between
suburbia, community and the cinema, I am spoilt for choice. However, Putnam's work prompted me to examine films through which I
can explore the idea of the decline, indeed the absence, of community.
Putnam's thesis clearly proposes that too little community is a problem.
But perhaps the question also arises: Can there be too much community?
To help address this question I have selected two films, *Pleasantville* (dir.
Gary Ross, 1998) and *American Beauty* (dir. Sam Mendes, 1999), each of
which is as iconic as those others listed above. Whilst these films share an
equally jaundiced view of suburban life, there is also an interesting and
important difference between them that centres on the argument identified by Zygmunt Bauman concerning the ambivalence of community
to which I have referred in earlier chapters. He argues that community
comes at a price that '[...] is paid in the currency of freedom, variously
called "autonomy", "right to self-assertion", "right to be yourself" ' (2001,
p. 4). If Putnam is certain that the absence of community is a problem,
then Bauman is equally certain that so too is its presence.

Pleasantville might be understood to be a film about the dangers of too
much community and the absence of the attributes of freedom described
by Bauman. Pleasantville's citizens have no idea that they are missing

anything. On the other hand, *American Beauty* appears to be a film about the dangers of too little community. Each of its major characters is, in one way or another, separated from the others. There is work and family and there are the obligatory roles of friends and neighbours, but none provide the basis for the mutual obligations that Putnam regards as important in the formation of communal life. There appears to be free-dom, of a sort, but no community. The differences between *Pleasantville* and *American Beauty* seem stark. And yet, there is, I will argue, more to the distinction between 'too much' and 'too little' community than meets the eye.

In summing up his discussion of suburbanization, Putnam confirms that it has made a considerable contribution to the decline in civic engagement since 1945 (2000, p. 214). It will be possible to gain a sense of the 'ideological' time travelled during this period if, before turning to *Pleasantville* and *American Beauty*, I pause to examine *It's a Wonderful Life* (1946).

It's a Wonderful Life: From Bedford Falls to Bailey Park

In the immediate pre- and post-war eras, Frank Capra's films presented American and international audiences with a series of idealized accounts of what he saw as the virtues of American popular or liberal democracy that have been built on the principles of self-help, mutual support, com-mon sense, pragmatism and friendship. Typically, these virtues were constructed and represented in direct structural opposition to the vices that might be thought as undermining democracy.[9]

In exploring these virtues and vices *It's a Wonderful Life* contrasts two ways in which finance capital can be organized. One, the bad way, is represented by Mr Potter (Lionel Barrymore) a businessman who plays Monopoly with people's lives by acquiring properties all around the board. Rather than providing the means by which the citizens of Bedford Falls, whom he describes as a 'discontented lazy rabble', can purchase their own homes, he prefers, instead, to pay them low wages so that they can only afford to rent the properties he owns. He has no moral scruples about foreclosing on debts. Potter's approach represents the 'unacceptable face of capitalism'.[10] It is the sort of capitalism that shapes the worldview of the characters of James Foley's film of David Mamet's play *Glengarry Glen Ross* (1992). Although Potter would not have used the same language, he would have approved of the sentiments expressed by top real estate salesmen, Blake (Alec Baldwin), to the tired and threatened junior salesmen desperate to close deals on what they call 'dead leads'.

Blake harangues them: 'Only one thing counts in this life; get them to sign on the line that is dotted. You hear me, you fuckin' faggots.'

The other, the good way, is represented by Peter Bailey (Samuel S. Hinds), the founder and executive secretary of the Bedford Falls Building and Loan, a mutual society dedicated to helping people save for a mortgage deposit to buy their own houses. Peter and Ma Bailey (Beulah Bondi) have two exceptionally able children, George (James Stewart) and Harry (Todd Karns), to whom they successfully pass on the values that have made the Building and Loan an integral and hugely respected part of Bedford Falls. The film centres on the life of George, who has an urge to travel, gain a serious education and become a building engineer, as he grows from being a 'good kid' to being a pillar of the community. First Peter and then George are deeply involved in the life of Bedford Falls and the lives of all its citizens. They seem to know everyone by their first names and are fully engaged by their civic responsibilities. Their social capital account could not be healthier.

At various points in the film Potter comes close to taking control of the Building and Loan, but fails. For example, at the outset of the film we see Peter resisting Potter who is not persuaded by the former's argument that the Building and Loan customers have children. Potter asks Peter Bailey, 'Are you running a business or a charity ward?'

George Bailey frequently appears to be on the verge of leaving Bedford Falls to travel, or to go to College or on honeymoon, however, at each point he is thwarted; thwarted by the death of his father or a run on the Building and Loans assets. As Potter appears to be grasping hold of the Building and Loan following Peter Bailey's death, George turns on Potter and speaks, in words that might have been uttered by his father, in support of the mutual mortgage principle:

> You know how long it takes a working man to save $5000? Just remember this Mr Potter, that this rabble you're talking about does most of the working and paying, living and dying in this community. Is it asking too much to live and die in a couple of decent rooms and a bathroom? Anyway, my father didn't think so. People were human beings to him. But to you – a warped, frustrated old man – they're cattle.

George stays in Bedford Falls for the next 20 years, marries Mary (Donna Reed) and they have children. Throughout this time he runs the Building and Loan which manages to help provide the mortgages that enables citizens to buy their own homes in the new Bailey Park suburb. He is not wealthy but he is happy. He and the Building and Loan suffer a number of crises, the final one of which looks like it could be terminal. It arises when, on Christmas Eve, 1945, $8000 goes missing from the Building and Loan accounts. His Uncle Billy (Thomas Mitchell) has mislaid some money that Mr Potter has found but 'failed' to return. Bailey fears that he will be imprisoned for embezzlement and, unable to face the shame, he contemplates suicide.

This brings about the intervention of Clarence (Henry Travers), angel second class. Heaven-sent Clarence, who is seeking to earn his wings, manages to convince George that although he might be frustrated because he hasn't satisfied his urge to travel and that the Building and Loan is in danger of collapse, he has made thousands of lives better by his staying. In spite of George's cry that it would have been better had he not been born, Clarence shows George otherwise and concludes, 'You see, George, you really had a wonderful life.' The film ends with all of George's friends and relatives, including his brother Harry, winner of a Congressional Medal, gathered at George and Mary's home. The members of the community to whom he had referred in one of his verbal assaults on Potter give their money to bail George out. Mutuality has proved that it has its place in the American economy. As if to underline the fact that George represents the American way, Clarence leaves behind a copy of Mark Twain's *The Adventures of Tom Sawyer* inscribed with a message:

Dear George:
Remember *no* man is a failure who has *friends.*
Thanks for the wings!
Love
Clarence
(Clarence's emphasis.)

It's a Wonderful Life is a beautifully realized film shot in black and white. Capra handles a huge cast of characters who grow old together over a period of around 20 years with great authority.[11] It is shot with both poise and energy. Bailey's roller coaster of a ride as he moves from pride, through frustration to despair, from moments of high comedy to tragedy is exquisitely paced.[12]

The film is also a highly manipulative, sentimental fairy story/morality tale that extols the virtues of pragmatism, friendship and community engagement. It reiterates the belief in the importance of home, a theme that is revealed in part through Mary's role in the story. This is the limit of the place allotted to women in *It's a Wonderful Life*. George's mother, Mary and servant Annie are all home-fire characters who have no function outside of faithfully supporting their men or families. Even Violet Bick, the 'pretty young thing' who pops up from time to time to flirt with George, decides that home town is best. Not only does the film deny an independent role for women but it also virtually excludes black characters altogether.[13]

The significance of the idea of the domestic life, of home, the small town, the future suburb and the idea of ownership is represented perfectly clearly. It is patiently crystallized by Peter Bailey:

> You know George, I feel that in a small way, we're doing something important – satisfying a fundamental urge. It's deep in the race, for a man to want his own roof and walls and fireplace. We're helping him get those things in our 'shabby little office'.

George's lot in life is to transfer the qualities of small-town America to the suburbs; from Bedford Falls to Bailey Park. Within months of *It's a Wonderful Life* opening, the first Levittown dwelling was sold and the post-war wave of suburban building was underway.[14]

American Beauty: too little community?

Film critics Leonard Quart and Albert Auster claim that '*American Beauty* is the blackest of comic portraits of American suburban life' (2002, p. 203). Set in a middle class, white (again) suburb, *American Beauty* presents absolutely no sign of a community or any form of civic culture. It presents only alienated or privatized suburban individuals existing in what Putnam, paraphrasing the words of ethnographer M. P. Baumgartner (1988), describes as 'A culture of atomized isolation, self-restraint, and "moral minimalism"' (2000, p. 210). Here, in *American Beauty*, the hollowness of the alienated and inauthentic life of the suburbs is chillingly represented.

American Beauty opens with a brief prologue, shot in low-grade video, in which a teenage girl assents to the offer by an off-screen male photographer to kill her father who apparently has become an embarrassment to her. The film cuts to a full-colour aerial shot of a suburb where the girl's father and mother, Lester (Kevin Spacey) and Carolyn Burnham (Annette Benning), live with their photographed daughter, Jane (Thora Birch).

As the camera's aerial shot moves towards the Burnham's subdivision, Lester begins to voice-over the story of the final year of his life as a chronicle of a death foretold. In deadpan tones he says,

> My name is Lester Burnham. This is my neighbourhood. This is my street. This is my life. [The film cuts to a bedroom, then to a shower.] I'm 42 years old. In less than a year I'll be dead. Of course, I don't know that yet and, in a way, I'm dead already. Look at me. Jerkin' off in the shower. This will be the highlight of my day. It's all down hill from here.

Lester hates his work in advertising sales. Carolyn sells real estate but compared with Kane (Peter Gallagher), the self-styled 'king of real estate', her business is small and she knows it. Jane, who is in high school, is alienated from her parents, has a very low self-image and a beautiful friend, Angela (Mena Suvari), who exudes sexual allure and talks incessantly about 'fucking' and 'boy's dicks'. Teenager Jane is already saving for cosmetic surgery. Lester, Carolyn and Jane are unhappy; unhappy with themselves and unhappy together. Lester and Carolyn's marriage is, according to Lester, '[...] just for show, a commercial for how we are, when we are anything but.'

The Burnhams have two contrasting sets of neighbours on their suburban subdivision. Gay couple, Jim Olmeyer (Scott Bakula) and Jim Berkley (Sam Robards), live on one side and newcomers, Colonel (Chris Cooper), Barbara (Allison Janney) and Ricky Fitts (Wes Bentley), live on the other. Jim and Jim are happy, outgoing, professionals. They are friendly and exist in the film both as a sign of contentment to the rest of the world and as a provocation to Colonel Fitts. The retired Colonel maintains a substantial gun collection, a Nazi-commemorative plate and a seriously aggressive attitude towards gay men or 'faggots' as he prefers to call them. Barbara is clinically depressed and mostly mute. Ricky, who has previously been placed in a mental institution by his father, lives a double life; the public life of a regular diligent student and reliable part-time worker and the hidden life of an obsessive video/digital photographer and drug dealer.

Lester's life changes from the moment he sees Angela perform as a member of Jane's high school's dance troupe. He begins to fantasize about her. His reappraisal of his hitherto mortifying life has a major knock-on effect on everyone around him and the film follows each of the characters as they undergo psychological and emotional journeys and either wittingly or unwittingly address their unhappiness. Lester decides to be honest with himself, his family and everyone else too. He takes control of the conditions of his own work redundancy by blackmailing his way to a good severance deal, he tells Carolyn what's on his mind, he buys cannabis from Ricky and he takes a low-paid job in fast-food retailing that doesn't require him to commit to anything. His new-found honesty is also revealed in his relationship with Angela who has responded to Lester's interest in her by casually flirting with him. Stimulated by this Lester begins to work out in his newly fitted garage gym.

Carolyn seeks to compensate for her now loveless marriage by immersing herself in her work by selling properties, by learning to shoot handguns and by starting an affair with Kane. She becomes an adept shot and she enjoys energetic and noisy sex. However, Kane ends the affair when Lester discovers it. Subsequently, taking the advice of a self-help tape she plays in her car, Carolyn repeats to herself the tape's mantra: 'I refuse to be a victim.'[15]

Jane's self-image problem begins to fade when she forms an attachment with Ricky. He deals in high-grade drugs, he's rather intense and, in Jane and Angela's eyes, his voyeuristic photography places him in the 'weird' category of young men. Yet Jane realizes, against her prejudices, that he at least is honest in his dealings with her, as indeed he is with everyone except his father. Ricky's relationship with Jane changes him too. Living with his parents he has to hide who he is. To make life easier for him and for them he lies and dissembles; he photographs the world – dead birds, plastic bags swirling in the breeze – instead of living in it. Ricky's last act of dishonesty with his father is to provoke him by telling him that he is a male prostitute and that Lester has been a client. With Jane he can be honest about himself. Colonel Fitts's obsessive 'anti-faggot' attitude leads him to misinterpret Ricky's behaviour with Lester. He assaults Ricky who decides he does not have to put up with this and can leave home. Jane falls out with Angela because Angela declares, to Jane's disgust, that Lester is sexy and she would like to 'fuck' him. Ricky and Jane decide to leave for New York where he knows people and will be able to earn a living by drug dealing if necessary.

Colonel Fitts continues to obsess about 'faggots' in general and about his son in particular. Angrily interpreting all sorts of behaviour as 'homosexual', he even thinks that Lester is gay and one rainy night, after his assault on Ricky, he approaches him whilst he is working out in the garage. He is crying and clearly upset and the 'new' Lester comforts him with a hug. The Colonel, misreading Lester's kindness, kisses him on the lips at which point Lester tells him gently, 'I'm sorry, you've got the wrong idea.'

Angela persists in masking her insecurity by adopting her cool, sexually experienced, confident and judgmental persona almost to the end of the film. Her cool, however, is disturbed by Ricky who, when leaving with Jane, describes her as 'Ugly, ordinary and totally boring and you know it.' For the first time, Angela appears unsure of herself and her mask begins to slip. When, shortly after, Lester begins to make love to her the mask slips completely and she is revealed to herself and Lester as being a 'normal' teenager who wants love and perhaps a father.

Thus, by the climax of the film, the main characters have begun to come to terms in some degree and in their own ways with the fact that they have been living alienated, inauthentic lives. Each character has been lonely and afraid and their loneliness and fear has been destructive. Two of the characters, Colonel Fitts and Carolyn, remain exposed. Colonel Fitts' rejected advance on Lester was humiliating. By kissing Lester he has behaved in a way that he has persistently and angrily denounced. Carolyn has also been humiliated. She has found Lester's behaviour incomprehensible and her attempt to deal with it by having an affair with Kane has led to further humiliation.

Both Colonel Fitts and Carolyn have access to guns and know how to use them. So when, at the final climax, the audience sees the barrel of the gun just behind Lester's head, it does not know who is holding it. As the camera pans to the tiled kitchen wall we see Lester's blood splatter on to it. Later director Sam Mendes cuts to Colonel Fitts who is covered in blood. Lester, so Lester tells us, remains contented. As he finds an authentic life, he dies; but he declares from beyond the grave that he wouldn't have changed a minute of his past.

Whilst *American Beauty* is not an existentialist philosophical tract I would argue that it can be understood in existentialist terms.[16] In its post-Sartrean guise, existentialism settles around the idea that no declaration of what it means to be human can take a generalized or abstracted form or be fixed in advance; meaning is what we make of ourselves in any particular situation through the process of existing itself. People cannot interpret the meaning of their lives by consulting psychological theories or biological facts nor by reflecting on the sociological roles or norms associated with being a father, husband, media salesman, bodybuilder or jogger. In leading an authentic, that is, a meaningful life, it is not enough to live as an outside observer of one's own life but one must be engaged by and in it. One chooses to act rather than simply feeling impelled to act.

In existentialist terms, Lester is an alienated man; an outsider observing his own life. He works in a job that controls him, he shares a marriage that is 'just for show', and he no longer knows how to act as a father does to Jane. 'This isn't life', he says, 'just stuff'. Living this 'life' is killing him, both figuratively and materially, and his alienation is expressed through his voiced-over first-person narrative. Lester is living an inauthentic life that is not of his own choice; Carolyn wants him to be like a 'normal' husband, Jane wants him to be a 'normal' father, his boss wants him to be a 'normal' employee – whatever 'normal' means. He could act like Carolyn, Jane and his boss want him to act and he could act out the roles well but these would be inauthentic acts because he would be acting according to a socialized notion of duty. Authenticity involves a kind of integrity, not of the sort that is defined in advance, that is a normalized notion of integrity, but one that is an attribute of a self-defined project. Shocking though it is to Carolyn, to Jane and his boss, Lester's project is to honestly and transparently pursue those things, including Angela, that will make him happy; to be the author of his own life and not only in his voiced-over narration.

The idea of the inauthentic life is explored throughout the film. It is apparent in Ricky's ethnographic digital and video photography by which he observes the world but keeps it at a distance. Inauthentic life is also found in the shots of the Fitts watching television, the Burnhams' dining and, of course, in the image of the red rose, American Beauty, the State Flower of Washington DC. In an early scene, Carolyn is cutting a full-flowered bloom. Lester introduces Carolyn to the audience: 'That's my wife Carolyn. See the way the handles on those pruning shears match her gardening clogs. That's not an accident.' One of the Burnham's gay neighbours asks Carolyn, how she cultivates such beautiful blooms. She tells him that her secret is a combination of eggshells and Miracle-Gro. Eggshells are a traditional organic material but the latter is a chemical mix, criticized by some organic growers because whilst it produces lush foliage and flowers it does not improve the soil structure for future gardening.

The central trope of *American Beauty*, as it frequently is in films of suburban life, is sex. Thus, for example, in discussing *The Graduate*, Robert Beuka, pinpoints precisely, '[. . .] the emasculating capacity of the suburban environment [. . .]', in which Ben Braddock has to define his manhood (2000, p. 14). In *American Beauty* sexuality is a synecdoche, a rhetorical device in which a part stands for the whole. The film does not present only one man's sexuality that has been sublimated, repressed or alienated, but everyone's and it is connected to the representation of the inauthentic life. Angela boasts constantly about her sex life but she doesn't have one and, until she meets Ricky, neither does Jane although she is constantly researching breast modification websites. Lester and Carolyn haven't had sex together in ages and certainly not in the film; Carolyn has enthusiastic sex with Kane, until he dumps her, whilst Lester prefers to 'jerk off'. Carolyn is particularly horrified to wake up one morning to find him masturbating in bed alongside her.

Carolyn's interest in growing roses also provides an obvious sexual image. The scene in which Lester observes Carolyn wielding her pruning shears to cut and trim her rose might be interpreted as him bearing witness to his own symbolic castration. It contrasts well with scenes in which Lester fantasizes about Angela, including one in which he is watching her opening her blouse and releasing thousands of red rose petals and another in which he watches her bathing, once more, in a tub of red rose petals.

Finally, Colonel Fitts appears to be a control freak but in his post-army service he has nothing, except Ricky and himself, to control. Whatever it is that has eaten him away is never made clear to the audience but it is possible to read his homophobic discourse as hiding a homosexual desire. When, finally he finds a gestural way – a kiss – to express his sexual desire, here projected on to Lester, it is firmly but kindly rejected. The Colonel proceeds to kill the new found object of his desire.

The synecdoche reaches its climax at the moment at which Lester is about to realize his fantasy by making love to Angela. Her pathetic and moving confession that she is a virgin profoundly effects him. The traditional lothario, a Don Juan, might have enjoyed the conquest even more. Lester's authentic response, however, is to rein in his fantasies and protect her by keeping her warm, making her a sandwich and giving her a hug. When she asks Lester how he is, he expresses pleasure with the sheer fact that, after years and years of living an inauthentic life, at last someone has asked him, 'how are you?' He says, 'I'm great.' Lester, who is a father, has chosen to act as a father not out of a sense of duty but because this is how he feels he wants to behave. This is his first act of love that isn't self-love; it is also his last for, just at the moment he has declared his happiness, he is shot dead. Love, sex and death are united by the visual image of the blood-spattered kitchen tiles bookended by a red rose.

Is there any room for optimism for the other alienated suburbanites presented to us in *American Beauty*? Although Lester, the deceased narrator, claims to have died 'contented' the other adults are in a mess. Colonel Fitts will go to jail, be placed in a mental institution or be executed. Carolyn, last seen recoiling in horror at the sight of the gun in her hand and hiding it in her closet, might tough it out; that would be a sensible thing to do. But what of the younger generation? In one sense Lester's choice, his project to pursue happiness, has shaken everyone up and provided them with opportunities to live authentically. Jane has found Ricky and is no longer in thrall to body fascism or Angela's self-assurance. Ricky has found Jane and has no need to photograph the world but can now live in it. Angela has found herself behind her mask, but is there anyone left to love her?

I have been making the case for the argument that *American Beauty* is a good example of an existentialist film that seeks to show the emptiness of modern life for white middle class suburbanites who are without social capital or community support. There is, it seems, just too little community. The highly stylized manner in which Mendes has presented this is sufficient for Jeffrey Sconce (2006) to suggest that *American Beauty* is an example of a phenomenon he calls 'smart cinema' and which forms a part of a larger postmodern or late-modern aesthetic project that emerged in Western culture at that time. The films were a product of a new generation of largely American, 'ideologically sympathetic' filmmakers as diverse as Todd Solondz, Wes Anderson and Quentin Tarantino who began directing from around 1990 and that stood in opposition to mainstream Hollywood (2006, p. 429).

Out of this complex mix Sconce identifies five elements of the ideal type of smart cinema, some of which are stylistic and others thematic: 'blank' style and incongruous narration, narrative 'synchronicity', interest in random fate, the dysfunctional white middle class family and '[. . .] a recurring interest in the politics of taste, consumerism, and identity' (ibid, p. 432).

By Sconce's measure, *American Beauty* is smart cinema. Stylistically, for example, Lester Burnham's 'blank' narration is both personal but somehow flat and disengaged; almost as if he is talking disinterestedly about someone else even when he is discussing himself. Thematically, it clearly focuses on the lifestyle of the middle class white family of the suburbs.

Sconce notes that the elective affinity of style and ethical issues evident in smart cinema has offended both the political right and the political left. The left is critical because such films do not address the underlying political motors of class, race and patriarchy (ibid., p. 437). The political right criticizes smart cinema films such as *The Sweet Hereafter* (dir. Atom Egoyan, 1997), *The Ice Storm* (dir. Ang Lee, 1997), *Donnie Darko* (dir. Richard Kelly, 2001) and *Election* (dir. Alexander Payne, 1999) because they seem to propose '[. . .] an irresponsible worldview where truth and morality are no longer of concern' (ibid., p. 437).

Most of the films described by Sconce do not have a big 'P' political agenda, indeed, much of Sconce's article is taken up with discussing the stylistic devices that mark out smart cinema's distance from films that do. However, the fact that many films produced at this time might be characterized as being stylistically 'blank' or disengaged does not mean, of course, that the films are neither politically interesting nor sociologically pertinent. Sconce, in the main, has successfully described the emergence of a new film aesthetic but has not adequately addressed what that emergence signifies. I would suggest that people turning to look at *American Beauty* or *The Sweet Hereafter* or *The Ice Storm* for specific moral or political guidance will be sorely disappointed. However, if on looking they saw films that somehow connected with a wider social issue, they should not be surprised because there is something 'going on' that is not just about style.

The sociologist C. Wright Mills (1959) once argued that when a married couple goes through a divorce, the individuals involved often find it a traumatic experience. This might lead to each to ask, 'What did I do wrong?' From the couple's point of view there is a personal problem. However, if looking up from the wreck of their marriage the couple noted that the rate of divorce in society was increasing rapidly, they might consider that there is not only a personal problem but a social issue too.[17] *American Beauty*'s Lester Burnham is not the only modern film character to be depicted as alienated. Countless other films from around this period have such characters including *The Ice Storm, The Sweet Hereafter, The Virgin Suicides, Ghost World* (dir. Terry Zwigoff, 2001) and *Garden State* (dir. Zach Braff, 2006). Perhaps, in addition to the personal problem there is a social issue if not an emerging structure of feeling, complexly expressed.

The directors of these films, and others, have found a way to express what Duany and Plater-Zyberk, to whom I referred earlier, described as 'the end of the authentic life'. In an America in which community, civic engagement and social capital is threatened by suburban sprawl, the dominance of the motor car, the privatized world of television, the rise and rise of consumerism fuelled by aggressive marketing in a neo-liberal economy, we should not be surprised if some of the most independently minded filmmakers want to represent it. What Sconce discerns as a retreat from politics in 'smart cinema' might, perhaps, be better understood as indicative of the malaise outlined so comprehensively by Robert Putnam; the collapse, but not yet the revival, of American community.

If Sconce is right to argue that American filmmakers are retreating from big 'P' politics then they ought to understand that not everyone else is retreating. The period of 'smart cinema', after all, is the era in which neo-conservatism and born-again Christian fundamentalism began to gather steam and became politically influential, setting itself against President Bill Clinton's liberal welfare-conscious administration. The Presidential election of 2000 served to confirm a significant fault line in US political opinion that has been confirmed by George W. Bush's presidency.

Pleasantville: too much community?

If *American Beauty* can be described as a film critiquing a society characterized as having too little community, then on the face of it *Pleasantville* presents the opposite case, too much community.

In the set up of *It's a Wonderful Life*, George, on the eve of leaving Bedford Falls for College, tells Bailey Sr 'I just feel like if I didn't get away, I'd bust.' Well he didn't get away but he didn't 'bust' either. He stayed to create Bailey Park, his suburban dream. However, some people, like his brother Harry, did manage to get away from Bedford Falls. Now roll the film forward 52 years and nobody, but nobody, leaves Pleasantville.[18] This is not just because *Pleasantville*'s Pleasantville is simply too pleasant to leave but also because there does not seem to be anywhere to go to.

Pleasantville is an allegorical satire of the dream of suburban life; the prosperous, God-fearing, patriarchal suburb has a white, homogeneous and content population and has high schools that are safe environments. Sex never 'rears its ugly head' in Pleasantville. *Pleasantville* is also a satire of the dreamt suburban life with its attendant clear gender roles and social rules as it was represented on 1950s and1960s' American TV in CBS sitcoms such as *Leave it to Beaver* (1958–1963), *The Adventures of Ozzie and Harriet* (1952–1962) and, especially, *Father Knows Best* (1954–1960).[19] The latter was set in Springfield, a Mid-West town, which, ironically, is the name of the town in which lives America's allegedly most dysfunctional family, *The Simpsons*. Springfield also appears on a road sign at the end of *Pleasantville*.

The immediate object of *Pleasantville*'s satire is 'Pleasantville', a 1950s black-and-white TV suburb sitcom, set in Pleasantville, that is being shown on end-of-the-century cable television and avidly consumed by senior high school teenager David (Tobey McGuire), who knows all the sitcom episodes inside out and back to front. As an allegorical satire, *Pleasantville* has no shame in engaging the services of a good fairy in the shape of a television repair engineer; a rather aggressive Clarence for the television age. His intervention enables David to be teleported back from the 1990s to 'Pleasantville', in the company of his sister, Jennifer (Reese Witherspoon), who happens to be around when the magic happens. If he is initially surprised by his travel, then she is horrified for she is decidedly not a TV sitcom anorak, has no interest in this sort of TV and has a date in her own time frame in anticipation of which she says, 'I've even bought some new underwear.' However, what is worse, at least for her, is the fact that David and Jennifer are not just observers of the sitcom but must assume the characters of Bud and Mary Sue, children of one of the sitcom's leading families, the Carter family.[20]

Initially, David/Bud and Jennifer/Mary Sue try to adjust their behaviour to this strange environment, but soon it is the citizens of Pleasantville who begin to feel strange. The initially unwitting, but later purposeful, interventions of two teenage time travellers enable the Pleasantville suburbanites to begin to see the limits of the world they inhabit. Together, David/Bud and Jennifer/Mary Sue reveal aspects of human personality and consciousness, for example, desire, curiosity, individuality, self-awareness of fallibility and aesthetics, to the two-tone sitcom characters. Subsequently, the latter begin to recognize their potential and to see the community that they had taken to be their real world was an illusion. As each character begins this recognition process, he or she turns from black and white to colour, and so does his or her immediate environment; Pleasantville's inhabitants finally find a use for umbrellas and the previously blank books suddenly appear to have texts and pictures. The CGI coloration techniques used by writer and director Gary Ross to demonstrate this effect are dramatic yet subtle and utterly convincing.

Much of *Pleasantville*'s drama arises because not all 'Pleasantville' characters achieve enlightenment simultaneously and some do not welcome the change. Those who have not, as yet, been touched by David and Jennifer's intervention want to keep Pleasantville 'pleasant' and therefore resist change. A meeting of the community is called to take action against David/Bud and his newly coloured and artistic boss, Mr Johnson (Jeff Daniels), but, as passions rise at the meeting, ultimately the action fails and all Pleasantville becomes coloured.

Pleasantville's narrative is occasionally loose, particularly so in the section concerning the way in which patriarchal forces within the town resist change. In 'real life' we might expect this to happen – there is clear and obvious motivation for men not to want to give up their comfortable lives. But in 'Pleasantville' there is no reason to suspect that the nice men of Pleasantville would behave in any other way than pleasantly and, as David would no doubt confirm, there is no precedence for it in the sitcom's back-story. Perhaps, we do not need to worry about this as allegories involving the intervention of magical television repair engineers do not need to obey 'real world' rules of sequence and logic. Audiences can take care of themselves and they need to for *Pleasantville* does require its audience to make sense of a double shift. David and Jennifer do not just travel back to a previous 'real world' but to a fictional representation of a 'real world'. Even *Blue Velvet*, a disturbing film representing the dark underbelly of an apparently friendly, suburban world does not require its audience to do so much work in suspending its disbelief. Nevertheless, *Pleasantville* retains its sense of purpose in exposing the way in which a 'fictional' community can create social conformity without destroying the audience's faith in storytelling. It does this by the careful way in which it handles the transformation of some of 'Pleasantville's' main characters; none less so than in the case of Bud and Mary Sue's fictional mother, Mrs Betty Carter (Joan Allen).

Betty Carter is a character taken lock, stock and barrel from the 1950s television suburban sitcom army of stereotypes. Middle class and white, she is always beautifully groomed, manicured, polite and smartly dressed. In total control of the domestic environment, providing meals on the table and cheery encouragement on demand, Betty is ready to slide into domestic action whenever her husband, Mr George Carter (William H. Macey), puts down his briefcase and newspaper, hangs his hat on the hall stand and calls out, 'Honey, I'm home.' She is, in short, precisely a woman typical of those who became the object of Betty Friedan's attention in her research informing the publication of her influential book, *The Feminine Mystique*; a book that disturbed a generation of American patriarchs when it was first published in 1963.[21]

According to Friedan, men did not really know much about women. They did not take an interest in them as women except in so far as they served their interests. Men knew that they could safely leave women to deal with domestic matters such as children and the home. In so far as men knew anything about women, what they knew was handed down to them from either their mothers or popular culture; in stories, through stereotypes found in jokes, in 'girly' posters and calendars pinned up in garages, office lockers and factories, in films in which good women baked cakes and in which 'strong' and independent women tended to get their 'just deserts'. Friedan argued that domesticity was the lot of most 1950s/1960s suburban women and such domesticity alienated women from their potential to be creative and fully engaged in society, under their own terms. Somewhat controversially, Friedan suggested that the types of mental and emotional adjustments that women had to make in order to serve the suburban family home were similar to those that inmates of German concentration camps had had to make (1965, pp. 265–8).

If this was the range of Betty Carter's experience then it was just about to change under the influence of Mary Sue, aka the worldly wise Jennifer. Betty had become aware that 'things' had been happening down Lovers Lane where Jennifer had initiated college basketball star, Skip (Paul Walker), in the joys of sex. At first Mary Sue/Jennifer hesitates to tell Betty but at her insistence informs her that what, indeed, happens is 'sex'. Mary Sue/Jennifer, reversing the parental role explains the facts of life to her Mom. Betty, taking her daughter's advice, and fearing George's ignorance in these matters, responds by masturbating whilst taking a hot bath. The pleasure she experiences is enough to set a tree on fire. It also changes her complexion from black and white to colour. At first she becomes anxious that this will be noticed so she allows David/Bud to help apply makeup to hide the change. But, the change is permanent with far-reaching effects and thus, one day, when George returns home, his call, 'Honey, I'm home', receives no reply.

Pleasantville's suburban good old boys feel threatened by the changes going on around them. They experience a thunderstorm for the first time whilst they are at the bowling alley. Declaring, 'We're safe now. Thank goodness we're in a bowling alley!', they agree to do something about the situation. Doing something means separating the 'things that are unpleasant from the things that are pleasant'. This involves the Chamber of Commerce setting out a code of conduct forbidding everything they do not like. The eighth and final point of the code reads, 'All elementary and high school curriculum shall teach the non-changist school of history, emphasizing continuity over alteration.'

The film's epilogue provides one further neat symmetrical twist to the tale. At the film's conclusion, Jennifer decides not to return to the present preferring instead to pursue a 1950s College career as Mary Sue Carter. David does return and finds his suburban mother, Mrs Wagner (Jane Kaczmarek), upset. David's Mom is the inverse of pre-liberated Betty Carter. Whilst Betty was a domestic goddess in a 'comfortable concentration camp', single mom Mrs Wagner is free but feels her life is empty and not as she had hoped it would be. In helping Betty Carter hide her newly coloured flesh and hence her new life, David had helped apply her make-up as a mask. In consoling his own mother back in the 'real world', David helps her remove her make-up so she can see the person she really is.

As we have seen, Robert D. Putnam expresses grave concern over the long-term decline in community, measured in terms of the diminution of civic engagement, social action and social capital. However, *Pleasantville* seems to be concerned with the consequences of the obverse of decline offering a critique of the excess of community that requires unquestioning conformity. Pleasantville is a suburb marked by comprehensive civic engagement. However, it is dull, unchanging, stultifying, two-tone in colour and culturally one-dimensional. The director and writers are also clever enough to suggest in the early part of the film, that is before David and Jennifer are teleported to 'Pleasantville', contemporary multi-coloured – although ethnically white – American community life might be conformist too.[22] For example, whilst Jennifer is clearly a highly popular figure, David is something of an outsider; his nerdish status, contrasted by his sister's popularity, sets him aside.[23]

Against the tyranny of Pleasantville's total community, David/Bud articulates a different creed that is less in keeping with the suburban dream and more in keeping with the American Dream. When called upon to defend himself before the Chamber of Commerce Town Hall meeting he says,

> I know you want it to stay pleasant around here, but there are so many things that are so much better like silly or sexy and dangerous. And everyone of those things is in you, if you just have the guts to look for them.

By the time that David/Bud leaves, the town and townsfolk are fully coloured.

Conclusion

I have suggested that *Pleasantville* seems to offer a critique of the excess of community that prioritizes security over freedom and conformity over difference. But what type of community is it that needs codes of conduct to police it? Surely, codes of conduct relate to clubs, secret societies, cults and sects? This suggests another reading of *Pleasantville* – that is, whilst Pleasantville, like William Whyte's Park Forest suburb, wears the drapes of community it is actually anything but one. Perhaps, contrary to my initial reading, *Pleasantville*/'Pleasantville'/Pleasantville suffers not so much from an excess but an absence of community. This apparently perverse reading is consistent with the ideas of the French philosopher and critic Jean-Luc Nancy, published in *The Inoperative Community* (1991).[24]

Nancy turns the received wisdom of what constitutes community on its head in two ways. The first concerns the impossibility of defining a

community in advance. The conventional way of thinking about community might be characterized as follows. When an outsider approaches
a community its members induct him/her into it. They inform the outsider that 'this is what we are, this is what we do and this is what
guides us; this is what defines our community.'[25] But, for Nancy, this
is not an articulation of community but of society. He argues that for
community, unlike society, there is no underlying foundational basis;
'community is presuppositionless' (1991, p. xxxix).[26] Community does
not need explaining and cannot be explained.

The second concerns a confusion between 'sameness' and 'in-
commonness'. Whilst community, as conceived by the inhabitants of
Pleasantville, is about the members' unity and their sameness, for Nancy
community is defined by 'in-commonness'. Within any particular set
or group – objects or people – 'in-commonness' logically implies difference but sameness does not; sameness implies identity. Acknowledging
'in-commonness' necessarily also means acknowledging 'difference' or
something that is not held in-common and the possibility of acknowledging that we share something 'in-common' requires a consciousness
of difference. There are, to be sure, differences in Pleasantville but these
are the social differences of gender roles, occupations or statuses. The
difference of which Nancy writes is the 'possibility of difference' itself;
'things' might be different. Pleasantville's citizens have no consciousness
that anything can be different and therefore, in Nancy's terms, it is not
a community.

Nancy argues that the ultimate evidence of the 'possibility of difference' can be found in the events of birth and death. He argues that '[. . .]
what community reveals to me, in presenting to me my birth and my
death, is my existence outside of myself' (ibid., p. 26). Births are planned
(sometimes) and anticipated (hopefully). Few people expect their lives to
be untouched – emotionally, cognitively, materially – by the arrival of
a child. Children are notoriously self-centred. When they are young the
world, and especially their part in it, seems ready-made and complete. It
is only as they grow up that they learn that there was a 'different' world
before them. Likewise in death; although the deceased's contributions
to life are remembered and, after a fashion, live on, new opportunities
for those surviving also arise. Birth and death, presence and absence,
reveal the possibility of difference and that means the possibility of or
for community.

An obvious, albeit by now a hackneyed, example of the significance
of death for community is suggested by the impact of the death of Princess Diana in a road crash in Paris on 31 August 1997 that produced a

major outbreak of mourning in Britain and elsewhere.[27] Prime Minister Blair described Diana as 'the People's Princess' and millions of people expressed their grief in public.

On the day following Diana's funeral, the British national Sunday newspaper, *The Observer*, ran the front-page headline: 'The nation unites against tradition' (*The Observer*, 7th September 1997, p. 1). Its editorial, echoed by those of other papers, warmed to this theme using phrases such as 'Princess Diana is and was a collective national property', 'the scale of the collective response and the feeling shared by her millions of mourners' and 'a new culture of intimacy'. The point being made here is not that the 'people' had lost someone, Diana, but they had found something; a collective response, a new culture of intimacy. This gain was not planned. Using Nancy's terms, the community – the collective – did not 'operate' or convert or translate Diana 'into some communal intimacy' (ibid., p. 15). Indeed, for Nancy, communities do not work, they cannot be instrumental or be instrumentalized. On the contrary, in the inoperative community, the community creates itself; here through Diana's death. Nancy writes, 'Community is revealed in the death of others; hence it is always revealed to others' (ibid., p. 15).

Diana's death brought about what Nancy, following Georges Bataille, calls an 'unleashing of passions'. This is not a private affair, far from it. Nancy writes, 'The presence of the other does not constitute a boundary that would limit the unleashing of 'my' passions: on the contrary, only exposition to the other unleashes my passions' (ibid., pp. 32–3). What *The Observer* calls 'collective response', the 'new culture of intimacy' and the 'new democratic spirit' are amongst countless other phrases used by and through the media that express the 'unleashing of passions'. Through the death of Diana, the British public recognized a new way of thinking about themselves.

However, it is not only death through which the inoperative community is revealed; the presence of the stranger can do this too. In *Modernity and Ambivalence* Zygmunt Bauman writes, 'There are friends and enemies. And there are *strangers*' (1993a, p. 53). He suggests that whilst friends and enemies share a colluding, 'cosy antagonism' (ibid., p. 55), the threat carried by the stranger is different. The stranger is an 'undecidable'. To the border guard's question, 'Who's there? Friend or foe?' the stranger might easily reply, 'I don't know, I'm a stranger here!'

David/Bud and Jennifer/Mary Sue are strangers in Pleasantville whose inhabitants cannot decide whether the youngsters are friends or foes; hence they cannot decide what to do with them, particularly since they have brought something to Pleasantville that had previously been absent. Instead of pleasantness they brought rain, fire, books, ideas, chance and sex. In short, David/Bud and Jennifer/Mary Sue unleashed a passion that coloured the suburb and the suburbanites' black-and-white lives and began to threaten, or so it seemed, the very possibility of their assumed social relations. To resist the threat posed by David/Bud and Jennifer/Mary Sue, the citizens define acceptable behaviour in a code of conduct. However, following Nancy's argument, paradoxically the very existence of a code of conduct signifies the presence of difference and that makes the possibility that community might just break out *more* not *less* likely. Community cannot be codified, it can only be created and lived. Nancy expresses the situation like this: 'So that community, far from being what society has crushed or lost, is what happens to us [. . .] in the wake of society' (ibid., p. 11). The point about the 'unleashing of passions' is that those passions are a creative force out of which new forms of social contacts, new possibilities of social relations can emerge and these are not predictable.

On these grounds, then, it might be argued that Pleasantville does not represent a society that might be characterized as having 'too much community'. By Nancy's measure, it actually has no community at all until the strangers, David/Bud and Jennifer/Mary Sue, arrive in town. By the time David/Bud leaves, Pleasantville has learned that community not only exists when people have the support of one another but the freedom to act as individuals.

Now, if we can use Nancy to invert the presumption that *Pleasantville* is about 'too much community' what can be said about *American Beauty* and the apparent absence of community? Here the possibility for community, it might be argued, emerges when Lester Burnham begins to act differently. Carolyn, Jane and Lester's boss want him to behave according to the rules that might never have needed to have been articulated before but were always present. They wanted him to be a normal husband, father and employee. Following Nancy's argument, the society in which the Burnhams, Fitts and Angela are living is predicated on 'sameness', in this case 'normality'. However, to reiterate, sameness and 'in-commonness' are not the same as only the latter logically implies separation and difference. Lester's behaviour challenges the presumed sameness that has been made possible by the characters living in bad faith, by leading inauthentic lives and by not 'unleashing their passions'. In *American Beauty* the death of the old Lester and the birth of the new Lester, even though it leads ultimately to his physical death, creates the possibility for the others to articulate their 'in-commonness'. This is too much for Colonel Fitts, although he did seek out Lester to kiss him, and probably for Carolyn Burnham too, although she seemed prepared to take a gun to Lester. There is, perhaps, more hope that the young generation, their passions unleashed, can sort themselves out, separately and together. There is an opportunity for community.

Thus by the end of the two quite distinct films two new communities have become possible. The releasing of passions that is key feature of each film has taken the characters of the conformist society of *Pleasantville* and the inauthentic society of *American Beauty* to the verge of community. Further, I would argue that these films are not only examples of 'smart cinema' but also, in the terms set out by Emmanuel Levinas and Zygmunt Bauman, ethical cinema as I discussed in Chapter 2 above. In each film moral responsibility '[...] the most personal and inalienable of human possessions, and the most precious of human rights [...]' has been reasserted in the suburbs (Bauman, 1993b, p. 250).

4
Class, Gender and Communitarianism

Introduction

This chapter explores a particularly significant moment in late twentieth-century British political history and culture. Between 1994 and 2000 a small but distinctive set of commercially successful British films were made, depicting working class communities facing a struggle to survive the macro reshaping of the heavy industry infrastructure taking place in the North of England. *Brassed Off* (dir. Mark Herman, 1996), *The Full Monty* (dir. Peter Cataneo, 1997) and *Billy Elliot* (dir. Stephen Daldry, 2000) presented not only a critique of Thatcherite individualism but also a reappraisal of traditional working class political action and an endorsement, either explicitly or implicitly, of the 'value of the community'. The timing of the production and release of these highly popular comedy dramas coincided with the politics of New Labour that came to the fore in the 1990s. The underlying themes of the films are the relationship between individuals and families, specifically with regard to the care of children, the place of the family in the community and the challenge to fatherhood and masculinity. The first two of these were also the key themes of the Blairite communitarian project for the moral regeneration of British society.[1]

I do not want to overstate the certainty of a relationship between the expression of an emerging dissatisfaction amongst the general public, the formation of the New Labour political ideology and the production and popular consumption of a number of films that emphasized community over individualism. However, there are some grounds for arguing that, taken together, these features constitute an emergent structure of feeling.[2] The films' stories do not simply reflect either the declining and emergent political ideologies or the personal experiences of worker redundancy. Nor does the popular success of the films reflect the truth of the stories. However, they are, I would contend, all part of a general interlocking process. Something was happening at this time in Britain and this chapter seeks to articulate just what it was.

From the moment Tony Blair became leader of the Labour Party, and before being elected Prime Minister in 1997, he set out to convert the Labour Party from a class-based party, close to the trades union movement, to a 'one nation' New Labour party. He and other prominent Labour leaders, including John Smith and Gordon Brown, argued that the Labour Party would never again achieve electoral victory if it continued to use the language of class, class activism and socialism. Blair understood that Labour had to attract the support of the middle class. In place of class, Blair emphasized the importance of community as the means for creating a moral regeneration of British society and he put this at the centre of New Labour's political programme.[3] His speeches emphasized the necessity for building a community, a moral community, at local, national and international levels. For example, in Blair's first speech as Party Leader to the Annual Conference of the Labour Party in 1994, 'A Modern Constitution', he said,

> We are the party of the individual because we are the party of the community [...] I want to build a nation with pride in itself. A thriving community, rich in economic prosperity, secure in social justice, confident in political change. A land in which our children can bring up their children with a future to look forward to.
>
> (MacArthur, 1999, p. 502)

Over the subsequent years Blair reiterated this theme, for example, in his Brighton speech, 'The power of community can change the world', addressed to the Annual Labour Party Conference in October 2001 shortly after the attacks on the World Trade Centre and the Pentagon. Blair reminded delegates in the conference hall and television viewers throughout the world that

> In all of this, at home and abroad, the same beliefs throughout: that we are a community of people, whose self-interest and mutual interest at crucial points merge, and that it is through a sense of justice that community is born and nurtured.[4]

For Blair the family is perhaps the crucial institution in the formation of a moral community. Nowhere, in any of Blair's speeches and writings is there the slightest hint that the family is anything other than a natural, and a naturally good, institution. In his 'The Third Way' speech to the 1998 Labour Party Annual Conference he said,

> I challenge us to accept a strong family life is the basic unit of a strong community. For strong families mean a strong Britain [...] the family is central to our vision of a modern Britain built on the kinds of rights and responsibilities that we learn in the home.
>
> (Tönnies and Viol, 2001, p. 144)

Blair regards community and the family as intimately entwined social forms of the utmost importance. Unfortunately, students of film, whether sociologically, aesthetically or historically oriented, have not shared his enthusiasm. As I argued in the introduction to this book, there is a dearth of academic studies of the relationship between community and the cinema and film. This is almost matched by the poor state of academic studies focusing on the family and the cinema and film. Of course, critical studies of melodrama have often examined families, quite rightly, through the prisms of feminism and 'women's films'.[5] There has also been some very interesting work on representations of sexuality in the cinema.[6] Additionally, family matters have been subject to sustained discussion in critical studies of filmmakers, most obviously British director Mike Leigh.[7] However, one has to look quite hard for other approaches. For example, interest in family life on the cinema screen is virtually absent from summary accounts of British films provided by, for example, John Hill's *British Cinema in the 1980s* (1999) and Robert Murphy's *British Cinema of the 90s* (2000).[8] Earlier Lester Friedman's *British Cinema and Thatcherism* (1993), another edited collection, did include a chapter on mothers but it did not substantively address families and family life. The book does, however, contain an interesting essay by Tony Williams (1993) on Terence Davies's films, in which he focuses on gender oppression in the context of the family. Davies's work has also inspired a brilliant and more direct account of family life by Geoff Eley (1995).[9] Deborah Chambers (2001) and Estella Tincknell and Deborah Chambers (2002) provide recent notable exceptions to the general indifference towards families and family life and the cinema.

From Thatcherism to Communitarianism

The collapse of popular support for Thatcherism became increasingly evident during the later years of Margaret Thatcher's government and subsequently throughout John Major's years in office between 1990 and 1997. The Thatcherite valorization of the individual and the spirit of capitalism in its neo-liberal guise became the object of widespread scorn and derision, and the 'yuppie' and 'dinky' lifestyles associated with greed and opportunism were frequently reviled.[10]

Although John Major offered a more emollient, avuncular image, his policies remained cast in the Thatcherite mould. Tony Blair, the New Labour leader and its chief ideologue, was prominent in the critique of Thatcherism. However, whilst Blair was critical of Thatcher's ideology of individualism, he was equally scornful of old-Labour style municipal socialism and left-wing liberalism especially with regard to the family.

> [The political left, in the 1960s and 1970s] developed a type of social individualism that confused, at points at least, liberation from prejudice with a disregard for moral structures. It fought for racial and sexual equality, which was entirely right. It appeared indifferent to the family and individual responsibility, which was wrong.[11]

Thatcher had been strangely ambivalent towards the family.[12] In 1982 she informed Britain through the Downing Street press office that 'Bringing up a family is the most important thing of all', and in 1987 she famously told readers of *Women's Own* (31st October 1987) that 'There is no such thing as society. There are only individual men and women, and there are families'.[13] The view of successive Thatcher administrations was that the role of the state, with its social work and social benefit systems, had taken away from the family the sense of the need to exercise responsibility for caring for children and the elderly. Men and women had to resume that responsibility. However, in policy terms Thatcher's administrations tended to use the idea of the family as a rhetorical hook on which to hang many of their domestic social policies. In practice, many policies, concerning for example freeing-up the labour market and creating the opportunities for 'flexible' employment, actually made it more not less difficult for families, particularly low income families, to function effectively.[14]

Blair's New Labour philosophy regarding the family differed from Thatcher's. Whilst he shared with her the belief that parents must take responsibility for caring for their children, he expressed this in a communitarian rather than an individualist discourse. At the outset of his leadership of the Labour Party Blair said,

> The Tories' view of the family is the same as their view of the individual: you are on your own. But the essence of family life is that you are not on your own – you are in it together. Families work best when their members help and sustain each other. The same is true of communities, and of nations.
>
> Community is not some piece of nostalgia. It means what we share. It means working together. It is about how we treat each other.
>
> So we teach our children to take pride in their school, their town, their country.[15]

Blair's politics begin with noting that the massive structural changes taking place in the world economy are challenging the United Kingdom's economic, political and cultural institutions and are having a direct impact on its citizens, including individuals, families and communities: an impact that the state can only ameliorate.

Drawing on the work of communitarians such as Amitai Etzioni, John Gray and particularly the Christian communitarian, John Macmurray, Blair argued throughout his premiership that the causes of many social problems, for example, crime and unemployment, lie not only with the major social changes taking place but with the absence of a moral community.[16] He argued that in a moral community all members balance an understanding of their social responsibilities with their own particular interest.[17] Blair identified the family as the crucial site on which the development of a moral sensibility crucial to the development of the moral community can be formed.

Paradoxically, whilst it is the case that families and communities are under pressure, it is, for Blair, these same social units that ought to be providing the resources of hope for the individuals and the United Kingdom as a whole. However, the problem is not simply a political or social one. Blair argues that the problem is, fundamentally, a moral one because it is the family, in particular, that forms the moral resource for a society. It is the family that is best placed to balance individual needs and rights with social obligations.

According to Blair, macro social changes inevitably create tensions between individuals, within families and communities. The legacy of Thatcherism is that some individuals, those whom Blair calls the socially excluded will struggle and, despite their best efforts, fail to overcome the problems that the social changes bring because their families and communities are under pressure. Blair was able to demonstrate to the middle classes that they were not immune from the impact of the decline of heavy industries and the restructuring of the service industries. Indeed, as Blair became Prime Minister the unemployment figure for the United Kingdom had risen above 3 million. The promise Blair made to the British voters was that his administrations would help construct the social and moral framework that would provide individuals, within families and communities, with the strength to achieve their ambitions and meet their social obligations and deal with the macro social changes.

This was a promise that British voters found attractive. Whether or not the voting public understood that Blair was offering them communitarian policies they nevertheless voted for them in 1997 and 2001, returning landslide three figure majorities in each case. Even at the 2005 general election, held in the wake of Blair's catastrophic decision to support US President Bush's invasion of Iraq, New Labour was able to secure a substantial majority in the House of Commons.

The films

Tony Blair's communitarian project sought to identify and implement the means by which to persuade parents and children who live in families, especially where the experience of family life has been made difficult by external macro social structural changes, that they are not simply victims. For Blair, families, for which key individuals take responsibility, are the key resource for the moral reformation of their communities and society as a whole. The relationship between individuals, family, community and macro social change articulated by Blair is depicted in a variety of ways in the films produced at this time and here selected for study.

Whether either the producers or audiences of *Brassed Off, The Full Monty* and *Billy Elliot* understood that they were contributing to a proto-communitarian discourse is unclear. Nevertheless, it is the argument of this chapter that they were.

The three films selected share a number of significant characteristics. They

1. represent in a substantial way the impact of macro social change, in this case the privatization of previously publicly owned heavy industries in the United Kingdom, on family life and family relations. The privatization of the previously state-owned steel industry began in 1986 and the coal industry was privatized in 1994;

2. depict a variety of family situations. Of the many families represented, one has a divorce, one is a single-parent family through death, one has a crossing-dressing father and son, one has a wife leaving with the children, one is deeply unhappy following infidelity and alcoholism and two are scarred by personal dishonesty and are childless;
3. represent the relationship between family life and paid work, or the lack or threat to it, as problematic;
4. are set predominantly in the North of England. This is significant in a country stratified by a North/South divide, a divide that Blair chooses to downplay. The cultural specificity is particularly important in the context of community identity;
5. achieved commercial success in the cinema and in the retail and rental video markets. Blair's unparalleled electoral success was matched by the huge box office success of the three films;[18]
6. inhabit a similar time frame in terms of both diegetic time and the time of production. Herman's script for *Brassed Off*, set in 1992, was offered to the producer Steve Abbott in 1994, and Lee Halls' script for *Billy Elliot*, set in 1984/1985 and the period after 1995,[19] was first presented to Stephen Daldry in 1998;
7. demonstrate two aspects typical of post-war commercial British cinema. First, they might loosely be described as having a realist form. Certainly they conform to Raymond Williams' criteria for naturalism, that is the characters, situations and language are all 'natural' although none of the films delivers realism 'straight'.[20] Except for one or two scenes in *Billy Elliot* the selected films do not score high marks for visual pleasure. Secondly, they focus very strongly on class;
8. fail to provide a coherent position for women, particularly middle class women, in the narrative of community construction.[21]

I have had to leave aside some very interesting and important British films from around this time and in which the working class figures prominently. For example, although Mike Leigh's *Secrets and Lies* (1996) and Ken Loach's *My Name is Joe* (1998) are amongst the best films of the 1990s, they do not focus directly on community changes wrought by macro industrial change in Britain.

Individuals and communities

In order to explore the structure of feeling that emerged around the shift in the public's political values, New Labour communitarianism and the films I have chosen to discuss have adopted a narrative-based analytical approach. I have done this not only because these are narrative films but also because each film pivots on moments at which moral choices are made that have both cause and consequence. Specifically, I examine two elements of each film: a key dramatic moment and the ending of each film. I argue that each element provides a potentially different prospectus for the Blair communitarian project in that although each key dramatic moment provides an optimistic reading each film closure is more pessimistic. I demonstrate that although each film resolves some issues about community, they each reveal a tension concerning class and gender, specifically regarding the marginalization of middle class women.

In so far as the films are predominantly realist in form and in thematic terms are saturated by the idea of class, they resemble the films discussed by John Hill (1997) in his important study, *Sex, Class and Realism: British Cinema 1956–1963*, first published in 1986. Hill notes that films of this period fall into one of two types: 'social problem' and 'new wave'. Although the particular qualities of these types need not detain us here, it should be noted that in films of both types the problems encountered by the characters are resolved by the standard conventions of commercial, narrative cinema. In particular, he notes that 'The movement from disequilibrium to a new equilibrium is not, of course, simply linear but also causal [...] For mainstream narrative cinema, it is *typically individual characters* that function as agents of this causality' (ibid., p. 56, my emphasis). Hill goes on to note that where class is a central figure of a film, then '[...] it is presented as *primarily an individual*, rather than collective, experience, a moral, rather than socially and economically structured condition' (ibid., p. 57, my emphasis).

This is the case in the films under review here. In each film, individuals not only 'function as agents of causality' they act on grounds that are personal and moral rather than class or collectivist. Specifically, it is important to note that in each film the action of the individual in making the 'right' moral choice precedes and triggers the support of the community. In *The Full Monty*, for example, the key character, Gary (Robert Carlyle), also known as Gaz, faced with having to make money to sustain his claims for joint custody of his son is prepared to exploit his body and sell it for display as a stripper. His action leads to the formation of a community response.

The situation is more complex in the more politically inflected films, *Brassed Off* and *Billy Elliot*. Both films attempt to reveal that industrial disputes between the National Coal Board (NCB), later British Coal, and the National Union of Miners (NUM), which form the environment of the action, constitute both a collective experience and a socially and economically structured condition.[22] It becomes clear, however, that the dilemmas involve moral decisions for individuals and these take precedence over political ones. In *Brassed Off*, we can see how Phil (Stephen Tompkinson), a character linking three generations of a family, accepts British Coal's redundancy offer rather than continue with the struggle to keep the pit open. His self-defined shame is palpable but he is not alone; the community rallies round. In *Billy Elliot*, we can see how Jackie (Gary Lewis), Billy's father, faced with either continuing with the collective action of the strike or breaking with the strike in order to aid Billy is prepared to opt for the latter. The shame he feels in taking this decision is overwhelming. Luckily his older son, Tony (Jamie Draven), finds a way for Jackie to rescind his action. However, the point is clear, Jackie was prepared to scab on his mates. When the community discovers the reason behind his action it rallies to support him.

Key moments

I define the key moment as the one at which a 'family' member, structurally presented as the central family member but not necessarily the main character of the film, shifts the direction of the whole film by taking responsibility for their family, particularly their children. In each of the films under review a character faces up to a moral dilemma, makes a moral choice and triggers a community response. However, the way in which the characters make the choice and how the community acts varies from film to film.

Brassed Off

Brassed Off is set in Grimley, a Yorkshire pit town, in 1992 when the NCB is seeking to close the mine and make the miners redundant. The redundancy terms are poor. The NCB is conducting an economic assessment of the pit's viability but we learn later that this is a public relations exercise and that it was always the NCB's intention to close the pit. The colliery has a first-rate brass band, represented as a symbol of the community, in which all main male characters of the film play.

The main family in *Brassed Off* is the Ormondroyds with widower Danny (Pete Postlethwaite) as its nominal head but Phil, who is married to Sandra (Melanie Hill) and with whom he has three children, is the one around whom the narrative flows.[23]

Phil is actually presented with a moral dilemma to resolve even before he gets to the 'key' moment I have identified. The dilemma concerns

Sandra and Danny, who is the Grimley Colliery Bandleader. Danny has told Phil to replace his old, battered trombone with a new one. The dilemma is this: should he buy the trombone and thereby support the band and through the band his father and the community, OR should he use what little money he has solely to support Sandra and their children? Now Danny is either oblivious to Phil's predicament or he does not regard it as particularly serious. This places Phil in a difficult situation because he is financially broke. Although he is in employment, he is paying off debts to loan sharks incurred during the 1984/1985 miners' strike. Sandra, who has become increasingly desperate as the family's financial troubles have mounted, becomes angry and distraught when she discovers that Phil not only has made a down payment on a newish trombone and favoured his father and the band but also, crucially, has lied to her. He has put his father, the band and the community before his wife and his children.

Phil's even tougher second dilemma involves him having to decide whether or not he should take the mining company's redundancy offer and use the money to repay his debts. He is conscious that this would involve betraying his union principles and his colleague's trust and, ultimately, might lead to the colliery's closure, his redundancy and the demise of the colliery band. The key moment, then, in *Brassed Off* occurs towards the end of the film. Sandra has left Phil. Phil's father has been taken ill with pneumoconiosis and he, Phil, has been unable to tell him that Grimley Colliery Band has folded. Additionally Phil has voted to take the colliery's redundancy offer and therefore broken ranks, or so he thinks, with his mates. Phil performs his act as a children's party clown, a part-time job through which he supplements the family income, but is clearly mentally unhinged. He tries to take his own life, an act which might be understood as an abrogation of his responsibilities to his family, but at the last moment he cries out for help and is saved by colliery security guards. He is taken to hospital where he meets up with his father. Phil at last addresses his moral dilemmas simply by telling the truth. At the very point when Phil faces up to his failings and the situation he is in, by 'telling the truth', he begins to gain the support of the community.

The Full Monty

The Full Monty is set in contemporary inner-city Sheffield, South Yorkshire around 1996. The main characters are six unemployed men of whom at least four worked in the steel industry. Some of the characters, inspired by a recent visit of the Chippendales to the working men's club, decide that forming a stripping troupe could earn them much-needed money. They persuade the other characters of the opportunities that stripping can offer. After a series of trials and tribulations, the men get their act together and their kit off as members of *Hot Metal*.

The film concentrates on three marriages of which only one involves a child, and it is the actions and motivations of members of this family that the main narrative presents. Gary, something of a late thirties jack-the-lad character, is the main narrative figure. He is shown to be idle, frequently thoughtless, intolerant and sexist; he 'fancies himself'. His wife, Mandy (Emily Woof), manages a local factory, is intelligent and resourceful but impatient with Gary. She has left Gary for Barry (Paul Butterworth), who has a comfortable home, unlike Gary's flat, on a middle class housing estate. Gary and Mandy have joint custody of their son Nathan (William Sharpe) but Gary is not contributing to Nathan's upkeep so she takes him to court in order to secure sole custody. Nathan is depicted as a sensible and sensitive lad who seems to love both of his parents. However, he is shown as being embarrassed by Gary's behaviour.

The film's key moment is that at which Gary, prompted by Mandy's justifiable expression of exasperation with him, begins to realize the seriousness of his predicament vis-à-vis access to Nathan. Gary confesses his inadequacy to Nathan and reassures him that he loves him and that he is serious about dealing with the situation. Nathan immediately rewards his father with a generous gesture, a cash gift from his savings. Initially Gary saw the problem of the joint custody for Nathan as one that threatened his self-interest. However, subsequently he appreciates that his bond with Nathan is a mutual one and its maintenance is in Nathan's interest too. From here on, Gary, with Nathan's assistance, builds *Hot Metal* as a micro-community, which then expands, mysteriously, to merge with the wider community at the film's ending.

Billy Elliot

Billy Elliot is set in Everington in the Durham coalfield during the 1984/1985 miners' strike. The community is shown to be struggling to survive but somehow managing. The film focuses on three families, of which the Elliots is the most important. Jackie, the individual who has to make the moral choice, is a fortyish miner whose wife has recently died. He lives with his two sons, Billy and Tony, and Gran (Jean Hayward), his mother-in-law, in a working class terrace house.

The other families are the Caffreys and the Wilkinsons. Michael Caffrey (Stuart Wells), Billy's best male friend, is depicted as beginning to explore his gay sexuality. The film strives hard to encourage the audience not to see Billy as gay just because he is interested in ballet and Michael's character is crucial in this respect. Billy's best female friend is Debbie

(Nicholas Blackwell), who is shown as fancying Billy but he has no romantic interest in her. Debbie is the daughter of Mrs Wilkinson (Julie Walters), who becomes Billy's ballet teacher. Mrs Wilkinson lives unhappily on a middle class housing estate with her unemployed husband who has had an affair and is a drunk. The special status given to Mrs Wilkinson is demonstrated in a very clever episode in the film in which the audience is encouraged to read her as tentatively assuming the role of Billy's stepmother. Mrs Wilkinson has asked Billy to bring some personal items that might be used to inspire him in an activity for a private ballet class. Billy brings a letter left by his dying Mother that had been intended for opening when he reached his 18th birthday. He has, however, already read it and knows it by heart. Mrs Wilkinson hesitates to read the letter but does so aloud although very tentatively. Her voice gives way to Billy's and then she reads it with him.

Billy's Mum has only recently died and is clearly missed by all the Elliots and particularly by Jackie who is depicted as a caring father but preoccupied by the strike. At first he fails to notice Billy's interest in dancing and even when he becomes aware of it he is not supportive. Tony, Billy's older brother, is decidedly hostile. However, Jackie finally recognizes how important dance is to Billy and, indeed, how talented he is. Mrs Wilkinson has been giving Billy private tuition and has tried to arrange for him to have an audition for the Royal Ballet School. Initially she is thwarted in this by a combination of events and by resistance from Jackie and particularly Tony. However, Jackie accidentally discovers for himself the extent of Billy's commitment and talent. For most of the film Jackie is not depicted as actually confronting a moral dilemma because he is more or less ignorant of what is going on. However, once he learns the truth he has to face a moral choice which he resolves by taking responsibility for Billy even though this might lead to him breaking with the strike and losing the respect of his mates, Tony and, indeed, himself. Tony manages to stop Jackie from scabbing and in doing so he too comes to accept that his father is right and that Billy needs support. This moment leads immediately to the community becoming involved. The family and community raise enough money to send Billy to London for an audition at which he is successful.

In summary, then, the key moment of each film offers itself to be read as involving an individual taking a moral stance that affirms the importance of the family and functions as a moral resource capable of rebuilding a moral community. At first glance, it seems that each film, taken as a whole, can be read as an affirmation of community life. However, a close scrutiny of conclusion to each film reveals that other readings are also possible.

Endings

The narratives of most commercial, popular films tend to come to a conservative conclusion exhibiting what John Hill, drawing on the work of Thomas Elsaesser (1975), has called an 'ideology of affirmation' in which the main problems encountered by the characters are solved (Hill, 1986, p. 55).[24] The films under review seem to be no exception; Grimley Colliery Band wins the National Finals to acclaim from a London Albert Hall audience, *Hot Metal* reveals its potential to the excitement of the audience in the working men's club and, finally Billy flies to freedom above the ballet stage to the awed approval of his father, brother and best mate, Michael. Like the fictional audiences in the Albert Hall, the working men's club and London theatre the cinema audience is positioned to share in the release of tension at the concluding performances. Each film, in short, provides the cathartic narrative pleasures so sought after in mainstream commercial cinema. However, the endings of the films are more complex and more problematic than they at first sight seem.

Brassed Off

The ending of *Brassed Off* is a complicated affair comprising three stages, none of which flout the rules of commercial narrative cinema. The first stage has a touch of magic about it. The band goes down to London to play in the National Finals without Danny, its conductor, who is very ill in hospital. The hospital has refused to discharge him even for the day. However, the band tries to 'do it for Danny'. During the final number Danny appears, as if by magic, at the back of the stage in his band uniform. There is another surprise appearance in the form of Sandra and the children. Sandra has made it all the way down from Grimley to arrive just in time for the band's performance. Through a series of edits the audience sees first Danny and Phil and then Phil and Sandra connected to each other. The suture provides the audience with a viewing position that works to integrate the action for the audience. The band wins and the film could have ended at this point with the family and community, in a sense, 'reunited'.

But it does not end here. When Danny steps forward apparently to receive the prize we are at the start of a second possible ending. Danny upbraids the audience in the Albert Hall, which represents the wider national community, for its indifference to the plight of the miners. He refuses the prize and leaves the stage promising to take the band out on the town. The film could have ended here with a statement of community solidarity and a gesture of defiance.

But the film does not end here either. As the band leaves the stage Jim (Philip Jackson), one of the main figures of the inner core of the band, takes the prize. The scene shifts to an open-top tour bus in the centre of London. A series of little exchanges between the characters indicate the possibilities of new beginnings, very tentatively expressed in the case of Phil and Sandra. The film moves to its end with an impromptu performance of 'Land of hope and (bloody) glory' as Danny puts it. This ultra-nationalist song provides the soundtrack against which two images are juxtaposed. The first of these is the background of the Houses of Parliament, where Thatcherite anti-labour policies had been legislated for the past 13 years. The second is a superimposed printed script outlining the destruction of the mining industry in the Thatcher era. The irony of this ending is clear. Phil's family might, just might, be alright and the community, with the band's victory, has had a welcome fillip. The 'truth' of the situation, as revealed by the script-over, is that the macro-restructuring has not stopped and its effects remain to be dealt with. The Grimley community faces a grim future.

The Full Monty

The night of the performance has arrived! There have been some last minute wobbles in which, for example, Gary is more or less blackmailed onto the stage by Nathan. And there have been some confidence boosting exchanges of trust and truth. But, at last, now, the lads get to perform, 'for one night only', a full monty strip. Magically, again, the performance looks quite professional. This is remarkable for a number of reasons. First, the lads have had little rehearsal time, and there has been no indication of them having the ready cash required with which to buy the appropriate outfit with the necessary Velcro fastening; they do steal some of it from a local supermarket. Secondly, two of the troupe have expressed anxiety about their 'equipment'. Horse (Paul Barber), the irony of the name is telling, confesses to having inadequate 'equipment'. Gerald's 'problem' is that he is easily sexually aroused and he fears embarrassment. Thirdly, and more importantly, ticket sales for the performance have risen above 400 and the club is packed out with working and middle class men and women. Someone, although we have no idea who, has made this possible. The audience includes a whole raft of people who have appeared in the film but who have not obviously helped the troupe, for example the police officers who arrested the lads during rehearsal, social workers and social benefit officers and brass bandsmen.

One reading of the ending is that these people constitute the community that has turned up to affirm the lads' efforts. However, the film gives no indication that these people do in fact constitute a community; they are simply people who live and work in the area. Thus, another reading is that the audience is there, just for the fun; this is a full monty strip after all. And what happens next, after the 'for one night only' full monty? We know that Gerald (Tom Wilkinson) has a new job but will Gary get a job and be able to maintain his maintenance payments? Will he stop resenting his wife's success? Will any of *Hot Metal* make it in the post-industrial world? Will the community provide the support necessary to enable Gary to contribute to Nathan's family life?

Billy Elliot

The technically adroit and affecting end to *Billy Elliot* seems, on the face of it, to be a prime example of the 'ideology of affirmation'. After Jackie has risen to the moral challenge regarding Billy's future and after the community has responded by making it possible for Billy to go to the audition at which he is successful, the film moves forward 10 years or so to a sold-out performance of an all-male Swan Lake in which adult Billy (Adam Cooper) is to dance a lead role. The film presents Billy in the way in which television sports producers present professional boxers. In the wings of the stage the broad-shouldered Billy, wearing a towelling dressing gown, jogs up and down on the spot and releases the tension in his muscles like the boxer his father wanted him to be. He is lit from the front by spotlights but the cinema audience sees him from behind with refracted light silhouetting his figure. In the auditorium Jackie and Tony are seated next to Billy's schoolboy friend Michael and through this magically contrived coincidence, the cinema audience can see the efforts of the community vindicated. But the community is not all present and correct; one character has disappeared from sight. Where are Billy's friend Debbie, and more importantly, her Mum and his teacher Mrs Wilkinson?

The characters who seem to connect most with Billy's aspirations are all female; his Gran,[25] his dead mother, a sympathetic member of the audition panel at the Royal Ballet School and Mrs Wilkinson. Mrs Wilkinson's intervention is pivotal in Billy's development for without her it is impossible to imagine how Billy might have become a dancer. At the point where Jackie tells Mrs Wilkinson that he is going to take responsibility for Billy, he thanks her for everything she has done but from that moment the film only allows Mrs Wilkinson two more brief scenes.

The day Billy leaves Everington to take up his place at school, he says goodbye to a number of characters, including Mrs Wilkinson. She seems cool and matter-of-fact and assures Billy that he'll soon forget her. He says goodbye and she turns to go back to her ballet class, passing through an iron doorway that clangs to after she has left. The audience's last view of Mrs Wilkinson is head down, standing alone in a dark room, backlit by a spot of light so that her facial features are obscured.

In the years between the end of the miners' strike and the *Swan Lake* performance, the audience might assume that much has happened in Everington. Most likely the pit, like the one in Grimley, has been closed down. Jackie and Tony seem fit and well but Gran, who was already very elderly, might have died. Michael seems content with his boyfriend, but who can tell? But what has become of Debbie and, more significantly, her mother, Mrs Wilkinson? Is she still married to her embittered husband? The cinema audience doesn't know and, perhaps, in the euphoric pleasure of the closing shots of the film it doesn't care. The Elliot family of Billy, Jackie and Tony are ok. The possible outsider of the community, Michael, seems ok; he has found a niche. The future is ok. But, what are we to surmise of Mrs Wilkinson's future? What has happened to her? Perhaps, a clue lies in a prophetic scene set on the spectacular 260 metre long Middlesbrough Transporter Bridge as it soars high above the River Tees in which Mrs Wilkinson tells Billy the tragic story of Swan Lake.

> *Mrs Wilkinson*: [. . .] and then one night she (the woman-cum-swan) meets this young prince and he falls in love with her and she realizes this is the one thing that will allow her to become a real woman once more.
>
> *Billy*: So then what happens?
>
> *Mrs Wilkinson*: He promises to marry her and then goes off with somebody else, of course.

My analysis of the films' endings, then, casts a shadow of pessimism over the possible success of Blair's communitarian project. In each case the viability of the community is unclear. In *Brassed Off*, any expressed optimism is undermined by the poignancy of Danny's bitterly militant speech and the ironic juxtaposition of the glory of the imperial past with the 'reality' of the industrial present. Danny's illness will, of course, claim him. The same coal that provided him with a living and an opportunity to play music and occupy a respected place in the community will kill him.

Likewise, in *The Full Monty* there is some optimism created by Gary and the lads working together to form a micro-community and achieving the magic of a professional performance. However, whilst the cinema audience can see that the wider community, such as it is, was present to witness the lads' triumph, it can also see it did not actually support the lads in their preparations. It might be argued that the wider community only performs the role of the audience member invited by the conjuror on to the stage to attest the validity of an illusion.

Finally, in *Billy Elliot* the cinema audience can see how Jackie's heroic gesture provides the community with the opportunity to support Billy and how that community is repaid by Billy's triumphant success. However, the audience is also privy to an outrageous cinematic sleight of hand when Mrs Wilkinson is conjured back to her place. The community can include Michael and his boyfriend but, it seems, neither Debbie nor Mrs Wilkinson.

Marginalizing middle class women

The film's treatment of Mrs Wilkinson's character resonates in the other films, where we can find further evidence of the marginalization of other middle class women. My close analysis of the relationship between key moments and endings of the films reveals that the two structural elements pull in different directions; the former is optimistic and the latter pessimistic. The films' equivocation or ambivalence creates some food for political thought, one aspect of which concerns the relationship between gender and class. As John Hill (1986) and others have noted, the theme of class has had a more or less constant presence in post-1945 British cinema and these films are no exception. This is hardly surprising given the significance of class to an understanding of British society and culture more generally. Since the 1960s, gender has become a focus of at least similar significance.

As I noted in Chapter 1, New Labour's popular political breakthrough came when Tony Blair appeared to be able to reach out to certain sections of the middle class. Blair demonstrated to the middle class that the macro social changes brought about by Thatcherite policies affected them too and, increasingly, for the worse. Additionally Blair also understood that whereas the Labour Party had its strongest roots in the male-dominated heavy industries of mining, steel manufacturing, ship building and so on, the decline of these industries would require New Labour to look elsewhere to garner support. This would involve constructing a cross-class political ideology that women, as well as men, would find attractive.

It is instructive, therefore, to examine how these three films represent middle class women. The central core of characters in each film is drawn from the male working class community; miners, brass band players, the unemployed and trades union members. Individual women are important but their status vis-à-vis the community is problematic. In each film, women take responsibility for children and motivate the children's fathers. In *Brassed Off*, Sandra takes the children from the family home both to feed them and also to protect them from witnessing serious marital strife and the violence of the loan sharks. In *The Full Monty*, Mandy asserts that Nathan's best interest is not being served by allowing dissolute Gary to have influence over his life. In *Billy Elliot*, Mrs Wilkinson takes responsibility for Billy's training and, through an exchange of a letter, becomes a surrogate mother. However, in these films it is not the women, but the men, who represent the link with the wider community.[26] Indeed, the women's actions might be seen as separating children from the community and might, therefore, be construed as divisive. In this regard, the films are unashamedly conservative and patriarchal.

I ended the previous section on the films' endings by noting Mrs Wilkinson's absence from Billy's triumphant performance. She is not the only middle class woman with whom the films' struggle. In each case the women occupy, at best, ambivalent places. They are represented as isolated, having little or no middle class extended family, friends or neighbours. The films do not allow the cinema audience to gain an understanding of middle class life except in the context of being the other to working class life. Despite the fact they are very important to the plots, they cannot find a secure place in the community and one woman can find no place at all. Perhaps this should not really be surprising. It certainly vindicates Iris Marion Young's scepticism regarding the presumption that community implies unity to which I referred in Chapter 1. Young writes that those motivated by community, '[...] will tend to suppress differences among themselves or implicitly to exclude from their political groups persons with whom they do not identify' (1990, p. 300).

Commercially successful, mainstream cinema has its share of films in which the narrative resolution is unsatisfactory. The classic genre most frequently cited in this regard is film noir. Annette Kuhn, for example, argues that in such films, '[...] there is always an excess of narrative disruption over resolution' (1982, p. 35). Although these films are obviously not examples of film noir it can, nevertheless, be argued that in each film it is the significant female characters who disrupt the narrative equilibrium by taking the men to the point of having to act and to act contrary to either a principle or a habit. The narrative problem, as it is for film noir, is what to do with women once they have done their narrative work.

Gloria (Tara Fitzgerald) is the leading middle class character of *Brassed Off* and the only substantially drawn female one. She is presented as an ex-working class local girl, the granddaughter of an esteemed Grimley Brass Bandsman and ex-childhood sweetheart of Andy, one of the inner core of the band with whom she strikes up an affair. She has returned to Grimley as a mining engineer engaged by the NCB to report on the viability of the pit but really, as she later discovers, as a public relations device to present a veneer of respectability and show 'good will' during closure negotiations. In narrative terms she is awkwardly placed. In addition to the fact that she provides commercial cinema's apparently necessary love interest, she can be understood as a Thatcher-child. This is certainly how she appears to Andy's mates.

Gloria sits within and beyond the community. She has local working class family roots and she is respected as a musician but she is young, upwardly mobile and 'management'. She causes problems for Andy (Ewan McGregor) as a member of the inner core of the band because she, in effect, tests his loyalty to them. The band's inner core identifies her as an important player in the pit's closure. She protests her innocence and confronts her bosses, who reveal that her report was immaterial to the negotiations as the decision to close the pit had been taken 2 years before. She is compromised by the management, rejected by the miners and guilty of her role in the decision to close the mine. She redeems herself in the eyes of the inner core of the band only when she provides £3000 of her own money to finance the band's performance at the National Finals. Her money is only grudgingly accepted. At the end of the film, this representative of the middle class is reunited with Andy and depicted, tentatively, as included within the band and hence the community. By this time, of course, the community has lost its material basis of existence.

There are two ways of interpreting Gloria's situation. The Blairite approach would be to argue that class is not important. The working class inner core of miners has been sold down the river by the bosses and so has the middle class as represented by Gloria. Everyone is in the same boat and everyone must act together to reach a safe mooring. Gloria has acted morally in offering to pay for the trip. This allows the community to come together. An alternative reading is that middle class Gloria was naive and lost. Her professional and technical approach to assessing the pits' viability was misplaced. She knew that the miners had an agenda, that is to keep the mine open, but had not realized the NCB also had one – to close it. The moral tale here is that people who leave their roots behind or aspire to live above their station are betrayed by their new bosses. Affirming her relationship with Andy and supporting the miners draws her back into her working class roots. Either way, Gloria's middle class status is, in effect, undermined.

In *The Full Monty* there are three middle class characters. Gerald, the ex-foreman at the steelworks, and his wife Linda (Deirdre Costello) live in a semi-detached house on a middle class housing estate, have expensive consumer goods including a home workout gym and enjoy ballroom dancing. He 'collects' garden gnomes partly because he thinks Linda likes them. He has not told her that he had been made redundant 6 months previously. Linda is only briefly present, sufficient enough to demonstrate that Gerald does not really know her and that his relationship with her is vulnerable. However, Gerald's relationship with the group moves from antagonism, through instrumentalism – the lads need a dance coach – to micro-communal mutual respect. The possibility of forming a community that includes the working and middle classes is affirmed by Gerald's participation; at least for one night.

However, *The Full Monty* struggles much more with Mandy, its second and far more substantial middle class female character, who is characterized as another woman causing trouble. Mandy and Gary are so different from each other that the cinema audience might wonder why they had married in the first place. Mandy might have once been part of the community but in terms of work, home and personal relationships she is outside it. Gary is depicted as feckless, boorish, sexist and disingenuous but Mandy is hardworking and honest. She is a successful, upwardly mobile professional who manages a factory. Gary is presented as a victim of Thatcherism whilst Mandy, like Gloria in *Brassed Off*, appears to be a meritocratic winner. Critics have not been shy in critiquing her character. Moya Luckett (2000, p. 95) has described Mandy's femininity as 'shrewish'. Deborah Chambers has described her as ' [...] bourgeois and materialistic' (2001, p. 107) and, with Estella Tincknell, as 'aspirational and economically predatory' and ' [...] a wholly one-dimensional character whose narrative function is to fuel his (Gary's) resistance to the "system" that has emasculated him' (2002, p. 150). I do not see Mandy's personality in the same way as do Luckett, Chambers and Tincknell. Certainly she is aspirational but neither particularly shrewish nor predatory. Nor do I agree that her narrative function is quite as Tincknell and

Chamber suggest. Her narrative function, as Nathan's Mum, is to provide Gary with the 'opportunity' to make a moral choice in favour of his son.

This disagreement not withstanding I do think Mandy's character is deeply problematic. Tincknell and Chambers are correct to argue that

> In *The Full Monty* the celebration of the homosocial seems at times to promise a new kind of masculinity that transcends class – precisely because class identities are linked to work structures that no longer exist. Yet the film's nostalgia for a safe past offers a *largely reactionary conception of community in which women are always on the boundaries and always a threat.*
>
> (2002, p. 150, my emphasis)[27]

Mandy, as with Gloria and as we shall see with Mrs Wilkinson, does exist on a social boundary and does constitute a threat. It is for this reason that I find her presence amongst the 'community' at the film's conclusion discomforting. Her place is as magically contrived as that of everyone else. John Hill (2000, p. 185) describes Mandy's appearance at the end of the film as a form of 'reproletarianization'. This, I am afraid, is to dignify lazy filmmaking with a clever rationalization as there is no hint that Mandy has any residual connection with the 'proletarian' community that she seems to be content to have left behind. It is just as reasonable to accuse Gary and the other strippers of 'deproletarianization', on the grounds they are prepared to form a micro-community – a small business? – to sell their bodies to make money. It might be argued that *The Full Monty* hints, through the character of Gerald, at the inclusion of the middle class within a wider moral community. However, its Blairite communitarian potential is undercut, as I have argued above, by the tenuous and wholly meretricious presence of Mandy in the final scene.

If the narrative resolution of *Brassed Off* and *The Full Monty*, in presenting the future of the female middle class characters as part of a community is unconvincing, then the narrative of *Billy Elliot* is even more so. If the former films offer signs of inclusion, albeit magically created and cosmetically realized, then *Billy Elliot* leaves the audience with no illusions. I have argued above that Billy's *Swan Lake* performance is in part a result of the efforts of his family and in part the efforts of the community. The appearance of Jackie, Tony and Michael at this performance is significant but so too is the absence of Mrs Wilkinson.

I have suggested that these films are patriarchal and conservative vis-à-vis women's place in community and society. It is difficult being a woman in these films, but being a middle class woman is doubly so.

Mrs Wilkinson is depicted as being emotionally separated from her husband and not having a base in middle class society. She lives on a middle class housing estate but she is presented as having no friends, nor neighbours nor extended family. She teaches ballet in the community rooms of the male working class community but she has no contacts with the community. Socially isolated, Mrs Wilkinson does not seek to serve the community, nevertheless, she does so. For it is Mrs Wilkinson who sees Billy's dancing potential, gives him private lessons, acts as a surrogate mum, argues his case with his family and even offers to lend the family money. In return Jackie and Tony are hostile towards her. She belatedly receives Jackie's thanks and, finally, Billy's too. But there is no room for her in the theatre-cum-community to witness his success. She begins the film estranged from her own class and a stranger to the working class community and that is where she remains at its end. She has unwittingly helped remake the community but there is no place for her within it.

The evidence from Tony Blair's speeches and policies is such that I think that he would be happy to see that these films represent male individuals taking responsibility for other family members and that this in turn helps provide the moral framework for the construction of a moral community. However, he might find the representation of middle class women much more problematic. The films reveal that Gloria, Mandy and Mrs Wilkinson are each stuck on the borderline between the privatized middle class and the working class community. This British class borderline is a sensitive one particularly for women trying to find a place in a traditional, industrial working class environment where the certainties of employment are being threatened by outside forces. Gloria, Mandy and Mrs Wilkinson's actions in their borderline places constitute, in Kuhn's terms, examples of 'an excess of narrative disruption over resolution' (1982, p. 35). As such, Mandy and Gloria's presence and, paradoxically, Mrs Wilkinson's absence are disturbing, not only to a cinema audience but also to New Labour.[28] The films locate family lives in 'real' working class communities in Sheffield, Grimley and Everington. They reveal tensions, particularly of class and gender, between those within a community, those who are sometimes in but sometimes out and those who are always out. The tensions or antagonisms provide Blair, and anyone attracted to the idea that moral family life can translate directly into moral community and national life, with a warning; it is not that easy. If there are cracks in the emerging communitarian structure of feeling then this, surely, is one of them. I'll return to the specific issue of women and community in the next chapter.

5
Leaving the Margins: Women and Community

Introduction

In the previous chapter I argued that the communal success, such as it was, of the largely working class male characters populating the com-munitarian films, *Billy Elliot*, *Brassed Off* and *The Full Monty*, was only achieved through the involvement of women. I also argued, however, that the process by which they formed their masculine collective identity and their subsequent action was achieved at the expense of the women's narrative marginalization.

In this chapter I shift attention to two films, *Calendar Girls* (dir. Nigel Cole, 2003) and *School for Seduction* (dir. Sue Heel, 2004), that locate women not only as the central focus of attention but also propose that women acting together can change their own lives in their own interest. Throughout *Cinema and Community* I explore the different ways in which the idea and practice of community has been conceptualised and used, at least as far as cinema representation is concerned. I do this here by drawing on the work of the Italian sociologist, Alberto Melucci, who has written extensively on the subject of self-realization, communication and collective identity and collective action. Working with *Calendar Girls* and *School for Seduction* enables me to explore a different way of thinking about community.

Calendar Girls, a largely US financed film with an 8 million pound budget, received excellent reviews and grossed £20.5 millions in the UK alone in 2004.[1] *School for Seduction*, a British financed film with a 3 million pound budget, had generally poor reviews and hardly registered on the British box-office radar in 2005. *Calendar Girls* had a huge cast of established character actors and two major stars, Helen Mirren and Julie Walters. *School for Seduction* had a cinema newcomer, ex-model Kelly

Brook, leading a cast of good but largely TV-based actors. Nevertheless, these differences should not mask their significant similarity for each film in its own ways presents a way of seeing women's collective action that is a country mile away from that projected by films, such as *Bridget Jones: The Edge of Reason* (dir. Beeban Kidron, 2004), that appear to set the limits of a woman's happiness and fulfilment at her right to get her man.

In discussing the communitarian films, I commented on the fact that the production and popularity of these films could, in part, be understood as being the cultural equivalent of the electoral success of New Labour. Together they signified an emergent communitarian structure of feeling. However, there is only a faint echo of this structure of feeling in *Calendar Girls* and *School for Seduction*. A further substantial difference between the two sets of films concerns the fact that the post-industrial environment which has a powerful presence that is worked into the narrative structure of *The Full Monty*, *Brassed Off* and *Billy Elliot* is entirely absent in *Calendar Girls* and *School for Seduction*.

There is a similarity, of course, in that all films deal in one way or another with gender politics. But even here lies a significant difference in that whilst the communitarian films are focused on notions of masculinity, *Calendar Girls* and *School for Seduction* are more concerned with femininity. For this reason, therefore, it will be useful if, before examining Melucci's ideas about women's collective identity, collective action and community, I briefly consider the relationship between feminism and femininity.

Feminism and femininity

The impact of second-wave feminism in the 1960s and 1970s has been considerable.[2] In the UK and in many other countries equal rights legislation and cultural attitudes more generally have begun to redress the imbalance of gender power a little towards women. Of course, many of the issues that fired second-wave feminism, for example female contraception, abortion and pornography, remain issues subject to debate and sometimes conflict. Nevertheless, 'women's rights' are now firmly on the social agenda and their advocacy constitutes a major force in democratic, political and capitalist systems.

The progress of gender equalization has not been plain sailing. For some feminists the speed of change has been far too slow and its impact superficial. Not everyone – not even all women – welcomed second-wave feminism and there have been numerous criticisms and backlashes. Some feminists have criticized second-wave feminism's tendency to assume a universalising discourse and project that does not take into account other cultural factors such as those associated with different religious belief systems. Indeed, they have queried whether or not it is possible or even desirable for everyone to be a feminist in the same way. It is no surprise, therefore, that second-wave feminism has been followed by a plethora of 'post-feminisms' – meaning either a rejection of feminism or simply 'after' feminism or a kind of disavowal of feminism.

Feminism, its past and future, its merits and demerits, has been the subject of arguments in academic and 'general reader' books, in journals, in political forums, homes and in the media across a range of cultural forms; anywhere, in fact, where people meet to discuss personal and gender relationships and political and economic power. The cinema and film criticism have participated in these arguments. In the UK, critics such as Charlotte Brunsdon (1997), Christine Gledhill (2000), Joanne Hollows (2000), Annette Kuhn (1982) and Laura Mulvey (1989) have produced exceptionally interesting and insightful work on women and cinema. In the context of this chapter, Brunsdon's work constitutes a useful starting point.

In *Screen Tastes* (1997), Brunsdon took issue with universalising feminist critiques of popular television and films' representation of women that do not take into account the way in which the life experiences of women, as audience members, shape their responses to them. Brunsdon was an early writer, Ann Gray (1992) and Dorothy Hobson (1982) were others, who wanted to discuss women's film and television consumption from where women are and not from an abstracted theoretical or political position. She argued, first, that film and television make important contributions, both positive and negative, to the complex ways in which women see themselves, their families and friends and their place in the world. Secondly, she argued, correctly in my view, that the way in which women engage with popular television and film has been influenced by feminism. This does not mean that women necessarily think of themselves as feminists or even in feminist terms, but it does mean that many women's life experiences have been formed in the context of the emergence and development of feminism. It should not be assumed, she argues, that merely because women do not think of themselves as feminists that they do not see the world through feminist influenced eyes.

In 'Post-feminism and shopping films', Brunsdon (1997) turned her attention to two major, successful star-studded Hollywood films that, on the surface at least, did not seem particularly feminist, *Working Girl* (dir. Mike Nichols, 1987) and *Pretty Woman* (dir. Gary Marshall, 1990). By the 1980s, many women felt they had benefited from the positive developments brought about by feminism but that they did not want to lose contact with aspects of femininity that they felt were attractive.[3] Some authors, such as Faludi (1992) and Walters (1995), argued that the adoption of this position, sometimes called 'post-feminism', was actually anti-feminist. Brunsdon rejected this argument and analysed *Working Girl* and *Pretty Women* to demonstrate her case. She described the films' heroines as post-feminist women; neither pre-feminist nor feminist but post-feminist. They choose to use feminism, in a historically post-feminist world, to achieve the things that they could not have achieved in a pre-feminist world but without either embracing all that feminism offers or rejecting everything associated with pre-feminism. They can get the man *and* get the job and achieve self-determination. Drawing on the work of Judith Butler (1990), amongst others, Brunsdon argued that '*Working Girl* and *Pretty Woman* are two films in which the performance of femininity was much foregrounded – to the evident enjoyment of huge audiences, but considerable ambivalence from feminist critics' (1997, p. 86). Thus, in both films, women used clothes and other material goods – and shopping for them – to construct themselves as the women who will be successful. Brunsdon suggested that in each of these films, '[...] something is going on in this girlie space' (1997, p. 101). And the something that is going on is a double movement in which feminism is drawn upon but also disavowed (1997, p. 83). For Brunsdon, this disavowal only matters if one understands feminism as a single, once-and-for-all historical moment, but she does not. She argued instead that the post-feminism of these films is not the end of feminism but a marker of the considerable distance travelled from the representation of feminism in the 1970s (p. 101). It is not the only marker but it is important because it is located at a point where the average filmgoer is actually living, thinking and feeling.

Joanne Hollows (2000), taking up Brunsdon's arguments, is impressed by the fact that Brunsdon's approach can offer '[...] a way out of the impasse of thinking of feminist and feminine identities as polar opposites' (p. 193). She advocates a critical strategy that explores not whether texts deliver the 'truth' about patriarchy to female audiences but whether they can provide a form of address and an account of the world that allows the audience to recognize themselves and their situation (2000, p. 200).[4] More recently, Hollows and Rachel Moseley, in reviewing approaches to the study of feminism in popular culture, have argued that 'Rather than coming to consciousness through involvement in feminist movements, most people become conscious of feminism through the way it is represented in popular culture' (2006, p. 2).

Whether or not *Calendar Girls* and *School for Seduction* might be classified as feminist films is open to debate. However, I think it is interesting to examine whether or not they have something to say to women about women's lives, particularly with regard to the relationship between feminism and femininity, at least as outlined by Brunsdon, Hollows and Moseley. It is also worth considering whether or not these films offer women something to think about in terms of community, collective action for social change and the place of the formation of collective identity. Perhaps they have something to offer men to think about too. More certain, however, is the fact that both films are clearly focused on women's collective action in a way that neither *Working Girl* nor *Pretty Woman* were.

In reflecting on what the films have to offer with regard to exploring the idea of women's collective action, it is useful to return briefly to Iris Marion Young's cautionary argument, to which I referred in Chapters 1 and 4; that is that feminists' dreams of community are idealistic and doomed to disappointment. She writes, 'The dream is understandable [...] because those motivated by it will tend to suppress differences among themselves or implicitly to exclude from their political groups persons with whom they do not identify' (1990, p. 300). To avoid the disappointment of the dreamy ideal of community, Young proposes a politics of difference; a politics that offers an 'openness to unassimilated otherness' (1990, p. 301). This, she argues, involves a radical politics that will '[...] develop discourse and institutions for bringing differently identified groups together without suppressing or subsuming the differences' (1990, p. 320). Her suggestions for a politics of difference provide food for thought, but unfortunately, she notes, the conditions for such a politics do not yet exist.

One way of moving from Young's cultural critique to a cultural politics is suggested by Alberto Melucci. In *Challenging Codes*, Melucci argues that women's experience of

> [...] subordination and entrapment in a body 'other' than that of the dominant culture makes a struggle for emancipation an important, and quantitatively perhaps the most significant, component of the movement's action. However, collective action by women is structured not only around the campaign for equal rights, but for the right to be different as well.

> (1996, pp. 140–1)

For Melucci, such a politics, with its emphasis on a self-reflective form of communication, is practical and achievable. It is not a politics predicated on an idealized or ossified idea of community but one in which community or any form of collective identity is always in the process of being made. It is, therefore, to Melucci I now turn.

Action defining community

I suggested above that, not withstanding the depiction of the formation of collective identities, the films might find it hard to meet the qualifying standard set by some feminists. The films, for example, do not present major set pieces in which feminist politics is discussed. Instead, they are happy to play with the idea of the female body in terms that seem to be quite consistent with dominant patriarchal discourses and present all the major female characters as white and heterosexual and so on. Whilst a number of the marriages depicted by the films are in serious difficulty, indeed in some cases they collapse irretrievably, the actual institution of marriage is not challenged. Despite this it is worth noting that all the major characters who drive the narrative forward are women and that the focus of each film is women, their relationships, their collective goals and the work involved in achieving them.

The feminism in the films, nascent though it might be, is not a finished politics but one that is in the process of being made. And it is constructed not in advance but as it is communicated, argued over, proposed, dissented from and even rejected. This idea connects with Brunsdon and Hollows' argument that we should consider popular or mainstream cinema, gender and sexual politics, not from a universalising feminist position forged in the 1970s, but as something that has to be argued for, negotiated over and engaged with in those places where women are actually located.

Melucci rejects claims frequently made in communication or social movement studies that we can understand people's actions simply by referring back to their 'membership' of a community. He argues that, in sociological terms, the manner in which actors inhabit collectivities including communities is neither as interesting nor as important as how they come to do so in the first place. In *Challenging Codes: Collective Action in the Information Age* (1996), he proposes instead a more processual or constructivist approach to understanding collective identities. The sorts of questions he pursues in his studies therefore are as follows: How do people begin to realize that their particular interest is one shared by others; through what processes do people gain/achieve a sense of collective identity and what meaning does this resulting collective identity have for themselves and others; how do people work together to translate this cultural identity into a social movement or community project?

For Melucci, collective or community action is a process in which communication is a crucial factor. The formation process, which proceeds from self-realization to community formation or collective action, is saturated with communication acts in which people articulate or define for themselves and for others the meaning of their actions. This process may be a very messy one because, as he wrote in an earlier article, 'The definition that the actors construct is not linear but produced by interaction, negotiation, and the opposition of different orientations' (1995, p. 43).

The formation of collective identity has both cognitive and affective or emotional characteristics. The process, by definition, involves networks of people in relationships and therefore in communication with each other to achieve, through various ways, calculated ends which, of course, may be reworked over time. In addition, Melucci argues, the formation requires an emotional investment. 'Passions and feelings, love and hate, faith and fear are all part of a body acting collectively, particularly in areas of social life like social movements that are less institutionalized' (1995, p. 45).

Melucci takes this argument further in *Challenging Codes*. In a chapter devoted to the women's movement, he considers the way in which gender politics involves a process of self-realization that frequently emerges out of daily life situations and experiences; out of what he describes as '[...] the slow and uniform repetitiveness of days and gestures, of many silences and few words.'[5] He continues,

> Women's collective action is nourished by these everyday experiences and does not express itself through public mobilizations; it develops through the shared apprenticeship of difference and resistance in everyday times, spaces and relationships.
>
> (1996, p. 134)

Melucci's undervaluing of public mobilization is unfortunate and wrong but his reflections on the many and various ways in which women come to collective engagement through life experiences, both affirmative and contradictory, which they share with other women are well made and pertinent for my analysis.[6] The women of Newcastle in *School for Seduction* and of Knapely in *Calendar Girls* are such women. By the end of each film none of the women have thrown themselves under the King's horse during the Epsom Derby or 'struck' in protest at the low wages paid by the large supermarket. They have, however, through self-realization and communicative action, begun a process of collective identification and they have defined their communities through making them. How they achieved this is the subject of the next section.

Calendar Girls

On the face of it, at the beginning of the two films, the female characters of *Calendar Girls* and *School for Seduction* do not belong to what might normally be thought of as distinct communities or social movements. However, by the end of each film the characters' collective identities, although remaining tentative, have coalesced well beyond the state in which they started. We can see this clearly in *Calendar Girls*.

The basic plot of *Calendar Girls* concerns the attempt by some members of a British rural branch of the Women's Institute (W.I.) to raise money for a new sofa for a patients' waiting room at a local hospital where one of the member's husband has recently died from cancer. They plan to do this by posing naked for their annual calendar. Despite the W.I.'s initial reluctance, permission is granted and the women go on to make over £500 000 of sales and thus wildly exceed their initial modest hope. They also gain national and then international fame. As the women take their increasingly commercial campaign to the United States, strains between the two leaders of the group begin to show and the women bring the campaign to a halt, at which point the two friends are reconciled.

The film, based on real events, begins in Knapely, a quiet village near Skipton in the Yorkshire Dales. The landscape, one of the most beautiful in Britain, is filmed by Ashley Rowe in a lyrical and sympathetic style that underscores the film's characters and events. The W.I. has had a reputation, largely undeserved, as a conservative organization that encourages good works in a rather low-key sort of way and that engages in 'traditional' and 'homely' activities.[7] The women of the film are regular contributors to these activities although it is immediately clear that they find some of them risible. The two main figures, Annie (Julie Walters), whose husband John (John Alderton) died from leukaemia, and particularly Chris (Helen Mirren), her best friend, are shown as quiet rebels. At John's death, Annie and Chris decide to raise money for a new sofa in the hospital's visiting room. Chris hits on the idea for the nude calendar after finding her son's 'lads mag' in his room and, later, spotting a 'glamour' calendar in the local garage.

At the onset of the film the women's collective identity, such as they have, is provided in part by the W.I. but it becomes immediately clear that this will not do. Indeed, the women's first task is to counter the W.I.'s scepticism, bordering on opposition, first at local and then at national level. Their action is consistent with Melucci's suggestion that we cannot simply look to membership of communities to explain the formation of a collective identity. The women are inspired to act not by the W.I.'s mission statement but by Annie and Chris's desire to link a formal recognition of John's life with a facility that will help other people who will, with dreadful certainty, need to make use of the hospital waiting room.

The experience of appearing naked in public or before the male photographer charged with producing the calendar images is new to each of the women. That the calendar is produced is due entirely to the support and encouragement the women give each other. Their hesitancies and changes of mind are resolved, as Melucci might note, by them talking to each other and reminding themselves of what they want the production of the calendar to achieve. It is through this process of providing mutual support, sharing, cajoling and persuading that the women not only produce the calendar but also produce their collective identity. And this process has its cognitive and affective aspects. Each of the women can compute the financial gain to be made from their participation and can take pride in this but they also experience the emotional cost of losing some element of privacy and even dignity. Much of the central section of the film is concerned with working out the fine balance involved between rational and affective human qualities and it does so with humour but also some regard for the nature of the commitment the women are making.

An unknown reviewer at Palo Alto Online claimed *Calendar Girls* ' [. . .] strikes a chord for post-menopausal feminism that rings loud and clear.'[8] I think there is something in this claim. If by feminist the reviewer means 'strong women' acting together to achieve a specific end in their own interest, rather like the 'miners' wives' did in the national coal strike of 1984/1985, then the film is a feminist one. The force of this argument might be countered by the observation that the means chosen to achieve the end, that is posing for a nude calendar, only panders to male curiosity or even prurience.

However, looked at in Brunsdon and Hollows' terms, even this point could be reversed. It might be argued that not only does *Calendar Girls* examine the relationship between feminism and femininity centring on sexuality and the body, but it does so in a way that allows the audience, at least the female component, to recognize themselves and their situation in the films. The director, Nigel Cole, and writers, Judith Towhidi and Tim Firth, take care to ensure that the female characters address the idea of nudity and the body. They discuss, sometimes in roundabout ways, the difference between pornography and art, the boundaries of taste and the commodification of the body. The actual calendar images are asexual, in that the poses struck bear no resemblance to the imagery found in the red top tabloids or in men's soft porn magazines. There are no crotch shots, no leg shots, no breast shots and no bedroom shots. The women are depicted watering their indoor plants or engaged in other domestic activities that illustrate Melucci's words concerning '[...] the slow and uniform repetitiveness of days and gestures, of many silences and few words' (1996, p. 134).[9] The women's hesitancies and reservations over their nakedness are clearly marked but collectively overcome.

This is particularly striking in the context of the fact that most of the characters and many of the female actors are in their fifties and sixties.[10] Whilst the film makes much of the potential frisson of excitement offered by the calendar's production it always undercuts this through humour, largely expressed by the female characters. Thus on being asked to appear in the calendar, Cora (Linda Bassett) a café proprietor, church organist and W.I. pianist, says, with typical Yorkshire bluntness, 'I'm 55 years old, so if I'm not going to get 'em out now, when am I?' Jessie (Annette Crosbie), an ex-primary schoolteacher somewhat older than Cora knows where she will draw the line. She says, 'What I mean is, no front bottoms. They're reserved for just one man in my life.' Asked if she thought her husband would mind, she replies, 'It wasn't my husband!' Celia (Celia Imrie), a determinedly middle class lady who golfs and who works out in the gym with a personal trainer, is concerned that her self-described 'magnificent breasts' will not get enough exposure. She also confesses that she hasn't ever appeared naked in front of anyone, not even her husband Frank. She points out, 'Frank's a Major. We approach nudity on a strictly need to know basis.'

The use of humour as a means of avoiding charges of voyeurism is reinforced by suitably discreet cinematography evident in the scenes in which the somewhat bashful and reluctant photographer is at work. These, in turn, match the discreteness of the calendar images. The audience is rarely given a privileged point of view shot that might undermine the integrity of the project. Only, when the women reach Hollywood does the direction slip a little as we see the women 'glamming up' for television. For example, Ruth (Penelope Wilton) is photographed pulling on a pair of black hold-up stockings in a manner typically framed for a male gaze. Even this might have a point in that the women are now operating in a different environment, where they are no longer in charge of the production of their images.

Ruth is actually one of the more interesting figures in the story. She was the most reluctant of the group to join for although sympathetic to the project she could not come to terms with the need for nudity. A sub-plot of the film concerns her growing awareness that her husband is cheating on her. Left, yet again, for a carpet convention her husband says he must attend, Ruth gravitates towards the group and agrees to be photographed. On discovering her husband's infidelity she throws herself wholeheartedly into the project and subsequently gains in personal confidence and, in turn, this serves to reinforce the group's strength.

The struggle involved in producing the calendar has required all of the qualities described by Melucci. The movement from each woman's self-realization of who she is and what she wants to achieve through to collective identity with all the negotiations, upsets and so on has been messy. The women's self-image as feminine has been held in balance with the necessity for them to be strong and purposeful, a necessity that has its cognitive and emotional components. The production of the finished calendar constitutes a strategic statement of the newly formed women's communal identity.

However, just at the point at which the calendar's success becomes apparent the group dynamics begin to change. For if Ruth's actions can be seen in a positive light in terms of the women's collective identity, the same cannot be said of the falling out between Annie and Chris. Although Chris has been the leader in the project – it was her idea and it was her speech to the W.I. national convention that won approval for the calendar – she begins to lose touch with the project's sentiment. For example, rather than obtain sponsorship with the seed company with whom John did business, Chris makes a deal with a brewer, even though John did not drink beer. When Annie mildly remonstrates with her friend about this, Chris tells her 'It's not about the beer, Annie, it's about the money.' Chris starts enjoying being in the public spotlight, she is proud that she has been the point of contact in setting up the US trip. Her redefinition of the project and her relationship with it is made all the clearer by the fact that her enthusiasm for the US trip seems to outweigh her concern for her 15-year-old son, Jem (John-Paul Mcleod). He has felt embarrassed by his Mum's activities and, indeed, his welfare has slipped below her radar. Jem and his pal, Gaz (Marc Pickering), are arrested for smoking weed but released by the police because the weed in question was not marijuana but oregano. Despite Jem's difficulty, Chris seems intent on going to the States until Annie persuades her that it would not be in Jem's interest to do so. She changes her mind yet again following an argument over a mix up between her husband and the tabloid press.

Chris pursues the money but the other women, and particularly Annie, draw the line at making an advertisement for washing powder that, once again, involves them being naked. The scene in which Annie walks off the set of the film studio where the advertisement is being shot brings the film to its dramatic climax. The visual framing represented by this development in the story is stark and contrasts with the way in which the production of the original calendar in Knapely was shot. There the women were at 'home', the country scenery was glorious and the interior set designs were in warm tones emphasizing the organic relationship between the women, their environment – both internally and externally – and their project. The integrity of their collective identity was expressed visually and it was reinforced by the humour involved in the amateurish but effective low-key photo shoots.

Hollywood looks different. The women arrive at the photo shoot against a fake skyline and they proceed to a large, brilliant whitelit, cavernous and empty studio. It is impersonal and the women look lost. The theme of loss is developed as Annie and Chris have a dramatic row in the backlot of the studio against the cardboard cut-out city sets familiar from every gangster and noir movie of the 1940s and 1950s. As Annie flees the pursuing Chris she reiterates her sense of being lost, both physically and in terms of the project. When Annie finally stops, the director presents them as two protagonists. Chris is angry with Annie, 'You can't stand that *I've* made this calendar a success.' To which Annie retorts, 'No, you see Chris, this calendar has made *you* a success.' As Chris's bewilderment and anger rises, she makes reference to the fact that Annie is constantly writing letters to those who have written to her about their own bereavements.

Chris: What's with all these letters, eh Annie? All this bloody Florence Nightingale turned agony aunt. Doesn't that smack just a little bit of being a star. You know loads of people lose their partners to this disease. I bet they don't get fan mail. Doesn't that make you a little bit of a success? A very successful bereaved woman? A celebrity widow? St. Annie of Knapely? Eh? Eh?

Annie: I'm not a saint because I'd rob every penny from this calendar if it would buy me just one more hour with him. You've got yours (husband) and you're in Hollywood. (She cries)

Here, then, is the crux of the drama. But it raises an important question mark about the film's credentials as one in which collective identity is explored. At what point did it happen that the campaign somehow got out of control and the emotional reason for campaigning became lost in the columns of the accountancy books? When did the women stop talking to each other honestly about the group? At what point did the women lose their collective coherence? And finally when did the possibility of constructing a social movement out of collective identity disappear?

By this stage *Calendar Girls* has long since stopped being a film about the construction of collective identity and become a buddy movie. The other women are still there but making smaller and smaller contributions to the collective whole. Effectively this transformation happened when the original calendar was published and Annie and Chris began to deal with the media and make plans for developing the project. The sub-plot concerning Ruth did give some strength to the collective but she did not join the women merely because they wanted her to but because her husband had, in effect, abandoned her. By the time we get to the end of the film, the focus of the drama is not whether or not the group as a whole has a collective identity but whether Chris and Annie will reform their friendship. Indeed, apart from a final Tai Chi coda, the film ends with the friendship patched up and the buddies cracking jokes.

The collective identity was formed through the process of the project, but once the project became 'uncertain' the possibility of sustaining the collective identity became uncertain too and the differences between Chris and Annie become tangible.

In Melucci's terms, then, the film does not quite fulfil its promise. A collective identity is formed, on the back of which the possibility of a nascent social movement is created. The Knapely women's self-realization is created in the world of 'everyday experiences' and *does* develop 'through the shared apprenticeship of difference and resistance in everyday times, spaces and relationships' to which Melucci makes reference (1996, p. 134). Nevertheless, it is stopped dead in its tracks as the ordinary life of Knapely is overwhelmed by the extraordinary world of tabloid newspapers, celebrity television and aggressive promotional marketing. In the face of all of this, the women's decision to return to the everyday life of the Yorkshire Dales and the re-affirmation of the integrity of friendship might be understood as a retreat from an engagement with the public sphere. However, the retreat does not have to be seen as a defeat. There is no blue print for self-realization and I think it is quite plausible to see their retreat as consistent with their initial decision to act. They recognized that through their actions they had been successful not only in achieving their material aim but in creating and sustaining themselves as a community.

School for Seduction

In his *Sight and Sound* review, Ali Jaafar notes that unlike *Billy Elliot* and *The Full Monty* with their '[...] shrewd insights into masculinity in the post-industrial north *School for Seduction*'s observations on gender polit-ics, by contrast, are at best inane' (2005, p. 69). I think Jaafar is wrong about *School for Seduction* for it is a film that does have something interest-ing to say about gender and sexual politics, particularly relating to social class, femininity and feminism. It is also interesting, perhaps surprisingly so, when looked at in the context of Melucci's ideas about collective identity and social movements.

School for Seduction concerns a group of mostly working class women from Newcastle, a large post-industrial city in the North East of England. The women for one reason or another feel their lives would be improved by attending the newly advertised 'Italia School for Seduction'. The School is run by Sophia Rosselini (Kelly Brook) who herself has recently graduated from a similar one in Italy before leaving her husband to go to Newcastle. The women gain self-confidence but Sophia is exposed as a non-Italian woman from Newcastle, whose real name is Gillian Hende-rson, and who has adopted a false persona to earn a living after fleeing from her abusive Italian husband. At first the women feel betrayed by Gillian's disguised identity but come to realize, through their new found strength inspired by her teaching, that they should support her and protect her from her husband. He is sent packing.

Too often British films concerning social class and particularly com-edies, such as *Up 'n' Under* (dir. John Godber, 1998) and *Little Voice* (dir. Mark Herman, 1998), present leading characters, both male and female, as stereotypes. Such characterizations, often in the traditional form of the theatrical grotesque, function to confirm audience attitudes towards ineffectual men and strong women in what are essentially filmic equival-ents of Donald MacGill postcards.[11] *School for Seduction* does indeed have its quota of stereotyped, grotesque male characters, only one of whom, the fish-and-chip shop fryer, has anything like a textured or nuanced identity. However, there is much more to the main female characters than this and most of them, in their own way, have the capacity to engage the audience in their everyday experiences and relationships at home and at work. These are characters that, for the most part, could step out of classic British realist TV dramas such as the soap, *Coronation Street*, and the series, *Clocking Off*. There is also earthy humour with some witty dialogue and sharp one-liners. With Geordie dialect and pronunciation to the fore, very rapid speech delivery and a strong emphasis on energetic group chat, the language sounds 'natural' and convincing. The writers,

Sue Heel and Mark Hebron, have also taken the trouble to provide the women with some back-story so that when events occur they do not leap out of character.

The visual power of the film, such as it is, lies almost entirely in its convincing capture of small group scenes in natural locations, such as clubs, pubs, living rooms and canteens. The camera serves the dialogue not only through the rhetoric of shot/reverse shooting, but by capturing the intimate and complex speech patterns particularly through the use of mid-shots. The visual editing style is frequently rapid and this also serves the highly charged dialogue very well. The film's audio style is effective but pedestrian. Non-diegetic music serves to signal location and mood. The now common use of popular songs as sound track works well enough, albeit very predictably. The predominance of vernacular and accented speech requires a recording sufficiently clear and clean to enable the audience to follow the dialogue and this is achieved. Sometimes sound is cut to precede visual cuts to provide a flowing introduction to new scenes. The strength of the film, then, lies in its naturalism, in terms of language, location and events.

In this context it is useful to compare the naturalistically presented 'fictional' Newcastle women with those who are the subjects of Beverley Skeggs' important longitudinal, ethnographic study, *Formations of Class and Gender* (1997). Skeggs conducted interviews with 83 working class women from the industrial North West of England over an 11-year period but mostly between 1983 and 1992. She discovered that the women's attitudes towards both femininity and feminism had been shaped in some measure by the various representations of femininity and feminism in popular media. Most of the women distanced themselves from the idea that they might be feminists. However, her research also demonstrated that these attitudes were refracted by their class position and Skeggs cited the particular significance of education, jobs, leisure opportunities and sustainable incomes. She convincingly showed that the discourse of class respectability was particularly important to them. The women interviewed were conscious of the fact that they were always being judged by their neighbours, by the authorities and by men in terms of their domestic arrangements, speech, clothes and respectability, a key feature of working class life. Some women embraced the discourse whilst others resented it deeply. Thus, for example with reference to clothes and respectability, one of the respondents, Anne, told Skeggs:

All the time you've got to weigh up: is it too tarty? Will I look like a right slag in it? what will people think? It drives me mad that every time you go to put your clothes on you have to think "do I look dead common? is it rough? do I look like a dog?"

(1997, p. 3)

In researching the women's attitudes towards femininity and feminism Skeggs asked her respondents about 'glamour', an important concern for women, particularly the young. A number of respondents spoke about this but Fiona's contribution was incisive:

You know it when you see it, sort of well put together and looking sexy but not tarty or obvious. There's nothing vulgar about being glamorous. It's good when it works, if it doesn't you just look stupid. I think it's also about attitude and the way you do it. I think you have to feel good to look glamorous. It's also then about how confident you feel. You can always tell glamorous women, they're dead confident about themselves.

(1997, p. 110)

I do not want to make too much of these remarks since I have selected them from Skeggs' own selection. However, Fiona's comments are convincing and are echoed loudly throughout the film. Sophia Rosselini's first conversation is with Clare Hughes (Dervla Kirwan) who has recently been promoted assistant manager at the Hotel that Rosselini is viewing as a potential venue for her 'Italia School for Seduction'. They strike up a conversation that turns to the subject of glamour:

Rosselini: I say not to be afraid of glamour. Time to bring it back. [...] Too long it has been the feminist or the feminine, eh? There's no need to choose. One can be both. This is what I intend to teach.

Clare tells Rosselini that if she went home and tried to seduce her husband, Craig, he would probably think there was something wrong with her. Rosselini responds in terms that echo de Beauvoir's famous aphorism quoted on a caption at the beginning of the film, 'One is not born a woman, one becomes one'[12] and resonates with Judith Butler's (1990) thoughts on performativity. She tells Clare 'You can be whoever you want to be. It's not up to others to choose for you.'

We can also hear Fiona's words later when, addressing the students attending the School's first session, Rosselini reflects on the relationship between seduction and confidence.

Rosselini: Seduction is not about pleasing men. It is about pleasing yourself. When, and only when, you are able to feel good in yourself then others around you feel good. Confidence, that is the true art of seduction. Confidence is the key word. It is a word I want you to repeat always in this class and to yourself like a mantra. Master this and the world is at your feet.

Skeggs' respondents revealed a whole tranche of attitudes towards men and masculinity. One woman sought legitimation or validation not by having a boyfriend but from the idea that she can get one. Another expressed the disappointment from a lack of validation because she fears her husband 'no longer "fancies" her' (Skeggs, 1997, pp. 111–13). These concerns and attitudes also resonate throughout the film. For example, Clare Hughes's husband Craig (Neil Stuke) belongs to a 'Spider Car Club'. He is much more interested in his red car which he keeps under a red light in his garage and drives wearing a red satin jacket. He speaks of the car in sexual terms, 'This is fifteen foot of absolute sex appeal. Someone will nick her out of pure lust.' Long-suffering and neglected Clare attends the class where she meets other heterosexual women who are all, for one reason or another, looking for some validation in their lives.

Clare's sense of disappointment and dissatisfaction are qualities experienced by the other three main working class female students, but for different reasons. Donna (Jessica Johnson) is single, likes a good time and is 'up-for-a-laugh'. She works as a supermarket checkout assistant, earning the money in the week that, she says in self-critical terms, 'She wastes at the weekend.' She possesses a keen wit, a sharp tongue and a belligerent disrespect for authority; parents, boss, anyone really. Her style of dress is what the women in Skeggs' study might call tarty. Nevertheless she is revealed as being dissatisfied with her lot and is looking for something better.

Her older sister Kelly (Emily Woof) dropped out of University when she became pregnant with Lucy, her now adolescent daughter. She is a single parent juggling two jobs, one at the supermarket, where she has junior supervisory responsibility, and the other behind the counter at the chip shop. Lucy (Nicola Blackwell) thinks Kelly 'Is the worst Mum in the world' because she won't give her everything she wants. Unfortunately Kelly's boss Brian (Nick Whitfield) is giving her more than she wants. On the one hand he wants to take her out but on the other he is fearful that she might pip him to the Deputy Store Manager's job that is just now being advertised. She is careworn and tired.

Irene (Margi Clarke), who is a generation older than the others, runs the successful fish and chip shop with her husband Derek (Tim Healy). She appears confident. Like Donna she likes a good time but finds Derek a little tame. Donna tells Irene about the class and she enthusiastically embraces the opportunity. Irene and Derek's son, Mark (Daymon Britton), is leaving for university but is intent on taking a gap year to 'discover himself' by working in Ghana. He asks Derek to lend him some money but Derek insists on him working in the shop for it. Here he meets Donna and they form a relationship, although not one without its difficulties.

As they attend the classes the women begin to gain more confidence. We see them talking about their problems and we see them trying to address them. They realize they are not alone and that other women are as unhappy as they are. The class becomes a site for their mutual support. As in *Calendar Girls*, the women of *School for Seduction* are trying to understand situations that are making them desperately unhappy. For each of them, the personal is definitely political. Thus, for example, Clare is desperate to make her car-loving husband notice her and take her seriously. No matter what she says or does he seeks to undermine her confidence. He blames her new job promotion for taking her away from the home and her domestic responsibilities. Clare says to Sophia, 'I shouldn't have to apologise for my success, should I?' She repays Craig by having his car crushed and dumped in his bed!

Donna tells Kelly of her despair about the way she's wasting her life and sees in Mark a person who has ambition to do something 'worthwhile'. She seduces him but they fall out when Mark seems to imply that his relationship with her is not worthwhile. He retrieves the situation first by apologising for his patronising assumptions and high-handed self-regard and second by offering to support her in her ambitions.

Brian steals Kelly's good idea for introducing a family friendly rota for the supermarket staff and, worse, tells her there is no point in applying for the Deputy Store Manager's job because he will tell the managers that she is a poor employee. Kelly takes courage and with the support of the other women turns the table on him by manipulating him into a compromising situation with Toni (Ben Porter), a male transvestite/drag artist, who also attends the seduction class.

Irene is a powerful personality who shapes the family home and life in her image; however, she is mortified and shamed to discover that Derek is unhappy because he feels left out by her. For example, whilst there are many photographs around the home the only one of him is kept in a drawer. He sees her attendance at the class as yet another situation in which she is putting herself first. She has the confidence to recognize that she is in the wrong and seeks to reassure him of her love.

However, more important than the separate developments in their lives the women begin to share a collective identity, not as victims, but as women who feel and think it is possible to take control of their lives. This is amusingly underlined by a scene in a pub, at which his classmates are present, where Toni performs his drag act and sings, 'Yes, I'm the great pretender.' The excessive performance makes it clear that Toni is not pretending to be a woman, but doing what Clare, Donna, Kelly and Irene are doing, that is performing as a woman. His friends comment with pleasure and pride on how much more confident he has become. Their emerging collective strength is first threatened and then demonstrated in a sequence of scenes shortly after they have played their trick on Brian and when they have to come to the aid of Sophia, their teacher.

During the second half of the film, Donna has developed a nagging doubt about Sophia's authenticity and this doubt is spectacularly confirmed when, at the class's graduation evening Sophia's husband, Giovanni, turns up out of the blue. His arrival creates a major crisis and during the chaos Sophia lets her Italian accent slip to expose her broad Geordie dialect. Donna immediately recognizes her and Sophia's personal history is exposed in front of her pupils.

> *Donna*: Oh my God, Gillian! Gillian Henderson! I knew you looked familiar. She was in my class at school. Friggin' 'ell. No wonder you couldn't get those specs off quickly enough the other night. She was a four-eyed little geek. And she was ginger. It's all been an act. What kind of person? Just having a good laugh at our expense.

All the women are angry with Sophia. Only Toni attempts to support her but Donna won't let him, describing Gillian as a liar and a loser. The women leave angrily and Gillian is taken away by her husband; humiliated, dejected and defeated. Ironically all the confidence she has instilled in the women has drained away from her. He is physically and emotionally violent towards her and is intent on taking her back to Italy.

However, thanks to yet another miracle of cinematic coincidence following Brian's humbling, Donna and Toni spot Gillian who has, in turn, been observing them from a car. He says, 'Was that who I think it was?' Donna looks knowingly. As he removes his hairpiece, he addresses her:

> *Toni*: What you've got to ask yourself is 'What would you have been doing tonight [supporting Kelly by tricking Brian] if you hadn't

answered that ad.?' There's more than one reason for putting on an act you know. And I should know.

This prompts Donna to gather the other women and together they drive round to Gillian's house where they arrive just as she and Giovanni are leaving. They implore Gillian to stay. They tell her what a good teacher she is, how she's changed their lives and it had all worked, because it was real. Clare reminds Gillian, who looks broken and confused, of her own words, ' [...] you can be whatever you want to be. Don't let anyone choose for you.' Still, it looks like Gillian is not strong enough to fight Giovanni and she goes off in their car. However, she tells Giovanni to stop the car and tells him 'You don't want a wife. You want a mother.' As she does so, the women assemble on the steps to her house and we see them all, for the first time since Giovanni's arrival, as a united group.

In terms of film quality, *School for Seduction* is distinctly modest. As it moves to a dramatic conclusion its narrative structure creaks and Sue Heel's directorial grip on characterization falls apart. That Sophia, who has had the courage to leave Giovanni once now capitulates so abjectly does not seem consistent with her character. The balance between naturalism and the grotesque – Irene's distinctly Ann Summers[13] approach to seduction, Brian's humiliation, Craig's car – has shifted towards the latter. Nevertheless, the film still delivers on the two fronts I have identified. First, the relationship between femininity and feminism has been broached in a popular form and along lines perfectly recognizable to the middle and working class women depicted in the film and described by Skeggs.[14] The scenes in which Sophia instructs her class in deportment, in being 'sexy' around the house and in undressing are handled with reasonable discretion and a touch of seaside postcard humour, but perhaps not the light-touch assurance of equivalent scenes in *Calendar Girls*. However, the issue of confidence that Fiona, one of Skeggs respondents, identifies is presented clearly as the central theme by the manner in which the women take a grip on their lives. It is a confidence that also allows the women to remain or perform 'feminine'.

Secondly, the women are depicted as forming a collective identity. They do not act because they are *from* a community but in acting together they *form* a community. Their process of self-realization leading to the formation of a collective identity comes out of everyday life; the everyday repetitive, habitual life of the home and work and, for Clare and Kelly, even the pleasure of work.[15] They know there is more to their lives than they are getting either through employment or with their respective partners. The women constantly ask themselves and each other what they are doing and what they can do. At various moments Donna, Kelly, Clare and Sophia/Gillian are at risk from responding to their situations with self-hatred and submission. That they do not is testament to the mutual support of the group. Their male counterparts either cannot help them – Mark and Derek are too confused – or will hinder them – Craig, Brian and Giovanni are bullies who feel threatened. Sophia is the outsider who provides the potential energy for change. But it is also Sophia who needs their collective strength to survive. The Newcastle women, who begin as isolated victims of their men's patriarchal dominance, expressed as disdainful incomprehension or bullying, transform themselves into a collective capable of resisting some aspects of patriarchal dominance. Whether or not they are capable of going beyond resistance to opposition is another matter but their transformation does constitute a victory.[16]

Conclusion

Melucci's approach to understanding collective identities and social movements has proven to be useful in the analysis of the two films. It has allowed me to argue that communal action and the formation of collective identities is a constructive rather than an essentializing process, in which community does not define the action but, on the contrary, the action – self-realization, communication, negotiation and so on – defines and makes the community. The women of *Calendar Girls* and *School for Seduction* began thinking about themselves differently and by communicating about this with each other they found ways to construct collective identities that enabled them to achieve a planned aim in the former case and a spontaneous one in the latter. Although the collective identity of the Knapely women fell away as they moved into less certain areas of promotional marketing and media exposure, the Newcastle women ended the film solid and united.

Understanding collective identification and community in this way addresses Young's concern for the tendency of community, both in principle and practice, to sacrifice difference in favour of a dream of unity. *Calendar Girls* and *School for Seduction* demonstrate that the assumed binary opposition of unity and difference is misplaced. It is possible not only to desire unity or in-commonness but also to accept difference too. Following Melucci, we can understand the formation of a collective identity as a tentative and fragile process with any resulting sedimentation, in the form of 'community', being understood as necessarily provisional but provisionally necessary. Neither film reifies or idealizes community but locates it firmly in a process of realization, communication and action.

Of course, neither *Calendar Girls* nor *School for Seduction*, in exploring the relationship between feminism and femininity at least as outlined by Brunsdon, Hollows and Moseley and experienced by Skeggs respondents, escapes the problem of representing women through patriarchal discourses. However, both films find ways to negotiate through and around those discourses in a manner that does not exclude the majority of a female audience but engages with it. As Ann Gray has demonstrated, women are not just 'products of discourse' (1992, p. 242) but have an active role in negotiating or resisting them.[17] For example, *School for Seduction*'s Craig and Brian are characters only too familiar to far too many women. The evidence from Skeggs, supported by Brunsdon, Hollows and Moseley, is that their 'come-uppance' would be devoutly desired and the pleasures derived from the women's collective success would be treasured.

6
Honour and Community in Multicultural Britain

Introduction

In recent years, British print and broadcast journalism has been consumed by a series of connected debates and arguments about the idea
of Britishness, ethnic and religious diversity and competing values in
a multicultural society. Al-Qaeda's 11 September 2001 attack on New
York's Twin Towers and the Pentagon gave added impetus to journalism's obsession with the debates whilst the London bombings of 7 July
2005 took British print and broadcast media to new levels of cultural,
occasionally racial, hyperbole, focusing on militant Islam in particular.

British cinema has been less exercised by the same debates. Indeed,
over the past couple of decades, only a handful of British mainstream
films, some of which have been commercially successful, have presented ethnic relations and associated issues as a prominent theme. Most of
these depict South Asian British characters, have involved a major contribution by South Asian Britons, usually as writers, directors and actors,
and have largely been family melodramas and comedies of manners.[1]

This chapter focuses on some of these films in the context of the
changing nature of Britain's multicultural society, and explores the ways
in which members of British South Asian communities, particularly
Muslims, have defined themselves and been defined by others in British
mainstream cinema. Although my attention is focused on films representing Britain's South Asian communities, it is important to remember
that Britain's multicultural society has a much more diverse composition. Unfortunately, mainstream, commercial films exploring the lives
and experiences of British citizens and their families and communities
of African and Caribbean descent are even scarcer than those depicting
South Asian ones. Important films such as Horace Ové's *Pressure* (1975),

Isaac Julien's *Young Soul Rebels* (1983), Julien Henriques' hugely entertaining *Babymother* (1998), Saul Dibb's highly prescient *Bullet Boy* (2004) and Amma Asante's critically acclaimed *A Way of Life* (2004) have all failed to achieve distribution deals that would lead to widespread exhibition outside art house cinemas. The latter example is particularly disappointing because Asante became the first Black woman director to win a BAFTA award for *A Way of Life*. Like Shane Meadow's also highly acclaimed *This is England* (2007), Asante's film depicted white racism but, unlike Meadows' film, it was not widely distributed.[2]

Britain: A multicultural society

Britain has long been a multicultural society whose cultural composition has changed dramatically over the centuries. Romans, Angles, Saxons, Jutes, Vikings and Normans have invaded, stayed and shaped Britain and joined Britons, Picts and Scots in laying claim to territorial, political and cultural hegemony over it. Since 1945 citizens of Britain's empire have 'come home' to live. More recently the expansion of the European Community has added considerably to Britain's cultural diversity. According to CILT, the National Centre for Languages, 307 languages are regularly spoken by London schoolchildren.[3] Contemporary Britain, then, is a multicultural society of great diversity (See Table 6.1 below). The fact that its diversity is marked by competing cultures that are organized, in part, around religious faiths has become, as I hope to make clear, a matter of comment and, in some quarters, concern.

Immigration to Britain in the second half of the twentieth century was largely a direct function of the 'legacy of Empire' and the need to manage it. The British Empire had succeeded in making people of much of Africa, North America, the Antipodes and South Asia subjects of the Crown. When the colonies gained their independence, Britain either could not or would not give up its legal obligations to those whom they had made its subjects.

Most immigration to the UK in the immediate post-1945 war period was from Poland and the Republic of Ireland. In 1945 there were probably no more than 30 000 non-white, ethnic minority people in Britain.[4] The first post-1945 influx of non-European immigrants comprised Black Caribbean citizens of the so-called Windrush generation.[5] The sanguinity of previous governments and electorates was less evident throughout the 1950s when Black Caribbeans and, later, Indians and Pakistanis, as British subjects, came to find work in Britain.[6] In subsequent years, successive governments sought to restrict New Commonwealth immigration and,

Table 6.1 Population by ethnic group in Great Britain, 2001*

White		
White British	50 366 000	
White Irish	691 000	
Other White	1 423 000	
All White		52 480 000
Mixed		674 000
Asian or Asian British		
Indian	1 052 000	
Pakistani	747 000	
Bangladeshi	283 000	
Other Asian	247 000	
All Asian or Asian British		2 329 000
Black or Black British		
Black Caribbean	566 000	
Black African	485 000	
Other Black	97 000	
All Black or Black British		1 148 000
Chinese		243 000
Other ethnic group		229 000
All ethnic groups		**57 103 000**

Social Trends, No. 35, 2005, Office for National Statistics. Adapted from Table 1.5, Population by ethnic groups and age, 2001.

only later, to address persistent and obvious forms of racism and racial prejudice against the immigrant communities.[7]

The settlement of New Commonwealth ethnic minority citizens in the UK has not been easy either for them or for the host population. Although post-1945 Britain escaped the worst excesses of racism found, for example, in the Southern States of the USA or in South Africa, there have been, nevertheless, desperate moments over the past half century that have brought shame on politicians and citizens alike. Particularly low points included: the 1958 'race riots' in Nottingham and Notting Hill,[8] the Smethwick political campaign in 1964,[9] Conservative M.P. Enoch Powell's 'Rivers of blood' speech in 1968,[10] the betrayal of the Kenyan Asians by the Labour government, also in 1968,[11] the Rushdie Affair in 1989 and 2007[12] and the murder of Stephen Lawrence and the subsequent failed murder investigation.[13]

Neither Labour nor Conservative governments enacted appropriate economic, social and housing policies to encourage the host population to be hospitable and the immigrant population to feel at home. Major cultural institutions, such as the BBC, the Universities and the Arts

Council, were slow to connect with the new citizens and, consequently, policies concerning equal opportunities and diversity were developed 20 years later than they should have been. Those discriminated against, and their representatives and social democratic supporters, have sought to use the instruments of local and national government to redress their disadvantaged social position. This activity, usually labelled multiculturalism, has been contested by those on the political right, including the largely right-wing tabloid British press, who argue that state support and encouragement of cultural and religious diversity undermines the traditional, national character of Britain. Most critics of multiculturalism claim to be against racism but nevertheless argue that it is the responsibility of immigrant communities to integrate.

Cultural identity and community

Historically, ethnic minority groups have sought to retain their cultural identities by forming proximate settlements, for example Pakistanis in Bradford and Punjabi Sikhs in Southall, London. More recently some settled immigrant communities have tried, with varying degrees of success, to protect or consolidate their 'traditional' cultural identities by other means. A good example of this has been the successful lobbying of Government by some Muslims to set up state faith schools.[14] Other means have occasioned controversy such as when some local Sikh community leaders and elders forced the cancellation of *Behzti*, a play by Gurpreet Kaur, a young Sikh woman, at the Birmingham Repertory Theatre in December 2004. Ironically, *Behzti* (Dishonour) is a 'black comedy' that deals with difficulties that arise when religious principles and other social and private values collide.

The ability or even desirability of ethnic and religious communities to sustain what they consider to be their cultural identity has been challenged from within the same communities. There is clear evidence of second and third generations of British Asians and Black Britons forming attachments through education, work, leisure and personal relationships, including marriage, in the 'mainstream' of British society.[15] Intergenerational community difference, typified by Gurpreet Kaur's experience, is a common, often complex and sometimes contradictory, theme of the South Asian British films I will examine later.

An important aspect of the development of post-1945 Britain society concerns citizen self-identification in a plural society of diverse, sometimes connected, even overlapping communities. The processes involved in citizens' attempts to recognize or make sense of their cultural identities are complex, especially when they involve a consideration of communal self-identity. This was clearly demonstrated by the Runnymede Trust's *The Future of Multi-Ethnic Britain* (2000), a report of a committee chaired by the distinguished political scientist, Professor Bhikhu Parekh. The Report's research drew on contributions from a wide range of ethnic minority British citizens, including this unnamed person:

> I could view myself as a member of the following communities, depending on the context and in no particular order: Black, Asian, Azad Kashmiri, Mirpuri, Jat, Kungriwalay, Pakistani, English, British, Yorkshireman, Bradfordian, from Bradford Moor [...] I could use the term 'community' in any of these contexts and it would have meaning. Any attempt to define me only as one of these would be meaningless.
>
> (Parekh, 2000a, pp. 46–7)

Developing this point, Parekh argued that the future of a liberal and plur-alistic, multi-ethnic Britain requires the recognition that British citizens should be seen as part of 'a community of individuals and a community of communities' (2000a, p. 48). Parekh and his colleagues also recognized that cohesion in this 'One Nation' idea of Britain had to be worked for:

> Cohesion in such a community (One Nation) derives from widespread commitment to certain core values, both between communities and within them: equality and fairness; dialogue and consultation; toler-ation, compromise and accommodation; recognition of and respect for diversity; and – by no means least – determination to confront and eliminate racism and xenophobia.
>
> (2000a, p. 56)

The Runnymede report can be read as a clear sign that multicultural Britain is not at ease with itself. This reading was aggressively con-firmed by the *Daily Mail*, a right of centre, middle class tabloid. After outlining the Committee members' profiles in demeaning terms, its edit-orial column described the Report's call to rethink 'the national story' of Britain as follows:

> Such were the means by which Stalin and Hitler twisted the past to suit their own political purposes. Now there is pressure for Britain to go through the same corrupting process – inspired this time not

by a savage dictator, but by those self-satisfied champions of liberal
orthodoxy, the Runnymede Trust.

(*Daily Mail*, October 11, 2000, p. 12)

The *Daily Mail* was angry because for the first time prominent and
influential ethnic minority representatives had dared to describe the
'community of communities', a phrase to which the *Daily Mail* took
exception, in its own terms. Bhikhu Parekh, in *Rethinking Multiculturalism* (2000b), argued that this self-reflexiveness marks out the new
multicultural Britain as distinct from that of the past. He suggests
that the diverse groups comprising multicultural society, aware of their
cultural differences and distinctions, including religious ones, are prepared to discuss the very idea of multicultural society and their place
in it without asking permission to do so. They believe they do not
have to accept their ascribed status position automatically and are prepared to challenge discrimination in all forms no matter from where it
emanates.

Such assertiveness challenges the view held by the dominant 'white'
society and typified by the *Daily Mail*, that new ethnic minorities can be
'tolerated' providing they integrate within the dominant culture. Where
there are important differences, for example in religious terms, people
of 'other faiths' are deemed free to practice them so long as they do
not impinge on the dominant culture. Richard Littlejohn, at the time
a highly influential journalist with the Murdoch-owned leading British
tabloid newspaper, *The Sun*, expressed the dominant culture's expectations of ethnic minority, post-immigrant communities in typically
forthright terms. Writing in the wake of a request from the Islamic Society of Britain for prominent Britons to sign a 'Pledge to British Muslims',
a request he declined, Littlejohn wrote,

All we should require is that people of all races and creeds who choose
to live here obey our laws, respect our traditions and beliefs and don't
expect special treatment.

(*The Sun*, Friday, November 9, 2001, p. 13)

The fact of diversity is the defining element of multicultural society but,
for some, it is the fundamental source of a problem: some people see
in diversity the potential for undermining the continuing existence of
a coherent, stable society. Usually this fear is expressed by those on the
political right either explicitly or implicitly. Indeed, Britain is used to having battles over the politics of race being fought in all sorts of places, for

example on the Website of the British National Party (BNP). Nick Griffin, the BNP Chairman, offers a typical expression of the right's objection to 'diversity':

> So now we know what the liberals, members of the CRE (Commission for Racial Equality) and other assorted 'Guardianistas' really mean when they talk about 'celebrating diversity'. No one can now doubt that the talk of 'enriched' and 'vibrant' communities is just code for deploring an excess of white people. The great crusade 'to fight racism' is nothing more than a vicious and systematic mechanism designed to destroy British ethnocentricity and ensure our demise.[16]

Given that cultural diversity is usually perceived to be a problem expressed by the political right, it was somewhat surprising, therefore, that the entrenched sensitivity of British public culture to 'diversity' was revealed in an article by David Goodhart (2004), 'Too diverse? Is Britain becoming too diverse to sustain the mutual obligations behind the good society and the welfare state?', and published in the impeccably left-liberal political monthly magazine, *Prospect*, of which he is the editor.

The complex article was written in the shadow of a number of events and activities that seemed to point to problems within multicultural Britain. One example concerned some street disturbances involving ethnic minority citizens in the spring and summer of 2001 in the de-industrialized English towns of Bradford, Burnley and Oldham. Subsequent official reports on these disturbances pointed to 'problems of segregation'.[17] Goodhart argued that for a liberal society to be at ease with itself requires that it possesses an optimum level of social solidarity. He speculated on whether or not a determinate level has been reached and whether solidarity is being threatened in Britain by increasing social and cultural diversity. In the tension between diversity and solidarity, the former, he claimed, can look after itself but solidarity needs to be managed by public policy. This important matter, he argued, presents a challenge to the left or the progressive groups who need to grasp it and not to abandon it to the extreme and nationalistic political right.

To Goodhart's surprise, the article created quite a stir and *The Guardian* newspaper published a collection of responses. Trevor Phillips, Chairman of the Commission for Racial Equality, wrote 'Nice people do racism too' (*The Guardian*, February 16, 2004). Gary Younge accused Goodhart of not so much as offering a challenge to the political left, but of rolling out '[...] the red carpet for the right' (*The Guardian*, February 26, 2004). This was a red carpet down which Peter Hitchens, a right wing political commentator, was happy to tread. He thanked Goodhart for '[...] grasping that a country cannot long retain consent, freedom and order unless it defends and respects its own culture.' Specifically he argued that 'Immigrants arriving here surely have a duty to become part of the culture that they have chosen to enter, so that its benefits can continue for their own children and grandchildren' (ibid.).

Goodhart's article, and the furore created amongst his liberal and not so-liberal critics, is a useful measure of the cultural and political environment in which any discussion of the cinema and multicultural Britain must take place. It is no less significant than the *Daily Mail*'s vitriol, Littlejohn's indignation and Griffin's sneering hostility.

Community in context

In previous chapters I have lamented the fact that the idea of community is shrouded in a rhetorical fog that is difficult to penetrate. The situation is little different in the context of writing about and discussing multicultural Britain. Once again the term is used by the political left and right, citizens, public spokespersons, academics, report writers and populists in a 'taken-for-granted', largely uncritical way. Even authors in scholarly texts, such as some of those contributing to the valuable collected volume *Muslim Britain: Communities Under Pressure* (Tahir Abbas (ed.), 2005), occasionally fail to define community although each particular context often clarifies its usage.

To a large extent I too shall have to follow the 'contextual' approach. In the films I have chosen to study, the meaning of the idea of community or communities is always presumed. Generally, it is taken to be Muslims living in the immediate locality, centred on a particular Mosque, between whom cultural values are shared and to whom obligations must be met. However, just as important in these films are the separations within communities, particularly regarding intergenerational differences, a subject to which I will return.

Representing multicultural society in mainstream British cinema

Until the release of *My Beautiful Laundrette* (dir. Stephen Frears, 1986), multicultural Britain was almost invisible in mainstream British cinema. Such ethnic minority characters as found their way on to the screen were usually in minor or supporting roles and were hardly ever shown as embedded in their own communities. It was, however, another 7 years before the release of the next major mainstream film to represent Britain's ethnic diversity, *Bhaji on the Beach* (dir. Gurinder Chadha, 1993). Multicultural Britain was much frequently represented by the independent, often avant-garde, small budget cinema that made challenging and vibrant films and videos.

In the 1980s, Channel 4 and the Greater London Council provided institutional support for ethnic minority, feminist and gay/lesbian independent film and video production companies or collectives to make films representing their experiences in Britain. The films and videos of the independent groups were not distributed in commercial cinemas but shown in art houses, on University campuses and, crucially, on Channel 4's *Eleventh Hour* slot.[18] In addition to producing an impressive body of work, independent ethnic minority groups facilitated the emergence of many talented filmmakers. For example, Gurinder Chadha made the independent documentary *I'm British But...* (1989) for distribution by the BFI before going on to direct mainstream feature films such as *Bhaji on the Beach* and *Bend it Like Beckham* (2002).

The majority of mainstream films focusing on British citizens of South Asian descent, like Chadha's films, over the past 20 years have used family melodramas and comedies of manner genres. Most have been set in contemporary Britain. A small minority have been political, but with a small 'p'. Some have been very successful at the box office.

Although British filmmaking has only belatedly paid attention to the ethnic diversity of British multicultural society, enough films have been made, nevertheless, for it to be necessary for me to restrict my close attention to just a few films. My chosen four films, *My Son the Fanatic* (dir. Udayan Prasad, 1997), *East is East* (dir. Daniel O'Donnell, 1999), *Ae Fond Kiss* (dir. Ken Loach, 2004) and *Yasmin* (dir. Kevin Glenaan, 2004), represent Muslim families in Muslim communities in non-Muslim societies. Set in the context of the social dynamics of more or less contemporary Britain, they were released within 7 years of each other. They have a striking contemporary resonance particularly for British Muslims. They share an emerging structure of feeling that connects with something decisive that is happening in multicultural Britain at the turn of the twenty-first century, as I will demonstrate shortly.

In selecting these films, I have had to omit discussion of a number of important and interesting films concerning Britons of the South Asian diaspora. First, I have omitted Empire heritage films such as *A Passage to*

India (dir. David Lean, 1984) and *Heat and Dust* (dir. James Ivory, 1983). Whilst such films do contribute if somewhat obliquely to an understanding of the development of multicultural Britain, they have little to say about contemporary community and cultural diversity issues and have therefore been excluded.

Second, I have only selected films that were made for cinema distribution. The distinction made between the film and television industries in Britain is clouded, for example, by the fact that television's Channel 4 and the BBC were major producers of film throughout the 1980s and 1990s. I have made a partial exception for *Yasmin* (2004), a film financed by Scottish Screen and Channel 4 and originally intended for cinema release.[19] It was exhibited at both Edinburgh and London film festivals in 2004, distributed and shown in cinemas in Europe where it was awarded the Templeton Film Prize in 2005 but ultimately was only released on television in Britain.

Third, the exhibition, in Britain, either in the cinema or in the home, by Video/DVD rentals or on terrestrial, satellite or cable television, of South Asian films made outside of Britain is socially and culturally important. It is, unfortunately, a highly specialized area of interest that is beyond the scope of this study.[20]

Fourth, *Bend it Like Beckham*, *Bhaji on the Beach* and *Anita and Me* (dir. Metin Huseyin, 2002) are lively films that address their serious topics with a light and sure touch and might, in other circumstances, have been included. Their success suggests there is clearly an audience for this sort of film. However, as I hope to demonstrate, they lack the urgency and prescience of my chosen films.[21]

Fifth, *My Beautiful Laundrette* (1986) is arguably the most critically acclaimed film representing Britain's South Asian citizens.[22] With a screenplay by Hanif Kureishi and directed by Stephen Frears it is the most hybrid of all such films; comedy, social critique, thriller, art movie. The main bloc of its characters is drawn from a Pakistani/British family but the film is far more interested in sex and moneymaking than in religion or community cohesion or diversity. It also belongs to a different historical conjuncture so I have reluctantly left it on one side.

Finally, Antonio Bird's *Hamburg Cell* (2004) and Peter Greengrass's *United 93* (2006) are also omitted. These compelling films made by British directors personalize the men who carried out the September 11 attacks. However, neither film addresses the main theme of this chapter. Indeed, their main characters are actually dissident Saudis rather than South Asian Britons.

From race to religion: The new inferential structure

If the number of newspaper column inches and hours of news broadcasts are any indication, British Muslims have become a prime focus of concern for the white British population. It is tempting to say that this began with the al-Qaeda attack on the World Trade Centre and the Pentagon in September 2001, and certainly that attack and George W. Bush's response by waging a 'War on Terror' pumped up the pressure on Muslims throughout the world. However, the shift of sensibilities in Britain regarding Muslims and especially in Muslim circles began much earlier, possibly as early as the initially inadequate response by NATO to the murder of Muslims in Bosnia-Herzegovina from 1993 and to the atrocities against Muslims in Kosovo and Chechnya. These events could be set in the context of the continuing assault on Palestinians and the long-standing dispute over the future of Kashmir. In addition, British Muslims began to realize that they were economically disadvantaged, their housing stock was poor and that their children were falling behind in educational attainment well before 2001.[23]

All four chosen films were released before the London bombing in July 2005 and the consequent heightening of civic tension. The bombing was shocking to most Britons, Muslim and non-Muslim alike, not only because of the scale of the deaths and injuries involved but also because some of the bombers, including the four thought to have detonated bombs, were British Muslims. At least three were raised and worked in Leeds, West Yorkshire where I am writing this book. With the bombing, a different way of thinking about multicultural Britain was created by the media and by civic institutions and counter-terror authorities. The public reaction to each subsequent event or action has been both shaped by and contributes to what Halloran et al. have called 'an inferential structure'.

> The development of an 'inferential structure' is not the development of a pro or con bias but is a process of simplification and interpretation which structures the meaning given to the story around its original news value. The story then takes its place as part of the information about events in society, which is all interpreted through the same communication process.
>
> (1970, pp. 215–16)

For most of the history of ethnic minority settlement in Britain, new events and actions were interpreted through the inferential structure of 'traditional' British cultural values that were frequently racialized.[24] However, the emergent inferential structure has begun to shift from race to religion and particularly to Islam, and this has found its expression in both private and public spheres. This was recently acknowledged, for example, by Irfan Ajeeb, a son of Mohammed Ajeeb, who was the first Asian Lord Mayor in Britain. Irfan, a Bradford actor, expressed his concern in these terms.

> In the community everyone knows what everyone else is doing, it's an extra weight on your shoulders [...] Our parents came from a different school of thought, the Pakistanis who came to Britain. We are British Pakistanis – I didn't choose to be born here. It's a very strange time to be living in the UK from the perspective of a British Asian, Pakistani Muslim, Bradford, Yorkshire, rich, poor – the list of labels get longer. We are being forced to see ourselves in terms of religion and our culture. It's claustrophobic.
>
> ('Looking at the bigger picture', *Yorkshire Post Magazine*, June 2, 2007, p. 10)

In the public sphere, issues such as Britain's social policies concerning cultural diversity, citizenship, the 'war on terror', the Middle East are now being read through a religious inferential structure that is frequently expressed in terms of a threat allegedly posed by 'radical' Islam or 'fundamentalist' Islam or 'militant' Islam. Recent examples of these include the prominence in the print and broadcast coverage of Muslim women wearing the Nijab in British public spaces, the arrest of 'radical' Imams preaching 'hate' against the British in Britain and Muslim protests at the repeated publication of satirical cartoons depicting the Prophet Muhammed in a Danish Newspaper.

The inferential structure has the power to draw everyone in. For instance, in the case of protests against the Danish cartoons, Fareena Alam, the female editor of *Q News*, a leading Muslim magazine, wrote,

> That the future of liberal democracy rests on defending the publication of these insulting caricatures is as ridiculous a claim as that Muslims can defend the honour of their prophet by unrestrained violence and rioting.
>
> Dressing up as a suicide bomber, waving placards calling on Muslims to butcher those who insult Islam and shouting '7/7' on its way – the inhumanity of it all is so utterly shameful. Clearly, it's not just Danish cartoonists and their apologists who are ignorant of the

Prophet. I wonder what the parents of the child wearing the 'I love al-Qaeda' cap would say had their son been on the number 30 bus that terrible day.

(*The Observer*, June 12, p. 29)

All of this, and more, is reported day after day in the news and through other media across the length and breadth of Britain. But what of the cinema? How has British cinema represented its 'community of communities', particularly its Muslim ones? The following discussion, intended to help answer this question, focuses on British films representing Muslim families and communities in Britain at the turn of the twenty-first century. The discussion takes as its starting point research by Tariq Modood and his colleagues who interviewed over 1000 British Muslim adults of Bangladeshi or Pakistani descent.[25] In particular, my analysis works around Modood's strong conclusion that

Religious affiliations may, therefore, slow down the rate of change in Pakistani and Bangladeshi families; *or the family may, alternatively, be a subject of discord between and within communities.*

(1997, p. 58, my emphasis)

The main site of discord within the family sits between the generations. In earlier research, Modood and his colleagues (1994) showed that whilst first-generation Muslims observed Islam strictly the second generation were less observant and said they observed Islam 'out of family and community pressure' (ibid., pp. 49–50). Further, they said that whilst they were likely to bring their children up in their community faith they would not pursue it strongly (ibid., pp. 51–2). Modood et al. also reported a clear difference between the generations concerning marriage. Thus, whilst the first generation strongly favoured marriage within Islam, the second generation was much more relaxed over mixed-religious marriages (ibid., pp. 73–4). The second generation-respondents were aware of the differences between themselves and their parents on this matter. Modood reports that in the case of mixed-religious marriages, they were concerned that their families might suffer a censure within the communities ' [. . .] and a loss of honour for the family of the defiant individual' (ibid., p. 74).

Modood et al.'s research (1994, 1997) was undertaken well before the riots of 2001 and the London bombings in 2005, and it reveals little of significance concerning the rise of a more radical Islam. However, Bagguley and Hussain's (2005) research undertaken in Bradford, predominantly with Muslims, reveals an interesting political distinction between the generations. Bagguley and Hussain's research shows that whilst second-generation Bradford Pakistanis regard themselves as ' [. . .] British citizens with the same "rights" as any other British citizen', first-generation Bradford Pakistanis regard themselves as having 'the status of being a denizen' (2005, p. 418).[26]

The younger generation revealed a self-confidence about their citizenship status consistent with that discussed by Parekh (2000b) and to which I referred above. The older generation was aware that changes had taken place between the generations. For example, Ramzan Latif, male, aged 64, commented, 'The Asian youths believe that this is their country and they should be given the same rights as the White people have. They do not want to tolerate anything anymore. They believe that they are just as British as the British are' (2005, p. 419).

In the broader context of the new religious inferential structure referred to above, the shifting balance of confidence and authority between the generations has become a highly significant social fault line, and it is one displayed in the films I have selected to analyse. In trying to explore this, my analysis will not follow the chronology of the films' production and distribution but will reflect the extent to which they engage with the wider social environment. Thus I begin with *East is East* (1999) which has the narrowest scope and conclude with *Yasmin* (2004), the broadest.

East is East

Daniel O'Donnell's highly popular *East is East*, adapted by Ayub Khan-Din from his own successful stage play and drawing on his own experiences, is a comedy. Released in 1999 it is set in 1971, when the South Asian Muslim population of Britain was around 250 000.[27] The fact that the film is set in 1971 does not undermine the films' contemporary relevance. The date of its exhibition is more important. The Khan family of two adults and seven children live in a cramped, chaotic and noisy terrace house in the largely working class town of Salford, Lancashire. The family also own and run a fish-and-chip shop nearby. In the film O'Donnell evokes, in a somewhat clichéd fashion, something of the working class 'community' we saw earlier in *Brassed Off*, *Billy Elliot* and *The Full Monty*; neighbours 'pop-in' unannounced, local white girls are 'up for it' and kids play football in the streets and chase after posh cars.

George (Om Puri), the father, is a Muslim with a mercurial personality. His mood swings from playfulness to anger when crossed and he appears to be constantly crossed. He regularly attends the Mosque to which he sends his reluctant children for religious education. Parvez swears and is prone to occasional lapses into violence. However, he also possesses a keen sense of personal pride and believes he knows what is right for him, his wife and his children. In principle his will is to be obeyed but, in most things, George is kept in order by Ella (Linda Bassett), his white non-Muslim wife. He has another wife in Pakistan whom he jokingly threatens to bring to Britain. Ella is patient, long-suffering, forgiving and loving to her children and, surprisingly, George. He is a frustrated and confused father who doesn't understand modern youth in general and his children in particular. He knows he has a duty to uphold Muslim values and, in particular, he wants to maintain the Muslim identity of his family and community in a non-Muslim society by creating marriages for his children. It is around arranged marriages that the plot revolves.

The film begins with some comical scene setting in which we see Ella and the children as 'flexible' in their religious observances; the children are happy to carry Christian iconography in a Catholic church confirmation street parade. However, the story takes off with Nazir's wedding. Nazir (Ian Aspinall), the oldest son, gets cold feet and leaves his arranged bride in mid-ceremony. Understandably, George, the bride and the bride's family are distraught for this is a dreadful insult to them and brings shame on the Khan household in general and George in particular. George disowns Nazir who has to leave the family home although Ella and Nazir's siblings try to keep in touch with him. George talks about his shame to a sympathetic mullah (Kaleem Janjua).

> *George*: Why he [Nazir] wants to do this thing see? And bring me shame on my family. I no understand. No understand. Maybe I should have taken family to Bradford long time ago.
>
> [Clearly upset by his experience and compromised by the shame, he seeks the Mullah's advice.]
>
> *Mullah*: Zaheed, until your sons join the community fully they will be a worry for you. But listen. I have a friend in Bradford, his name is Mr Shah. He has two daughters. He is eager they be married. Now, if you think any of your sons is suitable and ready, would you be willing to meet them?
>
> *George*: [Pause] No problem. They're ready. You arrange?

George has a secret meeting with Mr Shah and his two undesired and apparently undesirable daughters and agrees to commit to two marriage contracts for his sons, Tariq (Jimi Mistry) and Abdul (Raji James). Unfortunately, George does not tell them about the arrangements so that when they find out they refuse to comply with George's demands. They seek help from Nazir who returns to the family home to intercede. George physically attacks first Nazir and then Ella, giving her a large facial bruise. Ella persuades Tariq and Abdul to meet the Shah family, who are due to visit the Khans' house the next day. The family greets the Shahs. Ella puts up with their patronizing manner until an incident, involving a piece of obscene artwork belonging to another son, disrupts the meeting. Everything comes to nought but not before Ella vents her feelings against the Shahs. George is furious. He retreats to the fish-and-chip shop. Ella joins him, offers to make a cup of tea and takes his hand.

East is East is a lively film with plenty of good verbal and visual jokes. It is shot rather in the manner of a British television drama with a limited number of locations and a heavy use of studio sitting rooms. The central story is efficiently told and amusing sub-plots are cleverly worked in. It is well cast and well played. By setting the film in 1971, the writer and director allow the audience to view the casual and caricatured racism with amused distance. For example, the repeated joke about 'Pakis' seems like a museum piece. Tariq, faced with an arranged marriage to a Shah daughter says to his parents, 'You can both fuck off if you think I am getting married to a fucking Paki.' The term, however, is stripped of some of its potential to hurt by the double move of locating its use in the past, 1971, and giving it to the son of a Pakistani immigrant to utter.

Despite O'Donnell and Khan-Din's caricature of George, the representation of Muslim family life is in some respects convincing although viewers who have no knowledge of Muslim culture might not appreciate the fact. Expressed in the broadest terms, Islam regards the roles, responsibilities and character of fathers and mothers as complementary. The mother has responsibility for the home; caring for the children and cooking for the family and so on. The father is regarded as the material provider and family protector, and he has ultimate authority on family matters. However, his authority must be wielded in a considered way through partnership and neither arbitrarily nor capriciously. Commenting on the complementarity of husbands and wives in marriage, Shaykh Fadhlalla Haeri (1993) writes,

> Men can be brutally decisive and therefore wantonly destructive, while women tend to seek reconciliation and acceptability. When a man discovers the 'woman' within himself (that is, the qualities that predominate in and distinguish her gender), then he has reached a maturity that enables him to live harmoniously with any woman.
>
> (p. 123)

George's brutal decisiveness is frequently destructive; indeed, it is in danger of permanently splitting the family and damaging its standing in the community. Ella is constantly seeking reconciliation between George and the children but allows him to have his way on important family matters. This is made clear in the film in a conversation with her best friend, Annie (Lesley Nicol), about the youngest son's overdue and recently completed circumcision. Wondering about whether or not she was a good mother, she asks Annie

> *Ella*: Would you have put one of your lads through this, at his age?
> *Annie*: You had no choice.
> *Ella*: I did. I could've put me foot down and said no.
> *Annie*: And given yourself a load of bleeding grief. It's religion Ella and it's theirs, you know that. You knew that when you got married. [Ella falls silent.]

Later Ella bows to George's insistence on arranged marriages for Tariq and Abdul. She has witnessed George's humiliation over Nazir's wedding and now she steps aside knowing that the two young men do not want to marry the Shah girls. When the marriage meeting between the two families collapses into chaos, it is Ella who deals with the aftermath.

Liese Spencer (1999) correctly notes that as *East is East*'s narrative unfolds the film moves away from any pretence of naturalism towards farce. There is, of course, no reason why films about Muslims can not be farces but the problem in this farce is the representation of George, which, I think, raises difficulties for the audience. The farcical aspect of the film presents George as a buffoon; his English is decidedly pigeon; he buys 'ridiculous' presents for Ella, for example, a second-hand dental chair and he keeps secrets from her. It is only through Ella's intercessions and her conciliatory skills that George is repeatedly redeemed and the audience retains any empathy with him. Ella, the non-Muslim, behaves in the manner described by Shaykh Fadhlalla Haeri above.

George on the other hand behaves in a decidedly un-Muslim like way. His destructive behaviour and anger border on the pathological. He is foul-mouthed, volatile and occasionally violent towards his wife. He has no patience with his children, never talks to them, as the Qur'an requires, with gentleness and generosity. Shaykh Fadhlalla Haeri writes, 'The Prophet once said: "The best of my people is he who shows his family kindness and goodness"' (1993, p. 123). If George cannot persuade his children he cajoles, bullies, even strikes them, and he strikes his wife too.

By the end of the film, George is no further forward in his family planning; he has shamed himself and his family with two other Muslim families. His children are still single and not fully of the Muslim community and probably never will be, and so, as the Mullah suggests, they will continue to be a worry for him. George is destined to be an outsider in his family, his community and the wider world. *East is East* is a comedy but it is one built to a large extent around a tragic figure. It presents us with a representation of a Muslim father who is lost and ashamed.[28]

The history of filmmaking concerning ethnic and religious minorities has been dogged by a 'burden of representation' to which I do not want to add.[29] Filmmakers and critics, such as Kobena Mercer, Isaac Julien and Paul Gilroy, have pointed to the ambivalence or contradiction involved in, on the one hand, the desire to represent one's community and, on the other, the responsibility for doing so. Because so few films focus on multicultural Britain each, in some way, takes on the burden of representing it and of providing the definitive view. In this context, then, we should be wary of drawing any 'conclusions' regarding the particular representativeness of George's character. However, I shall return to George's experience of loss and shame at a later point after I have explored the other three films.[30]

Ae Fond Kiss

The British section of the 2004 Edinburgh Film Festival included three films that dealt, albeit in different ways, with the relationship between Muslims and the wider society: *Ae Fond Kiss*, *Yasmin* and *Hamburg Cell*. I have explained that *Hamburg Cell* falls outside of my brief and I will turn to *Yasmin* in due course. Here I discuss Ken Loach's *Ae Fond Kiss*, a family melodrama/romance that, like *East is East*, explores Muslim intergenerational relations. However, it is more ambitious than the latter in that it deals more explicitly with the theme of cultural diversity. Story lines concerning the film's three children are more nuanced and varied than those in *East is East*, but nevertheless each returns to the dilemma facing George; how to sustain Muslim family life in a Muslim community in a non-Muslim Britain, in this case Glasgow.

Loach directs in his normal style, emphasizing naturalistic dialogue, locations and language delivered in a semi-improvised fashion.[31] Long and complex speeches are delivered convincingly by actors who respond to carefully structured directions that provide them with opportunities for actor spontaneity based on intimate character familiarity. Paul Laverty's dialogue is witty and passionate with passages of great warmth and quiet tenderness contrasting with scenes of spite and anger. The narrative has some holes and some important character information is glossed over. However, the film convinces that the issues with which it deals are serious and weigh heavily on the minds and emotions of the characters. In an interview given at the 2004 Edinburgh Film Festival, Loach explained how he seeks to make ordinary lives extraordinary and by doing so give the audience something to reflect upon.[32] The Khan family is in this sense an ordinary family.

The title sequence begins with a scene of a lively disco packed with young South Asians and whites dancing to Bhangra rhythms. It cuts with the same music to a sweeping pan across industrial Glasgow to a corner shop. Loach then cuts to and fro between the disco and shop to introduce three of the film's major characters: a shopkeeper, a young woman and a disc jockey (DJ). The shopkeeper, Tariq Khan (Ahmad Riaz), is trying to stop dogs fouling his newspaper placard, on which is written, 'Church tells Celtic fans "No nookie in Seville." ' He attaches car jump-leads to the placard's metal frame whilst his mid-teens daughter, Tahara (Shabana Bakhsh), watches in bewilderment. Casim Khan (Atta Yaqub), the shopkeeper's son, spins the discs.

Loach cuts to a new scene, a secondary school assembly where Tahara is speaking in a debate. In a typical Loach manoeuvre Tahara is address-ing the thorny issue of cultural identity in terms that Parekh would recognize. It is worth quoting in full.

> Imagine someone lumping George Bush, the Pope, Henrik Larsson and Willy Benjani together in one person. You'd laugh. Why? Because it's dumb. But that's exactly what the West has done with Islam; as if one billion Muslims in fifty countries with hundreds of different languages and countless ethnic groups were one and the same. Take my family. My sister considers herself Muslim and because she has a political streak, calls herself black. My Dad's been in this country for over forty years and is one hundred per cent Pakistani. Or so he thinks. I reject the West's definition of terrorism which excludes the hundreds of thousands of victims of state terror. I reject the West's claim of moral high ground after two of its main Jesus lovers tore up the UN charter. But above all I reject the West's simplification of a Muslim. I am a Glaswegian, Pakistani, teenager, woman of Muslim descent who supports Glasgow Rangers in a Catholic school. 'Cos I'm a dazzling mixture and proud of it.
>
> [As she speaks she puts down her notes and removes her tie and undoes her blouse to reveal a Glasgow Rangers football shirt.][33]

Empire India was partitioned in 1947 and Pakistan and India gained their independence. Tahara's Muslim father, Tariq, finding himself on the wrong side of the partition line in an India dominated by Hindus and Sikhs had to migrate to the newly formed Pakistan to avoid the communal violence to which he and countless others became subjects.[34] During the move he lost contact with his twin brother, Casim, who he presumed was killed. Subsequently emigrating to Scotland, Tariq and his wife, Sadia (Shamshad Akhatar), had three children: Rukhsana (Ghizala Avan), the eldest, her younger brother Casim, and Tahara, the youngest child. Tariq and Sadia have a very strong, close and loving family that is well-respected in Glasgow's Muslim community.

The dramatic turning point of *Ae Fond Kiss* film occurs when Casim meets Roisin (Eva Birthistle), an Irish Catholic part-time music teacher at Tahara's Catholic school, and they fall in love. Casim is formally engaged, by family arrangement, to Pakistan-based Jasmine (Sunna Mirza), a fact he neglects to tell Roisin until they are on holiday together in Spain. Roisin, in turn, is also married but separated from her husband. Roisin and Casim argue but get back together; not for the last time. It is clear throughout, particularly when explaining his Muslim world to Roisin, that Casim loves, respects and admires his parents.

Casim and Roisin's love, which is romantic, passionate and turbulent, stands in marked contrast to Rukhsana's family-arranged engagement to Amar (Pasha Bocarie), which is steady, respectful and quiet. The contrast goes further, right to the heart of the film and, indeed, to the heart of many intergenerational relationships for Muslims in multicultural Britain. Rukhsana and Amar's marriage has the power to bind their two families together and consolidate the community. On the other hand Casim and Roisin's relationship, if it persists, will break up Casim's family, destroy Rukhsana's chance of marriage to Amar and bring dishonour to the family in the eyes of the community. On hearing of Casim's feelings about Roisin and marriage, Sadia says, 'How can I tell your aunt now? This is not good. What will Jasmine do? This will shame us.'

Sadia's point is consistent with Modood's (1994) research that showed that both first- and most second-generation Muslims disapprove of Muslims living with a non-Muslim outside of marriage (1994, p. 74). It also showed that, whilst most second-generation Muslims were not against mixed-religious marriages in principle, in practice parental wishes and authority are serious considerations. Modood reports, 'Several interviewees speculated that if they were faced with a head-on-clash between romantic love and love for one's family, they would forsake

the former' (ibid., p. 73). Interviewees were concerned that their families might suffer censure within the communities 'and a loss of honour
for the family of the defiant individual' (ibid., p. 74). Rukhsana makes
this general point very clear and very personally to Roisin when, at
Rukhsana's request, they meet. Rukhsana patiently explains,

> Casim's left home and he's living with you and as far as my family is
> concerned and my community is concerned it's brought a great deal
> of shame on all of us. You see we have this concept called *izzath* which,
> I guess, is family honour and that's really important to people. And my
> parents all through their lives have worked very, very hard to main-
> tain that, to keep that and they've built up respect and trust in the
> community. And what Casim has done is that he's taken that away.

Ae Fond Kiss is a more satisfying film than *East is East* because its understanding of the issues at stake is more complex and the characters are
more rounded. For instance, Loach and Laverty take time to show us
Roisin's own problems regarding cultural identity. Roisin's head teacher
wants to offer her a full-time, permanent contract but points out that
as her 'Certificate of Approval' has expired she should contact her par-
ish priest to renew it. In a verbally violent and threatening scene, Father
Chambers (Father David Wallace) refuses to renew her certificate because
she is living with a man who is not her husband and because she has not
been attending mass regularly. The Priest tells her she can marry a Muslim
provided that both she and he agree to bring up any child they have as
a Catholic. Roisin's dilemma is that her personal happiness and career
is being threatened by the intransigence of 'fathers' from two different
religious traditions.

The film climaxes in the Khans' new home extension that represents
both a material space and a narrative device. Loach has shown the audience the progress of the extension throughout the film, and by the final
scenes it is complete. Tariq sees the extension as the means by which he
can keep his children, particularly Casim and his fiancée Jasmine, close
by. The home extension symbolizes the family extension. It is beautifully appointed and, like the family, built with pride. The dramatic
climax arises when Rukhsana, in one final desperate act, seeks to show
Roisin the effect of what Rukhsana regards as Casim's foolishness. She
tricks Roisin into visiting the house. Sitting in Rukhsana's car outside the
house, Roisin sees the Khan family, Amar, Jasmine and Jasmine's mother,
recently arrived from Pakistan, all gathered to present the extension to
Casim. When Roisin realizes what is happening she rushes from the car,

away from the house. Tariq tries once more to persuade Casim to give up Rosin:

Tariq: I may not be as clever and educated like you are, but I'm your father.

[Increasingly desperate he continues]

Tariq: Listen, don't let a cheap goree come between us. They throw you out in the street. She'll find another man. What about values? Right? What about your culture? Your religion? Right? Listen to your Mum. We're your parents. We'll die for you. You're our only son. You're our future.

Casim rejects Tariq's appeal and rushes off to find Roisin. In either anger or frustration or both, Tariq smashes the extension's windows and front door. The family like the extension is damaged. Tariq's sense of loss and shame over the public humiliation that Casim's decision will bring the Khans in the eyes of the community is palpable.

In *Ae Fond Kiss*, Loach and Laverty direct our attention to two ways of thinking about cultural diversity. The first way is separation; embrace Islam or be prepared to step away from it. Rukhsana desires to sustain her Muslim faith and cultural identity by staying close to Muslim traditions including that of maintaining family honour. Casim knows that if he wants to live with Roisin then he risks separation, even exclusion, from the family he loves and respects. In this way the boundary lines of diverse cultures are fixed.

In the second way, Tahara's way, cultural diversity is presented as negotiable and flexible. She has difficulties with her father's expectations regarding her career choice, she wants to study journalism but he wants her to study medicine. He also wants her to stay in Glasgow but she wants to go to Edinburgh. Describing herself as a 'dazzling mixture', she wants to be one and the other. Tahara tells her parents that she will try to work something out.

My Son the Fanatic

Just as *Ae Fond Kiss* set its scene wider afield than the immediate environment of George and Ella Khan's street in *East is East*, so *My Son the Fanatic*, directed by Udayan Prasad and written by Hanif Kureishi, is set in an even broader social context. However, Prasad's visual style, which is sombre and restrained, undercuts the openness of the story line to direct a film with a distinctly claustrophobic atmosphere. Parvez (Om Puri) and his wife, Minoo (Gopi Desai), live with their son,

Farid (Akbar Kurtha), in a working class terrace house in Bradford.[35] Parvez has been a taxi driver for 20 years. Farid is training to be an accountant.

The film begins with Parvez, Minoo and Farid being entertained by Farid's girlfriend Madeleine's family at their expensive house in the country. Despite Madeleine not being a Muslim, Parvez is hoping that the young couple will marry. In so far as the scene provides some embarrassment for Farid and Madeleine as Parvez misjudges the sincerity of Madeleine's parents' hospitality, *My Son the Fanatic* looks like its going to be a culture clash, comedy of manners film. This is deceptive, as the film quickly plunges the audience into Bradford's dark and depressing underworld with the arrival of Mr Schitz (Stellan Skarsgård), a businessman from Germany looking to set up some contacts in Bradford and, at the same time, to enjoy himself with women. Parvez meets Schitz at the airport and suggests, as taxi drivers do, that when Schitz needs a taxi he should call on him.

Parvez is not a Muslim father in the manner of either George Khan or Tariq Khan. He does not observe his faith strictly and his leisure pursuits include listening to American jazz and drinking whisky. He is an open and generous person who takes people as he finds them. He is happy for his son to marry a non-Muslim. He is particularly friendly with Bettina (Rachel Griffiths), a prostitute, who, like Schitz, prefers to call on Parvez to drive her. Bettina and Parvez are very relaxed together. Through him we learn something of Bettina's background and see that for her prostitution is a job, a source of income that does not define either her identity or worldview.

Although the film tells Parvez's story, it is partly organized around Bettina. First, Schitz is looking for a woman and, wanting to put some work Bettina's way, Parvez introduces them to each other. Bettina has a commodity to sell and Schitz, the businessman, is keen to buy. Indeed, Schitz wants to buy more than Bettina's services for a party he is arranging for local businessmen. She agrees to supply women and Parvez arranges the food and drink.

Second, Farid also takes an interest, although a very different one, in Bettina and her colleagues. Following the meeting between the two families, Farid rejects Madeleine and the accountancy training which his father is so proud of Farid for taking. In their place he begins to take his Islamic studies more seriously. He persuades Parvez to allow a Maulvi, a holy man, to stay at their house. Parvez reluctantly agrees and becomes dismayed at the way in which the Maulvi is moulding Farid's mind. As Farid and his friends develop their strict, in Parvez's eyes fanatical, views they take violent action to rid the streets of the prostitutes including Bettina.

Third, by the time of Schitz's party and Farid's initial actions, Parvez and Bettina have begun to forge a closer friendship that ends with them sleeping together. Farid has learned of their involvement through gossip in the Muslim community and from Parvez's colleagues at the taxi company. His concern is heightened in several scenes involving Bettina at Parvez's oldest friend Fizzy's restaurant. Parvez had helped Fizzy (Harish Patel) set up in business so that when Parvez realizes the huge cost of putting the Maulvi up at his house – telephone bills and so on – he goes to Fizzy for financial help. Fizzy agrees, but only if Parvez agrees to give up seeing Bettina. He refuses.

Finally, Minoo becomes aware that Parvez and Bettina have become very close. Marginalized in her family home by Farid and the Maulvi – she is allowed to cook for them, but not to eat with them – she becomes lonely, frustrated and angry.

The breakdown in the relationships between Farid, Minoo and Parvez becomes inevitable. Farid and his colleagues try to burn down the brothel. Parvez discovers this and helps rescue Bettina and drags Farid away before the police can arrest him. Minoo, humiliated by Parvez's public attachment to Bettina, has decided to return to Pakistan, possibly forever. She accuses him of 'putting self before family'. Parvez admits he has a 'friendship with one of those women'. But, he insists,

Parvez: Friendship is good, Minoo. I think it can be found in the funniest places.
Minoo: All this time I stayed here to serve you and you were out laughing with low class people. What a fool I've been made into. What a waste.

Farid, for his part, disgusted by what he considers his father's profoundly un-Islamic behaviour is leaving too. After he has dragged Farid away from the arson attack, Parvez starts to throw out the Maulvi's things and tells Farid:

Parvez: He could be Jesus Christ himself, but he is leaving.
Farid: If you shame me I'm going away too.
Parvez: Alright! I won't stand for the extremity of anti-democratic and anti-Jewish rubbish. And he eats too much!
Farid: Is it too much for clearing our corrupting streets for our goodness?

Parvez: There is nothing of God, spitting on a woman's face. This can not be the way for us to take.

[Farid continues to attack his father's morals and referring to the rumours flying around Bradford he says]

Farid: It makes me feel sick to have such a father. I never thought you are such a man. You are a pimp who organizes sexual parties.'

[Parvez slaps Farid, who turns on him.]

Farid: You call me a fanatic, dirty man. Who's the fanatic now?

[Farid spits in his father's face.]

Parvez drinks alcohol, plays jazz, pays insufficient attention to his faith, commits adultery, drives prostitutes to parties and pays them Schitz's money, and he humiliates his wife. He is not a model Muslim. But he is generous, protects women and respects friendships irrespective of faith. As Farid stalks off, Parvez's final words to him are

Parvez: Remember two things. There are many ways of being a good man and I will be at home. Will you come and see me?

Parvez's strengths are, in the minds of his son and his wife, his weaknesses and he pays dearly for them. He has become a lost figure. He neither saw the harm Schitz and others were doing to him nor Farid's embarrassment at it and where this might lead him. He did not recognize Minoo's humiliation or that he had lost what respect his community might have had for him. Losing sight of all this he knew only that he was lonely and that Bettina was a good woman who liked him, perhaps loved him. He did not recognize the accumulation of shame felt by the people he loved.

The taxi, his source of income and the means by which he entered a wider social world, perfectly symbolised his life. He was not 'at home' in his home, at the Mosque, at the taxi company or even at Fizzy's. He was at home only between places, in his taxi driving around the city. After Minoo and Farid leave he returns to his house, drinks his whisky and plays another jazz record; 'Please send me someone to love.' A pathetic coda to a lost man's life.

In *East is East* and *Ae Fond Kiss*, Tariq Khan and George Khan railed against their children's actions, fearing their behaviour would bring shame on the family and community. In *My Son the Fanatic* the accusations of shame are reciprocal. Of course, Parvez was ashamed of Farid for behaving so badly to Bettina and corrupting the principles of a peace-loving religion for violent ends. However, his shame is not expressed on behalf of his family or community but on a personal level because, quite simply, he feels that Farid should not behave like he did towards any other person. Farid, on the contrary was ashamed of his father's wilful, in his eyes, disregard for Islam; abusing alcohol, adultery and pimping prostitutes are not compatible with Islamic values.

Yasmin

The reversal of the dynamics of intergenerational relations and loss of honour found in *My Son the Fanatic*, in contrast to those in *East is East* and *Ae Fond Kiss*, is repeated, in part, in Kevin Glenaan's *Yasmin*. Likewise, the opening up of Muslim family and community life to wider social values and forces presented in *My Son the Fanatic* continues in Glenaan's film. Made 7 years after *My Son the Fanatic*, *Yasmin* introduces, for the first time in British cinema, the theme of the impact of the attack of 9/11 on British Muslims and the implications it might have for cultural diversity.

Although it lacks the passion of *My Son the Fanatic* and the psychological depth of *Ae Fond Kiss*, in social and political terms *Yasmin* is a more complex film. Glenaan adopts a social realist style with natural dialogue, grounded locations and 'real' situations. *Yasmin* is filmed without glamour and pretension. The characters are, for the most part, rounded and convincing, and Glenaan provides them with suitably authentic dialogue and speech patterns.

Like the other films, *Yasmin*, focuses on members of one Muslim family who live in Keighley, in the Bradford district once again. The family occupies Khalid Hussain's two-terrace houses that face each other across the street of an old working class estate. Khalid (Renu Setna), a widower, lives in one house with his teenage son Nasir (Syed Ahmed). The other is occupied by his daughter Yasmin (Archie Panjabi) and, in a separate room, her husband, Faysal (Shalid Ahmed), a rural Pakistani who is in the UK for a marriage of convenience that will allow him to gain British citizenship. As soon as Faysal's papers come through Yasmin intends to divorce him, although Khalid has other hopes. Khalid runs a television and video repair shop with Uncle Hassan (Badi Uzzaman), who is a friend of the family originally from India. Yasmin, who is in her early twenties, is a day care social worker involved in collecting young people from the locality and taking them to a care centre. As the film begins, she seems to be on good terms with her colleagues and particularly John (Steve Jackson), her driver. Nasir, Yasmin's younger brother, does not appear to have a job or go to school. He sings the call to the faithful to pray at the local Mosque, for which Khalid is the caretaker, but also deals in drugs, particularly weed, and enjoys casual sex with a white girl of the same age. He is a 'bit of a lad', prone to bouts of personal exaggeration, self-certainty and cockiness.

The film's initial focus is on Yasmin who, we discover immediately, inhabits two different identities. As she drives from her house she is wearing her salwar kameez and hijab, but in the countryside en route between her home and work towns she changes into Western style dress; tight jeans and jumper. As Miranda Husain notes,

> The image symbolises her daily struggle to balance the different dimensions of her being: the independent 'westernised' working woman and the dutiful daughter and sister does what is expected of her. It also highlights how Muslim women's choice of dress has become synonymous with the battle between tradition and modernity.[36]

This is everyday life for Yasmin; sharing a joke with John about not wanting to buy a TP – Typically Paki – car, experiencing quiet and sullen hostility in a pub and a minor brush with the police. One day she arrives home to find that Nasir has failed to switch on the oven in which the evening meal had been left. This leads to a brief but important confrontation with her father through which intergenerational differences are declared for the first time in the film. Yasmin takes the meal across the street to Khalid's house where we see Khalid, Nasir, Faysal and Uncle Hassan.

Yasmin: [To Nasir, in a strong Bradfordian accent] I work, I cook and you can't even switch oven on!

Khalid: If you hadn't been out, buying fancy cars you could have done it yourself.

[The ensuing argument about Yasmin's car gets out of hand:]

Khalid: Flaunting yourself in that thing. You bring shame on the family. Is that what you want, disgrace the family name?

Yasmin: [Pointing at Faysal] I married him for the family didn't I? Bloody thick Paki.

Khalid: I will not have the language of the gutter in this house. Do you understand me?

Yasmin: Yeh. I'm sorry.

Khalid: Now say it like you mean it.

Yasmin: I'm sorry.

Khalid: You think your father is a stupid old man? I know what goes on, I know. Out there you will do what you will do. But in this house you will show some respect. Too much freedom. [To Uncle Hassan] See what happens. I'm sorry you had to see this.

Here, then, we see repeated the intergenerational frustrations expressed by both father and child that we saw in *East is East* and *Ae Fond Kiss* and the familiar parental accusation of family shame. However, there is a further turn of the screw not experienced in any of the other films. This is provided by al-Qaeda's attack of 9/11.

Glenaan shows us members of the family and others watching the 9/11 and post-9/11 events unfolding on different television screens. Scenes of obtrusive police activity on the streets and aircraft trailing across the sky become common and we hear speeches by US President George Bush and British Prime Minister Tony Blair declaring the 'war on terror'. Yasmin's relationships with her colleagues begins to break down; she finds a picture of her defaced by a Osama bin-Laden beard, a Post-it note on her locker declaring, 'Yas loves Osama' and the words 'Tehran van' written in her van's dust. John tells her, 'Don't let it get to you, it's just a joke.'

September 12 sees another family argument over dinner; this time Nasir is in trouble. Khalid is worried over whether the attack will lead to the British government repatriating citizens to Pakistan. Referring to the attack, Nasir says,

Nasir: You got to admit it's got style.

Khalid: Why did you say that, boy?

Nasir: I mean nobody is going to forget that in a long time, are they? Not for years. Boom! That's a calling card alright.

Khalid: Style? You know something, what you call style, I call shame! I am ashamed, that's what I am. I am also ashamed that I brought up a son who thinks that killing thousands of people is style. Was it the Qur'an I taught you all those years or was it some comic books? Huh? Get out of my sight boy.

The lives of the Hussain family are changing. The film shows Khalid as fearful, without cause, that he will be repatriated.[37] Yasmin draws back towards her father and his traditional, orthodox Muslim values, whilst Nasir shifts from drug dealing and casual sex right across the Muslim spectrum past Khalid's values to those held by militant Islamists.

Yasmin, already the victim of discrimination at work, suffers a violent armed police raid of her house looking for a terrorist suspect whilst John was visiting her. Roughly handled and arrested, she is taken to a police station and interrogated about a terrorist, who it transpires the police thought might have been Faysal. She is ultimately released without charge. At the police station John hears about Yasmin's husband for the first time, but does not hear the full story. At the same time as Yasmin's release, Faysal is taken in for questioning. Although it is clear he is an innocent abroad and not political he is held for a while. Yasmin locates where Faysal has been taken and approaches the police so that they can get him to sign the divorce papers that have come through. The police detain her in a police cell for a while where she reads a copy of the Qur'an that has been left there. After release she decides to wait at the police station for Faysal's release too. She takes him back to her house and looks after him. Although, she still wants a divorce she is much more conciliatory towards him. The film indicates, not too convincingly, that her experience of the way in which the authorities have treated Faysal and herself, the reaction of her workmates and her reading of the Qur'an have helped her appreciate the vulnerability of herself, her family and community.

Meanwhile, Nasir has begun meeting some Muslims who do not share the quiet, orthodox views of Khalid and his generation. He and other young Muslims receive instruction from Kamal (Amar Hussain), an outsider recently arrived in the area, about the injustices in Palestine and Chechnya and how they can be 'good Muslims'. Nasir's religious/political reeducation intensifies and it is not long before he visits Yasmin to tell her that he is going to Pakistan for training and from there he will go to Palestine.

> *Yasmin*: What do you think goes on there? Eh? Putting leaflets under the door. Knock and run with the BNP? It's dangerous out there Nas!
> *Nasir*: I've been asleep for a long time, Yas. I've been doing bad things. Now I've got a chance, a chance to do good.
> *Yasmin*: That's good is it? I preferred you as a drug dealer.

Nasir asks Yasmin for her blessing, but she calls him a 'selfish bugger' and refuses. He departs, leaving a note for his father. On reading it Khalid tells Yasmin, 'I'm growing old, Yasmin.' She hugs him.

Khalid, then, has felt ashamed of both of his children, but he has become reconciled with Yasmin. Her behaviour, commonly found amongst the second-generation Muslims as described by Modood (1994, 1997), stemmed from her interaction with a diverse world at work and leisure. Khalid had not thought his daughter was Muslim enough. The problem he had with Nasir is that Nasir had adopted a different form of Islam. Khalid tells Kamal's followers including Nasir, 'I am not your brother.' Nasir's decision to follow Kamal's Islam has led to his separation from his father and to Khalid's shame.

Conclusion

Each of the nine main younger-generation characters depicted in these four films is confronted with a series of choices, the outcome of which will affect not only themselves but also their families and the Muslim community. They are all, at one time or another, situated on borders between Islam as defined by their parents and either the non-Muslim world or an Islamist world. Of the nine young people only one, Tariq and Sadia's oldest child, Rukhsana, seeks to embrace Islam and Muslim culture in the way in which she has learned from her parents. She is happy to enjoy the non-Muslim world so long as it does not conflict with her Muslim values. She is confident to freely embrace the security that the Muslim community she knows can offer her. Each of the other eight young people takes their own path away from the Muslim world in which they were raised into the future. Some, like Casim, Rukhsana's brother, do so reluctantly. He steps away over the border into the liberal non-Muslim world where he found his partner. Others, like Parvez and Minoo's son, Farid, grasp the opportunity when it is offered to step across into an Islamist world.

The majority of these fictional young British Muslims have exercised their citizen rights to form romantic attachments with whoever they like or pursue their chosen career or embrace a more fundamentalist Islam. But where does this leave their parents? As noted above, Modood's research had identified the potential loss of family honour that might follow such independent behaviour, and this is precisely the situation depicted in the films. Each of the fathers of the families at the centre of the films' actions experience loss and feel shame over the behaviour of their children and each fear for the future of their family. In addition each, except for Parvez, is fearful for his family's honour in the eyes of their community. In *Ae Fond Kiss*, Rukhsana refers to this as *izzath*. Bano Murtuja writes, 'As a concept, *izzath* denotes honour, reputation and standing of the individual, family and/or community at large' (2006, p. 303). Murtuja conducted in-depth enquiries with 43 Pakistani Muslims in Britain and Germany to study the 'processes of social exclusion from within diasporic Pakistani Muslim communities' (p. 295). Her research revealed that for many respondents *izzath* is an extremely important aspect of Islamic community life. However, some of her respondents were concerned that *izzath* is too 'unnegotiable'. Zoe (UK, female) for example, says,

> I think our community latches on to that word (*izzath*) too strongly, I don't think we really know the meaning of it. Sometimes they will lose their family and their loved ones for the sake of *izzath*. They'll lose everything for *izzath*. But at the end of the day are they being good Muslims? No. They don't question that. They get stuck on the word *izzath* and then some will not move on at all.
>
> (Murtuja, 2006, p. 308)

Zoe, like many of her generation, might interpret the actions of the parents depicted in *East is East*, *Ae Fond Kiss* and *Yasmin* as being 'stuck on the word *izzath*'. But it is not just parents who are stuck, for in *My Son the Fanatic* and to a lesser extent, *Yasmin*, children think that it is their parents' behaviour that threatens *izzath*.

To this extent, then, I would suggest that the films are articulating, in the senses of both expressing and connecting, another potential emergent structure of feeling. Against the backdrop of major social changes and action in Britain and the inferential structure through which the news media reports them, the films show the vulnerable position of fathers who are not securely placed within the national culture and fear their loss of honour in their faith community. The ability of George Khan, Tariq Khan and Khalid Hussain to keep their children in the faith and in a manner that is broadly accepted by their local Muslim communities has been tested and, in the most part, found wanting. Parvez simply wanted his son to be a decent person, irrespective of faith, but he too has found disappointment. The final images of the fathers in each of the films except *Ae Fond Kiss* are also the final images of the films, and they show defeated or at best resigned figures. In *Ae Fond Kiss*, Tariq's resigned defeat is also clear.

Taken together it is interesting and important to see that through these four films British cinema has been able to pinpoint an absolutely key moment in what might be seen as an emergent structure of feeling. The fact that the films, focusing on British Muslim families and community, have coalesced around the same, deeply felt issue of honour/*izzath* provides some pause for thought. It is connected to the general concern to which Goodhart drew attention when he asked his readers to reflect on the dynamics of the relationship between social solidarity and cultural diversity. In these films the social solidarity of the Muslim community, initially represented by the first generation of denizens, is challenged by a second generation of citizens who see the world differently, in terms of marriage, career or the fundamentals of Islam. This is not cultural diversity defined by the BNP or the right-wing press but by Muslims themselves.

In *East is East* and *Ae Fond Kiss* the issue centres on the domestic sphere of marriage, whilst in *My Son the Fanatic* and *Yasmin* the issue has moved beyond the domestic sphere and become political and global. In these films, religious figures represented by the Maulvi in *My Son the Fanatic* and by Kamal in *Yasmin* have come from outside the community and represent a different authority from that of the fathers, Parvez and Khalid Hussain.

The depiction of the influence of Muslim 'outsiders' might be thought of as pessimistic, in that they are shown as undermining the efforts made by British Muslims to find a way of living in a non-Muslim environment. It is a local form of the more generalized pessimism Samuel H. Huntington articulates in his highly provocative 'Clash of Civilizations?' thesis. Huntington hypothesises,

> That the fundamental source of conflict in this new world will not be primarily ideological or primarily economic. The great divisions among humankind and the dominating sources of conflict will be cultural. Nation states will remain the most powerful actors in world affairs, but the principal conflicts of global politics will occur between nations and groups of different civilizations. The clash between civilizations will dominate global politics.
>
> (1993, p. 22)

He hypothesises further that as the seven civilizations he identifies – Western, Confucian, Japanese, Islamic, Hindu, Slavic-Orthodox and Latin American – appear at this stage to be incommensurable entities, they will have to learn to coexist with each other.

Huntington argues that a civilization is 'the broadest level of identification with which he [a person] identifies' (1993, p. 24). Thus, for example, Huntington might say of Yasmin that once she has stripped away any personal identity she might have developed through her work, lifestyle, regional affiliation and national allegiance, her broadest level of identification would be Islam. His thesis is stimulating but riddled with elisions, generalizations, contradictions and category errors. For example, Huntington claims that the most important criterion of difference between civilizations is religion but, strangely, whilst he identifies Islamic and Confucian civilizations, he does not identify a Christian civilization but a Western one.[38]

However, academic disputation alone does not always disturb the deep waters of international politics. Since the publication of his thesis and his subsequent expansion and defence of it, the realpolitik of world events seems to have sharpened the division between the Western and Islamic 'civilizations' that he alleges to exist and to which he draws particular attention. Many ex-Cold War warriors looking for a new enemy have converted a thesis into a fact. On the other hand, it might be argued that 'Learning to coexist' does not appear to be on President George W. Bush's agenda nor on that of Islamists who seek to impose a cross-national caliphate.

Such a pessimistic politics, expressed in the most global terms, is in stark contrast to the positive proposals and conclusions of *Our Shared Future*, a report published by the Commission on Integration and Community on 14 June 2007. The independent commission was set up by the British Secretary of State for Communities and Local Government and chaired by Darra Singh, Chief Executive of Ealing Council. The report received generous media coverage and, in stark contrast to Goodhart's *Prospect* article (2004), was widely welcomed by the Commission for Equality and Human Rights (incorporating the ex-Commission for Racial Equality) amongst others. Following extensive consultation, the Report presented a long list of practical proposals related to four key principles. These are the need to focus on 'what binds communities together', to build 'a new model of rights and responsibilities' and an 'ethics of hospitality' emphasizing mutual respect and civility and, finally, 'a commitment to equality that sits alongside the need to deliver visible social justice' (2007, p. 7).

Huntington versus Singh? Pessimism or optimism? Today I am feeling optimistic. Who knows what tomorrow might bring?

7
Globalization, Mobility and Community

> Simply put, globalization denotes the expanding scale, growing magnitude, speeding up and deepening impact of interregional flows and patterns of social interaction. It refers to a shift or transformation in the scale of human social organization that links distant communities and expands the reach of power relations across the world's major regions and continents.
>
> (David Held and Anthony McGrew, 2000, p. 4)

> The tourists travel because *they want to*; the vagabonds because *they have no other bearable choice*.
>
> (Zygmunt Bauman, 1998, p. 93, Bauman's emphasis)

Introduction

The will to survival and power motivated human beings to communicate with and migrate beyond the confines of their immediate local environment and communities well before intellectuals began to characterize contemporary society as 'global' and the processes involved in shaping it as 'globalization'. Long before Marx and Engels described the internationalization of capital (1952) or Marshall McLuhan (1962) coined the phrase the 'global village', people travelled across continents and oceans to explore and sometimes settle in or colonise foreign lands.[1] So what is different about present times?

The new global world is characterized amongst other things by the high speed of physical movement and ease of mediated communication by multitudes of overlapping networks of people each spreading beyond the village, the town and the nation state. It is also characterized by the importance given to international organizations through which nation states and other corporate entities organize their relationships, sometimes immediately and sometimes virtually. However, perhaps the most telling feature of globalization is the fact that global society has become an ordinary, everyday experience but by no means for everyone. Of course, the new global world is as stratified as previous ones and many of the forms of stratification are similar, although the manner in which they present themselves might have changed.

Whilst most social scientists might agree with the general outlines of Held and McGrew's description of globalization quoted above, they frequently differ in their analyses of globalization's dynamics, particularly concerning power relations. Wallerstein's (1984) account, for example, privileges capitalism as its driving force. Giddens (1990) in his more complex account acknowledges the continuing power of capitalism but he also identifies three additional drivers of change: militarism, industrialism and inter-state systems. Manuel Castells' trilogy, *The Information Age: Economy, Society and Culture* (1996–98), also offers a multi-causal account in which he notes the ways in which the metropolitan centres such as the White House, Beijing and the London Stock Exchange dictate the initial terms of globalization. Castells also demonstrates that the metropolitan centres cannot control the ways in which local societies, interest groups and social movements respond and shift these terms in their favour. Venezuala's Hugo Chavez's intervention in the global oil market and al-Qaeda's actions anywhere provide distinct, but equally compelling, examples of this.[2]

Chavez and al-Qaeda's actions are precisely targeted at the metropolitan hegemony but they do not, perhaps, pose its main threat. The major risk in the global world, global warming, not only threatens metropolitan society but every person in every village and street of every society. The overwhelming body of environmental scientists and climatologists now argue that global warming, the self-made catastrophe of the industrial age, requires immediate action. The problem is that the carbon emissions creating global warming are produced locally, particularly by the USA and increasingly by China and India, but experienced globally. Thus, for example, even if the USA was to reduce its carbon emissions today, unless China, India and others act to eliminate or significantly reduce their emissions then global warming will continue. And so mountain glaciers and ice flows will continue to melt, sea temperatures will rise further, and one day, not too long from now, Manhatten could disappear below the waves.

Global warming is at the extreme end of the relationship between global and local interests and perhaps international action will be taken to address it, although Nobel Laureate Al Gore who made the film, *An Inconvenient Truth* (dir. David Guggenheim, 2006), precisely about this issue should not hold his breath in waiting. My task, far more modest than Gore's, is to pose and address a question: 'How is mainstream cinema contributing to an understanding of the impact of globalization on the idea and practice of community?' In addressing this question, it is important to note that globalization is not just something that exists outside of us, that is you and me, and bearing down on us, although it can feel that way. It is better understood as a process that we are involved in making and for which we, academics, filmmakers and audiences, bear some responsibility. This does not mean that everyone experiences it in the same way, or is equally responsible for the process or is equally damaged or benefited by it.

In his analysis of globalization, Giddens argues that 'time-space distanciation' is altering the forms of social relations through which we live (1990, p. 14). Giddens is arguing that for many people space has 'shrunk' because the time taken to move through it has decreased; materially by jet travel and virtually by IT systems including the Internet. The increasing speed of travel and communication enables politicians, business operatives and bankers to treat the world as their backyard. Once, Scots moaned that London had too much control over their lives; now control is increasingly exercised in Delhi, Moscow and Singapore. All of this leads to what Giddens calls the 'disembedding' of social relations, in which the terms, norms and parameters of social relations in the family, at work, and at leisure are influenced not just locally but globally. Materially, this might mean that a Japanese company could rescue an ailing British car manufacturer but it might also mean the introduction of new work practices that are more akin to Japanese social norms than British ones. Virtually, this might mean that Internet chat rooms rather than the family breakfast table will provide the means by which young people learn about the world, for good or bad.[3]

How, then, in the face of the disembedding forces of globalization are people to live together? What are the social resources on which they can depend? The family has been one resource and the community a related other. Yet, as I demonstrated in Chapter 4, both the family and the community are amongst those forms of social relations from which individuals are becoming disembedded.

I am concerned in this chapter with the means available to people who are experiencing global social change at a local point to maintain some control over their own lives in their own communities. Craig

Calhoun's ideas are helpful here. Calhoun has explored the idea of community, seeking to redefine and secure it as a 'radical' concept, valuable for social action. His understanding of community is not one that looks back to mythical or golden age notions of community as a binding force in itself and nor is he wedded to a notion of community as an unmediated, small-scale social formation (1988). Rather, Calhoun, like Robert D. Putnam whose work I discussed in Chapter 3, argues that community is a form of interrelationship or social network that works, and is acknowledged as working, as a means of mutual support and a resource for collective behaviour. Such interrelationships do not have to be immediate but can be achieved, at least in part, through mediating and increasingly globalizing forms of communication, for example the telegraph in the nineteenth century, the telephone in the twentieth and the Internet at the turn of the twenty-first. In this respect, Calhoun's approach is similar to that of Benedict Anderson (1983) who famously argued that the demotic appropriation of the print medium helped construct what he called the 'imagined community' of the nation. Following Calhoun, perhaps, we can see that globalization, despite its disembedding tendencies, does not necessarily eradicate community in principle but challenges it in practice whilst offering new opportunities too.

Ordinary people experience these challenges and opportunities every day. Our experiences are not, of course, universal but marked by difference, and it is the varying experience of global society that I want to explore in this chapter. Doreen Massey has argued that the global changes of the sort described above require everyone involved, including social commentators, to develop an appropriate sense of place and of movement. The flows and interconnections of the global society are organized through power relations that stratify individual and group access to mobility and connectivity. She writes,

> Different social groups have distinct relationships to this anyway differentiated mobility: some people are more in charge of it than others; some initiate flows and movement, others don't; some are more on the receiving-end of it than others; some are effectively imprisoned by it.
>
> (1997, p. 234)

In order to examine the way in which major socio-cultural change is impacting on the idea and practice of community, I have selected films for this chapter that relate directly to Massey's theme of mobility and explore some of its properties. Many of the characters of *Monsoon Wedding* (dir. Mira Nair, 2001) are cosmopolitans who are as 'at home' in Delhi as they are in Houston or Sydney. Mobility is not a problem for them, indeed it provides them with opportunities for personal and social development. The main characters of *Lost in Translation* (dir. Sofia Coppola, 2003) are also cosmopolitans but do not seem to be at home in their hotel, or Tokyo, or Japan or anywhere. They have taken advantage of opportunities for mobility, but it has not brought them happiness. The characters of *Last Resort* (dir. Pawel Pawlikowski, 2000) and *Lilya 4-Ever* (dir. Lukas Moodysson, 2002) have homes, of a sort, in Russia but choose to leave them to seek a better life elsewhere. The decisions they have taken to move prove problematic, fatally so for Lilya. The Afghan characters of *In This World* (dir. Michael Winterbottom, 2003) have also had to abandon their homes and live in a refugee camp just outside of Peshawar in Pakistan. However, whilst *Last Resort* and *Lilya 4-Ever* focus on the motivation for and, particularly, the consequence of migration, *In This World* pays meticulous attention to the conditions of the journey itself.

Cosmopolitanism

In this section, I want to consider how recent mainstream cinema has represented the cosmopolitan milieu of those for whom access to mobility and connectivity is easy and sometimes pleasurable. Cosmopolitanism is not a new phenomenon either in 'real life' or on the cinema screen. The upper classes of the French Riviera (Alfred Hitchcock's *Rebecca*, 1940) and Rome and the Amalfi coast (René Clément's *Plein Soleil*, 1960 and Anthony Minghella's *The Talented Mr Ripley*, 1999) have long known of its pleasures. However, the character of cosmopolitanism has changed dramatically in recent years as transnational capitalism has pushed its way into every nook and cranny of the developing economies from Rio to Bangkok. The days when cosmopolitanism was strictly a genteel affair only to be found in Harry's Bar in Venice or Raffles' Hotel in Singapore have long gone. The modern form of cosmopolitanism has been explored by Zygmunt Bauman in two recent books, *Globalization: The Human Consequences* (1998) and *Community: Seeking Safety in an Insecure World* (2001), and I will draw on his ideas here.

In *Globalization*, Bauman argues that 'access to global mobility' is now the 'topmost rank among all stratifying factors' (1998, p. 87). He develops his argument by contrasting two types of people on the move in the global society: vagabonds and tourists. His discussion is fascinating and worth quoting at length:

> The tourists stay or move at their heart's desire. They abandon a site when new untried opportunities beckon elsewhere. The vagabonds know that they won't stay in a place for long, however strongly they wish to, since nowhere they stop are they likely to be welcome. The tourists move because they find the world with their (global) reach irresistibly *attractive* – the vagabonds move because they find the world within their (local) reach unbearably *inhospitable*. The tourists travel because *they want to*; the vagabonds because *they have no other bearable choice*.
>
> (1998, pp. 92–3, Bauman's emphasis)

The tourist as a type of cosmopolitan is a theme Bauman develops in 'Secession of the successful', a brief chapter in *Community* (2001) in which he argues that those who have been ascribed status or have achieved success retreat to spaces that are separate from everyone else. These 'cool' people (2001, p. 52) can exile themselves, at home or abroad, in gated communities. Cosmopolitans can play the game of musical gated communities but with planes and boats and trains instead of chairs. When the music stops the cosmopolitans are able to leap for the nearest gated community; the company condominium or the executive hotel. Whether in Hong Kong, Mexico City or Cairo, these cosmopolitans can secede from the world and 'escape from community' (ibid., p. 57).

Bauman's account draws on research undertaken at the Institute of Advanced Study in Culture of the University of Virginia (2000), in which US executives were asked about their globetrotting lives. The study reports,

> Wherever they [the globetrotters] go, the hotels, health clubs, restaurants, offices, and airports are all virtually identical. There is a sense in which they inhabit a socio-cultural bubble that is insulated from the harsher differences between national cultures [...] They are cosmopolitans to be sure, but in ways that are limited and insular.
>
> (Quoted in Bauman, 2001, pp. 55–6)

This is the world inhabited by the two main characters that feature in Sofia Coppola's critically acclaimed film, *Lost in Translation*. Bob (Bill Murray) and Charlotte (Scarlett Johansson) are alienated characters in a Tokyo hotel that looks like every other five-star hotel in every other business city. The difference here is that neither Bob nor Charlotte fully understand what they are doing in the hotel or Japan. Charlotte, a Yale philosophy graduate, is with her new husband John (Giovanni Ribisi), a 'Rolling Stone' type photographer, who is pre-occupied with his shoot-ing project. Bob is an 'on-the-slide' film actor who is in Tokyo to shoot a Japanese 'whiskey' commercial. She is bored and he is confused; confused by the shower, the gym, the commercial shot in Japanese and the prosti-tute sent to his room by the ad agency. Bob and Charlotte get together to share their experiences of alienation and visit the city which they find bewildering. They do meet up with some young Japanese people who take them to karaoke, a very popular entertainment form in Japan, which is in a way another sign of alienation as it involves singing someone else's songs. Coppola captures through long, slow-moving takes, particularly of Charlotte in her room, Bob on the phone to his wife and the hotel generally, a general air of ennui which can be the lot of the constant traveller. However, through a more active editing style Coppola captures Bob's confusion as he fails to cope with the cultural differences between Japan and the USA.

Lost in Translation, then, can be seen as a critique of the 'socio-cultural bubble' described in the Virginian study. However, whilst the film offers a critique of the hollowness of the cosmopolitan world it does so in a strangely cosmopolitan fashion, in that it is curiously indifferent to mod-ern Japanese culture. For Kikai Day, a Japanese artist, this indifference borders on racism. She writes of the film,

> There is no scene where the Japanese are afforded a shred of dignity. The viewer is sledgehammered into laughing at these small, yellow people and their funny ways, desperately aping the western lifestyle without knowledge of its real meaning. It is telling that the longest vocal contribution any Japanese character makes is at a karaoke party, singing a few lines of the Sex Pistols' 'God Save the Queen'.
>
> ('Totally lost in translation', *The Guardian*, January 24, 2004)

She has a point and it connects with mine. Following the Second World War, modern Japan, as much as any other Asian country, has been shaped by the USA – economically, politically and socially. Clearly, Japan has retained some aspects of its pre-capitalist culture, as Charlotte discovers on a trip to a shrine. However, for the most part, the film shows the Japanese as 'ridiculous people' (Day, 2004) embracing, often mimicking, a hollow version of cosmopolitanism. It is the 'reflective' Americans, Bob and Charlotte, who see through it and turn their back on it. Of course, Charlotte might have been bored in an identical hotel in Bombay or Jakarta and Bob confused by the culture shock experienced in Nairobi or Lahore. However, in *Lost in Translation* all of this is filtered by the director through a lens that portrays hackneyed stereotypes of the Japanese. Cinemagoers who are looking for a more nuanced account of the relationship between Japanese and global culture might do better to view Masayuki Suo's Japanese Academy Award winning *Shall We Dance?* (1996). It is less than ironic that the distinctive international dimension of Suo's film is almost entirely lost in Peter Chelsom's (2004) American remake with the same title.

Bauman's account, then, is useful in thinking about cosmopolitanism but his is a strangely one-dimensional one, looking, as it does, at cosmopolitanism from the point of view of a self-described cosmopolitan intellectual fearing the spread of consumer global capitalism and its attendant 'flight from the "messiness of real intimacy"' (2001 p. 52). It is a point of view that I recognize but it is partial and easy to make from a metropolitan centre. However, there is another account to examine and this is the one offered by post-colonial writers such as Stuart Hall (1987) and Paul Gilroy (1993), who celebrate the different cosmoplitanism found in the cultural diasporas of, for example, Afro-Caribbeans living in Paris, London and New York. It is also the account offered by Hamid Naficy in *An Accented Cinema* (2001), who writes with authority about the ways in which exilic and diaspora filmmakers have translated their work across the world to address both home and host audiences alike. I wish to turn to one of the filmmakers he discusses, Mira Nair, to show how her film, *Monsoon Wedding*, offers a very different view of cosmopolitanism to that found in *Lost in Translation*.

Mira Nair was born in Orissa, India, and studied sociology at Delhi University and filmmaking at Harvard. She has directed in India and the United States making both documentaries and feature films. The two films for which she is best known are *Salaam Bombay!* (1988) and *Monsoon Wedding* for which she was awarded the Golden Lion Prize at Venice in 2001. *Salaam Bombay!* depicts young, orphaned, abandoned street children in Bombay trying to survive by whatever means possible. It is shot in a cinéma-vérité, ethnographic style. To someone such as myself who has not seen the world the film depicts, it looks realistic and compelling. It appears sentimental but not manipulative. Naficy notes that US and UK critics admired these aspects of the film but he also points out that Indian critics were less sympathetic to the film's 'politics'. Naficy writes, 'Because it elides power relations and targets foreign audiences,

Nair's cinematic gaze upon her native home is considered [by Indian critics] touristic, voyeuristic, and superficial [...]' (2001, p. 69).

Naficy suggests that Nair could have avoided this sort of criticism of the film if she had been 'more self-reflexive about its own status as a diasporic rumination about India, and had it highlighted Nair's own in-betweenness [...]' (ibid., p. 70). Whatever, the merits of Naficy's argument this point could not be made against *Monsoon Wedding*. *Monsoon Wedding*, made in English, Hindi and Punjabi, enthusiastically embraces the cosmopolitan world of the upper middle class families of Delhi, and Nair, the child of such a cosmopolitan family, knows precisely of what she directs and lets the audience know it too. The dialogue that slips effortlessly between languages has the effect of keeping the monolingual English-speaking audience on its toes and constantly aware of the hybridity of this segment of Indian culture.

The plot is quite conventional. The film opens four days before Lalit (Naseeruddin Shah) and Pimmi (Lillette Dubey) Verma's daughter Aditi's arranged marriage with Hemant Rai (Parvin Dadas), the son of another wealthy Delhi family, who has flown in from Houston for the wedding. Aditi (Vasundhara Das) has been having an affair with Vikram (Sameer Arya), a star TV presenter who she cannot resist meeting again, although the wedding is imminent. She knows that Vikram is married. Finally, discovering that he is a scoundrel Aditi tells Hemant of her affair. Initially Hemant is very angry, but he forgives her and the wedding goes ahead. Nair weaves several other sub-plots into the main story, of which two are particularly important. The first concerns Tej (Rajat Kapoor) the very wealthy senior male of the extended family who supported Lalit after he was forced to move to Delhi following partition. Tej is revealed to have sexually abused Ria (Shefali Shetty), Lalit's niece and ward, when she was young. Ria exposes Tej when she discovers that he is now abusing her cousin, Aliya (Kemaya Kidwai). Lalit has to decide what to do about this. He chooses to send Tej away. The second sub-plot concerns the romance between Dubey (Vijay Raaz), the wedding planner, and Alice (Tilotama Shome), a family servant. Dubey, a comic figure who is always on the make and the possessor of a colourful repertoire of obscenities, is smitten by Alice's beauty, gentleness and kindness, despite her lower caste status. At the end of the film Lalit makes a point of choosing to dance with Alice.

The film is about a family and community and how ideas of the family are changing in modern India, especially in the context of globalization. Whilst the family wedding is deeply rooted in Hindu culture and the Verma family is shown as being committed to Hindu family values, Nair shows the audience how India is changing. This is seen in small ways; Pimmi smoking, Mrs Rai (Roshan Seth) drinking whisky in public, tea vendors discussing customers who want to drink American style, 'sweet and low' coffee, cousin Ayesha being very forward with another male cousin and so on. There is also one extended metonymic scene, positioned very early on, indicating the major scale of the change that is taking place. Nair shows Vikram chairing a TV panel discussion about Indian culture in which handloom weaving and spoken Hindi are contrasted with American culture. Vikram manipulates the discussion by introducing one of Delhi's top Bollywood dubbists who proceeds to demonstrate her traditional skills by speaking the lines of a porn movie.

However, the most important trope indicating change concerns the fact that four young members of the family either work or want to work outside of India. The groom Hemant works in Houston, Rahul (Randeep Hooda), son of C. L. (Kulbhusan Kharbanda) – a Muscat businessman – lives in Melbourne, Umang (Jas Arora) another of C. L.'s sons is due to fly in from the States and, finally, Ria wants to study creative writing in the USA. *Monsoon Wedding* represents a new generation of young people who are family oriented but also comfortable in the wider, cosmopolitan world beyond India. Mira Nair, the cosmopolitan filmmaker dedicates her film, 'for my family'. The final dance sequence, like many of the earlier ones, is a riotous affair in which all generations and social castes and classes, including Alice and Dubey, are pulled into a single community.

Monsoon Wedding draws on a number of film traditions. On the one hand, the music and dance sequences draw on Bollywood style although the explicit theme of sexual abuse does not. On the other, as Lalitha Gopalan (2003, p. 364) demonstrates, the latter theme and the potential impact it has on the family bears a striking similarity to the denouement in *Festen* (dir. Thomas Vinterberg, 1998), the Dogme film. However, unlike in *Festen*, Lalit Verma deals with the charge of abuse positively. The similarity with *Festen* can also be seen by Nair's extensive use of hand-held camera technique. Nair's reasons for choosing this technique are interesting:

[Nair chose the technique] Mostly to achieve mobility and fluidity that would link the multiplicity of Indian life, the hybridity that is in our music, our location and our languages. India is a fantastic place because we have opened our doors to people from all over the world – before the British, after the British – and now, with American globalization. We absorb, we borrow, we assimilate, we plagiarise and we steal, and somehow twist it all to make something that is inimitably Indian.

This is the mood I wanted to capture in the multilayered stories, and this kind of camera can take us fluidly from a five-star hotel to the crowded streets of old Delhi; it's a way to link the family's intimate drama to the world.[4]

In this fashion, and in clear contrast to *Lost in Translation*, *Monsoon Wedding* portrays the cosmopolizing tendencies of global culture very positively. No doubt, Delhi has its share of Park Hyatt, Raddisson and Hilton style hotels and no doubt Vikram would be at home in them all. However, Nair's film is an attempt to demonstrate that it is possible to take the qualities of globalization and 'to make something that is inimitably Indian'. There are tourists and vagabonds in Delhi, but there are other cosmopolitans who are as at home with their families as they are doing business in Houston, Melbourne and Muscat.

In the sheltered corridors of cosmopolitan hotels any hope for community, of building a network of mutual support, must rely on the accidental, casual, serendipitous meetings of alienated characters such as Charlotte and Bob. However, to its credit *Lost in Translation* does not end with Charlotte and Bob setting off to build their little home on the prairie but in an acknowledgement that they must part. The hopes for community in *Monsoon Wedding* are much higher. The film seems to share Calhoun's optimism that the new forms of information technology – the telephone and Internet – can help sustain the dense level of interrelationships that was on view in the Verma household. Unfortunately, the grounds for optimism for community in our contemporary global society raised by *Monsoon Wedding* are challenged by the evidence provided by the next section of this chapter.

Leaving home (i) Looking for love and work

The rejection of state communism in the former USSR and its East and Central European satellites has produced some stable governments and some stable economies and civil societies. It has also created the potential for civil wars and that potential has been realized, for example, in former Yugoslavian states between Serbs, Croats and Bosnians and in Chechnya. It has also created economic and civil turbulence in many countries, not least in Russia itself. Each country has a new generation of people who see in existing Western-style democracies a world that they want to inhabit or economic fortunes they want to make. The recent expansion of the European Community to encompass some former Soviet bloc countries has brought a little stability to the region but over the past 15 years for many citizens trying to make their own way in the world the only way has been out.

If the central characters of *Monsoon Wedding* and *Lost in Translation* are, in Bauman's terms, tourists then those of *Last Resort* and *Lilya 4-Ever*, who 'have no bearable choice' (Bauman, 1998, p. 93) are better understood as vagabonds.[5] The latter films depict the plight of three Russians, a woman and her son and a girl who all, for one reason or another, leave Russia. They form an interesting contrast of how mainstream cinema has sought to represent the experience of people journeying across the physical borders of modern nation states, and the psychological border of hope and despair. Neither film can be described as self-consciously being about the mechanics of globalization but they are concerned with its effect, specifically related to a sense of place and movement, and how this is experienced by ordinary people. The social changes involved in the collapse of the former Soviet Union has disembedded each of them from a world that, whatever it strengths and weaknesses, provided a measure of certainty.

Last Resort, directed by Pawel Pawlikowski, the son of an émigré Polish mother who settled in the UK in the mid-1970s, tells the story of Tanya (Dina Korzun) and her son Artiom (Artium Strelnikov) on their arrival at an airport in the UK. Tanya has left Russia to join her fiancé but he fails to meet her. In desperation and confusion she applies for asylum and, together with her son, is taken to a refugee holding centre in Stonehaven, an English seaside town. Mortified to discover that it will take between 12 and 16 months to process her application for asylum, Tanya tries to escape but is caught and returned to the centre. Tanya meets Alfie (Paddy Considine), an amusement arcade manager and bingo caller, who seeks to help her. Alfie falls for Tanya and aids her escape. Ultimately, she decides not to stay with Alfie but to return to Russia to start again.

Tanya's home-seeking journey to the UK became a journey of homelessness before ending as a journey of home-returning to Russia. For a while Tanya and Artiom had been in danger of becoming long-term refugees, a part of what Bauman describes as 'the human waste product of the global frontier-land' (2004, p. 80). The holding centre is a strictly liminal space and its liminality is emphasized by it being located by the sea in a town in which the railway station has been 'closed until further notice'.

Last Resort is not a didactic film. Pawlikowski constructs no easy targets. Of course, there are immigration officials, police officers and security guards but none are shown to be dishonest, brutal or hostile. Even the pornographers that offer Tanya some work are depicted as having some sort of basic sensitivity – for pornographers. Pawlikowski does not overly concern himself with all the practicalities of the asylum management process. Nor does he make any attempt to romanticise the society Tanya has left and to which she will return. Finally, Pawlikowski resists any temptation to make Tanya a representative figure – she does not 'stand' for anyone or anything.

Running only for 79 minutes, *Last Resort* is a very compact film about love and ethics in personal relationships. Tanya and Artiom have come to Britain on the promise of love but it is a love that disappears on landing at the airport. From that moment the real love story is focused on that of Tanya for her son. Although it is clear that Alfie has formed an attachment to her, this is somehow secondary. We can better understand Alfie's role in the ethical terms provided by Levinas. Alfie behaves in the manner of the sisters in *Babette's Feast*, discussed in Chapter 2. His commitment to both Tanya and Artiom is an open one. To him they are strangers to whom he offers hospitality. He seeks no reciprocation from Tanya.

That Pawlikowski manages to convey this non-didactic representation of migration is in part due to the quality of the acting but it is also achieved through the delicately phrased script and particularly through his visual style and his choice of poetic tropes and narrative devices. Pawlikowski and his director of photography, Ryszard Lenczewski, alternate intimate hand-held camera close-ups with very still, distant and mid-shots on both internal and external locations. This enables the audience to experience not only the tension of Tanya and Artiom's personal traumas but also the isolation of the liminal space they occupy.

Various visual tropes are deployed throughout the film. First, *Last Resort* begins and ends with shots of Tanya and Artiom travelling on a conveyor through a tunnel connecting airport terminal buildings. The image is clear; the characters are borne along as if by fate but at the end of the tunnel they will have to make decisions. Secondly, Pawlikowski contrasts the drab and formal geometry of the tower block refugee holding centre with the bright lights of the amusement arcade, bingo hall and the fairground, which is visible from it. Yet neither of these places are where Tanya and Artiom belong; the fairground, Alfie's environment, does not offer a means of escape from the holding centre. Thirdly, Tanya, who is a children's book illustrator, has brought with her from Russia a picture she has painted of a magical boat. When, later, we see a boat anchored on the seashore the audience can begin to imagine that this will form part of her return journey.

Each of these tropes provide the audience with a sense of engagement with Tanya and Artiom. However, there is one further trope that seals the audience's commitment. Apart from Alfie, Tanya's most important relationships with adults are through media; the telephone answering machine of her fiancé, the surveillance CCTV equipment that watches her every move when she first tries to escape and the pornographers' webcam. Contrary to Calhoun's optimism for the communal possibilities offered by media, Pawlikowski shows how each technology objectifies her. The CCTV surveyors and the pornographers do not need to be shown as evil; it is enough that they are shown as ordinary. The audience, taking up the viewing position the media technology offers, witnesses this alienation. Thus whilst the film is not a didactic one, its ethics are apparent and they raise political questions. Perhaps, the most important of which is, 'in whose interest is it that a democratic society, such as Britain, should treat strangers in this way?'

Pawlikovski presents Tanya and Artiom's future as uncertain but her new-found realism provides the audience with some grounds of hope for her. Such grounds are not to be found in *Lilya 4-Ever*. The narratives of both *Last Resort* and *Lilya 4-Ever* are sparked by acts of betrayal, but the effects of the betrayal in the latter are distinctly darker. Moodysson, who directed and wrote the screenplay, returns to his interest in representing children's lives, but whereas the children of his previous films *Show Me Love* (1998) and *Together* (2001) end up happy, teenager Lilya (Oksana Akinshina) and her young friend, Volodya (Artyium Bogucharsky), end up dead.

Following the collapse of the Soviet Union, Lilya is abandoned by her mother, who had in turn been abandoned by Lilya's father, when she moves to the United States with her new partner. She breaks her promises to send Lilya money and to arrange to have Lilya come to her. Lilya is destitute and survives through prostitution. Her one friend is an 11 year-old-boy, Volodya, who is even more vulnerable than she is. Lilya meets Andrei (Pavel Ponomaryov), an apparently good man who says he works in Sweden, and they form a close relationship. Lilya is pleased when Andrei suggests they go to live in Sweden where, he says, he can find her a job too. Volodya warns Lilya about trusting him. However, she accepts Andrei's offer and leaves Volodya, who feels betrayed. He kills himself. Volodya is right about Andrei who passes Lilya on to a pimp who imprisons, rapes and offers her up to a succession of clients. She kills herself.

Moodysson helps the child actors produce wonderful, fresh performances in complex roles. Oksana Akinshina as Lilya is outstanding as she
manages to convincingly portray childish playfulness and bewilderment,
adolescent confusion and young adult anger and hurt often in the same
scene. This is necessary because one of the key themes of the film is how
her experience of betrayal by everyone except young Volodya robs her
of her childhood but does not prepare her for adulthood.

Moodysson adopts the same cinematic style that he used in his previous film, *Together*.[6] He uses tripod-mounted cameras placed as far away
from the actors as possible in order to provide room for them to move
freely in the confined spaces. However, here he makes much more use
of hand-held camera work, particularly to indicate Lilya's sense of loss,
firstly in Russia and then in the Swedish rooms where she is repeatedly
raped by the 'clients'. In these scenes the claustrophobic atmosphere of
her imprisonment is palpable. Moodysson gives absolutely no encouragement to the viewer to enjoy these scenes by focusing largely on the
grunting, sweaty men. The film is shot throughout in mostly muted col-
ours, with grey and blue tones predominating. The exterior shots are
utterly depressing. Moodysson leaves the audience in no doubt about
the quality of the environment in which Lilya and Volodya have been
trying to live.

Lilya 4-Ever differs from *Last Resort* in a number of respects. First, it
is less poetic. Moodysson's visual tropes are not always successful. The
imagery works, for example, in the scenes when her mother (Lyubov
Agapova) leaves. Lilya initially refuses to acknowledge her departure, but
finally runs outside to hug her before she disappears. Lilya refuses to let
her mother go but is forced to do so. As the car speeds away, she chases
after it but falls on her knees in the grey mud. The metaphor perfectly
anticipates the life that Lilya will find as she slides, inexorably into a
descent from which not even her prayers and religious pictures will save
her. Less successful is the scene in which Lilya is visited by the ghost of
the now dead Volodya, resplendent with angel wings.

The sense of inexorability marks a second difference with *Last Resort*.
In the latter, Tanya's relationship with Alfie is open with Pawlikowski
offering evidence of Alfie's good intentions. The narrative structure of
Lilya 4-Ever is much more deterministic and the audience is aware of
this from the very beginning of the film. At the outset, Lilya is shown
running from something or someone along busy city roads. The audience
does not know what she is running from, but as she stands on a bridge
overlooking a road it is clear that she is battered and bruised. The picture
fades to black and the narrative goes back 3 months to somewhere in

Russia. It becomes obvious that the film is not about what might happen to Lilya but how it happened.

And this leads to a third difference. *Lilya 4-Ever* is a much more didactic film than *Last Resort*. The representation of the housing estate on which Lilya lives is given greater texture than is Tanya's refugee clearing centre. We are introduced to other people, particularly youngsters whose lives are all damaged by grinding poverty and squalor and by personal impoverishment. All the estate's adults are old or tired or both. None of them have the time, money or interest to help Lilya and Volodya. The estate, the apartments and their inhabitants are burnt-out shells. The only young adults who have money are the men who frequent the disco to pick up young girls. Lilya is of school age, but her school doesn't care whether or not she attends. The social services know that she is destitute but they afford no protection; they have no protection to offer. Her only source of income is to be made by following her aunt's advice, 'Go up to town and spread your legs'.

It is difficult not to see Lilya as a representative figure; someone who 'stands' for something. This is achieved, partly, by Moodysson adopting a realist film rhetoric. But more importantly he achieves it by showing that Lilya is not alone. He introduces the audience to Lilya's young friend, Volodya, and to her girlfriend, Natasha (Elina Benenson), and to the lads of the estate with whom she drinks alcohol, sniffs glue and hangs around. These lads eventually gang-rape her. Lilya had once talked Volodya out of throwing himself off a bridge. By the time Lilya actually jumps she does not know that Volodya has also killed himself by taking an overdose of pills. Lilya's tale is an exemplary one.

The fact that Lilya's case is only too common has been made clear by many studies and reports on human trafficking. The summary report of the London School of Hygiene and Tropical Medicine's study *Stolen Smiles* (2006) estimates that many thousands of women are trafficked within Europe each year. The study was based on the experiences of 207 women, of 15 years of age or older, who gave private interviews in numerous European cities including Kiev, Prague and London.[7] *Stolen Smiles* reports that

> Trafficked women have very different experiences while in the trafficking setting. Some are held captive, unremittingly assaulted and horribly violated. Others are less abused physically, but are psychologically tormented, and live in fear of harm to themselves and their family members.
>
> (p. 5)

Julian Graffy has correctly argued that Moodysson's depiction of Russia is convincingly 'abject and doom-laden' (2002, p. 22). He also argues that Moodysson's depiction of Sweden, frequently regarded as a beacon of liberal values, is equally devastating. It is not just Russian men who want to steal the lives and smiles from young Russian women; Swedish men want them too and are prepared to pay and they have more money than most Russians with which to do so. The United Nations' 2006 Report 'Trafficking in persons' identifies the Russian Federation as a 'very high source of origin of humans trafficked for sex' and Sweden as a prominent point of arrival.[8] Sex trafficking for prostitution is big business and no country has the moral high ground from which to criticize others.

The abandonment of disembedded children and cruelty towards them by adults and parents are not new horrors. We cannot simply hold 'modernity' to blame nor can we blame the 'space-time' compressed ambivalences of postmodernity. Every generation abandons children in its own way whether to the mines or factories of the new industries of the nineteenth-century Industrial Revolution or the use of children in armies of some contemporary African states. However, it is always shocking and not least so in its present manifestation as part of the globalization of sex crime.[9]

When the former Soviet bloc collapsed, commentators such as the distinguished journalist Misha Glenny predicted that the path to political, economic and civil stability would not be smooth. Writing, somewhat prophetically in 1992, Glenny argued, 'As Russia continues to decline (at the moment we are at the very start), its negative influence will be felt ever more on large parts of Russia and the Balkans [...] The Russian morass must provoke grave concern both within the republic and in those states surrounding it' (p. 265). Of course, economically Russia is no longer in decline although the distribution of its wealth is massively unequal. Tanya, Artiom, Lilya and Volodya are depicted as characters caught up by the massive forces of change that swept and, indeed, continue to sweep across Russia. The collapse of social structures of government, employment, family, social security and even of religion in the aftermath of the collapse of communism provides little opportunity for the growth of the sort of community relationships described by Calhoun. It is possible that the spread of demotic new technologies might create the conditions for a more revitalized community built on different terms. However, it is just as likely that the same technologies will be put to work by the pimps and traffickers not only in the unstable ex-Soviet countries but also in the stable, secure and liberal older democracies of Western Europe and the USA.

Leaving home (ii) Seeking refuge and asylum

> Refugees (are) people who are outside their country and cannot return owing to a well-founded fear of persecution because of their race, religion, nationality, political opinions or membership of a particular social group. This has been subsequently expanded to include people who have fled because of war or civil conflict.
>
> (UNHCR Founding Mandate)[10]

> Refugees, the human waste of the global frontier-land, are 'the outsiders incarnate'. The absolute outsiders, outsiders everywhere and out of place everywhere except in places that are themselves out of place – the 'nowhere places' that appear on no maps used by ordinary humans on their travels.
>
> (Bauman, 2004, p. 80)

Filmmaking was banned in Afghanistan under the Taliban regime, and during the subsequent, frequently terrifying years, it has not generally been a priority for the Afghans.[11] However, films about Afghanistan have been made by directors from other countries, for example from Iran, which shares a border with Afghanistan. Both Mohsen Makhmalbaf's *Kandahar* (2001) and his daughter Samira Makhmalbaf's *At Five in the Afternoon* (2003) explore Afghan experiences during the Taliban years. Mohsen's film particularly gives shape and form to the distress of that time.[12] However both films are in a sense local films. To explore Afghanistan in a wider context, a global context, I want to look at Michael Winterbottom's *In This World*; a film about refugees, economic migrants and asylum seekers; the worlds' flotsam and jetsam.[13]

The main vagabond characters of *In This World* cross the borders of several nation states. It sounds banal, but true nevertheless, to say that nation-statehood is under pressure from globalization. The ability of a nation state to maintain the integrity of its borders has become as critical to a nation's survival as it is difficult to achieve. Although it is nigh on impossible to keep out unwanted electronic communication, unless as with China, you have the power to negotiate with internet service providers, it should be easier to keep out unwanted 'real people'. Nation states spend much time and money on attempting to do just that.

If border control management is hard even for the USA with apparently unlimited funds available for homeland security, then how much more difficult is it for Pakistan, Iran and the other four countries with which Afghanistan shares its border? Human Rights Watch claims that in the immediate aftermath of the US-led occupation of Afghanistan, 3.5 million Afghans sought refuge with Pakistan and Iran.[14] *In This World* tells the story of two such refugees, Jamal and Enayat, who travel along the Silk Route from the Shamshatoo refugee camp outside of Peshawar, Pakistan, to seek asylum in the UK.[15]

Afghanistan, a country more than twice the size of the UK, has a population of around thirty million people of whom 97 percent and 3 percent are Sunni and Shi'a Muslims respectively. Its ethnic mix is very varied with Pashtun, the largest ethnic group. According to the World Health Organization, the life expectancy at birth of both men and women in Afghanistan is 42 years.[16]

Massey, discussing her idea of a global sense of place, argues that despite all the shifts to our conception of place brought about by globalization, it is important to remember that places do have a uniqueness. Such uniqueness owes much, she writes, to '[...] the accumulated history of a place, with that history itself imagined as the product of layer upon layer of different sets of linkages, both local and to the wider world' (Massey, p. 240).

This should be kept in mind in thinking about Afghanistan, which has always been a part of a global society at least in the older sense of the term. Afghanistan wears its frequently turbulent history in everyday life. In distant times, it was invaded by Macedons, Huns, Persians, Arabs and Mongols. More recently, the Ghaznavid dynasty (962–1186 AD) established the Sunni Muslim basis of the country and thereby helped stop the spread of Shi'a Islam from the Middle East to the Far East. Afghanistan's crucial geographic location was recognized by Marco Polo who travelled through Afghanistan in 1273 in his attempt to establish the Silk Route from China to Venice. Its strategic position was well understood by European imperial powers. Thus, more recent history involved two nineteenth century wars with Great Britain and the late twentieth century invasion by the Soviets striving to fulfil the hegemonic dreams of previous Russian Tsarist regimes. The Soviets were defeated by the Mujahideen resistance fighters who were, in turn, defeated by the Islamist Taliban group. The most recent attempt to control Afghanistan has been led by the United States, which, in the wake of the 11th September 2001 attack on the New York's World Trade Centre, alleged a link between the Taliban and al-Qaeda.

The Afghan refugees are in a situation that Michel Agiers describes as 'liminal drift',[17] for the Afghan refugees of 2002, or of 2008 for that matter, had or will have no conception of whether or not there will ever be a home for them again in Afghanistan. As such, those that can change their status from refugee to economic migrant or asylum seeker might as well do so and, having done so, set off westward along the Silk Route to seek personal and economic security.

The United Kingdom is at the other end of the now extended Silk Route. According to the United Nations High Commissioner for Refugees (UNHCR) in 2002, the year in which *In This World* was completed, the UK was host to 20 305 Afghan refugees and asylum seekers, an increase of approximately 5 000 over the previous year.[18] Many of the refugees and asylum seekers sought entry to the UK via the village of Sangatte which, situated at the French end of the Euro rail tunnel, is also the site of a Red Cross refugee holding centre. By 2002, despite the noise from the bellicose and frequently xenophobic British popular press, 28 000 people, mainly refugees or asylum seekers, had passed through Sangatte by legal or illegal means on their way to the UK.[19]

Some refugees have tried to enter the UK by paying human traffickers to carry them in ferries or through the tunnel in lorries, sometimes successfully but other times not so. Thus it was that on 18 June 2000, 58 Chinese migrants who had been ferried from the Belgian port of Zeebrugge were found suffocated to death in a container lorry at the English Channel port of Dover. These migrants would have paid a large financial price for their transportation, but they had not anticipated the greater cost they would ultimately pay. Their deaths, in part, inspired Michael Winterbottom to begin work on his film.

In This World follows adolescent Jamal (Jamal Udin Torabi) and his older cousin, Enayat (Enayatullah), as they seek to travel from the Shamshatoo refugee camp to London. Enayat's father has paid for their journey. He has also organized the chain of 'fixers' who will facilitate the cousins' progress as they cross the huge distance between Shamshatoo and the Sangatte camp through Iran, Turkey and across the Mediterranean to Italy and on to France. Their journey by bus, lorry, pick-up truck, container ship and train and on foot across the Iran/Turkey mountain border is hazardous and only Jamal survives. After smuggling himself under a lorry on which to ride through the Eurotunnel he is refused asylum. However, the British Immigration Office does grant him 'exceptional leave to enter' the UK on condition he leaves the day before his 18th birthday.

Winterbottom, shooting on digital video mostly with available light, contrives to give *In This World* a strong documentary look and sound. With this relatively simple equipment, he manages to provide an impressive visual style. The vast, empty looking landscape with an occasional tent, camel or burnt-out vehicle is recorded at length and shot in muted tones. This is in marked contrast to the camp and city life that he films in a lively, sometimes vibrant, fashion, except in those sequences when the cousins are waiting for their 'fixers' to set up the next section of their journey.

The film's documentary effect is achieved in a number of ways. First, the occasional use of voice-over provides information about the lot of refugees in general and Jamal and Enayat in particular. Second, their route is shown visually on maps on which key towns are marked. Third, Winterbottom takes time to show everyday events and activities of the people in whose world he is, in a sense, intruding. These include horse training, dancing, slaughtering a bullock for meat, playing football, at work, washing and praying. Winterbottom does not try to integrate these sequences in the central narrative. Fourth, the performances of Jamal Udin Torabi and Enayatullah, who are non-professional actors, are entirely without artifice or conceit. Fifth, the use of available light dramatizes the scenes. The border crossing over the mountain range between Iran and Turkey in heavy snow uses only reflected light and creates the appropriate tension. Finally, Winterbottom also takes time to provide some identity to the cities and towns through which Jamal and Enayat travel. An exception to this documentary style is the manner in which Winterbottom records Tehran. It is initially presented through rapidly cut, bright, night-lit images of the paralyzingly heavy traffic that emphasize its metropolitan status and the fact that Jamal and Enayat will have never seen anything like it before. He then shifts back down to a much slower pace as the cousins settle in for a long wait.

There is much more to be said about the way Winterbottom manages to represent Jamal and Enayat's experiences as they cross the thousands of miles towards a safe haven to a diverse, global audience. To do so requires a brief excursion to discuss some developments in world cinema.

One of the features of globalization is the fact that the cinema is no longer simply dominated nor even defined by Hollywood, or Bollywood for that matter. Shahini Chaudhuri argues that the term 'world cinema' '[...] encapsulates the dispersed and decentred model of film production and distribution that increasingly prevails, especially if it is used to emphasize the interplays between national, regional and global levels of cinema' (2005, p. 12). Whilst this points to an important and obvious fact, as a term 'world cinema' masks a variety of film production forms and distribution methods. For example, Chaudhuri has little to say of the place of new technologies, such as digital video as used by Winterbottom in *In This World*, nor of the relationship between the cinema and television. *In This World* was a joint production between the Film Consortium, the UK Film Council and the BBC. The latter is, of course, one of the largest television and radio corporations in the world but it has invested quite heavily in films that have been made, initially, for cinema release before airing on TV.

In the following pages, I will draw on the work of Hamid Naficy (2001) whose contribution to an understanding of the idea of world cinema is, as Alison Butler (2002) suggests, very important. Within world cinema can be found what Naficy calls an accented cinema; a cinema of exiled and diasporic filmmakers. Denying that accented cinema constitutes a unified cinema, he nevertheless argues that it is '[...] an increasingly significant cinematic formation in terms of its output, which reaches into the thousands, its variety of forms and diversity of cultures, which are staggering, and its social impact, which extends far beyond exile and diasporic communities to include the general public as well' (2001, p. 4).

The range of styles Naficy identifies is as wide as the modernist and postmodernist movement in the arts generally, and the variety of their subject matter emphasizes the fluidity of movement associated with the exiled and diasporic communities found globally. The filmmakers themselves, he argues, are artisans and bricoleurs using whatever means are available for their work, including those stolen or borrowed from the mainstream. They do not work in a cinematic bubble, but '[...] in dialogue with the home and host societies and their respective national cinemas, as well as with audiences, many of whom are similarly transnational, whose desires, aspirations, and fears they express' (2001, p. 6).[20]

By Naficy's definition, Winterbottom is clearly not an exile from the UK where he was born and has made many of his films. Nor is he a member of a diasporic community whether defined in victim/refugee, imperial/colonial, labour/service, trade/business/professional or cultural/hybrid/postmodern terms (Robin Cohen, 1997, p. 178). However, perhaps Naficy's definition is too restrictive. Stuart Hall, probably the most influential proponent of cultural studies in the UK, has taken a more radical approach to the idea of diaspora and marginality. Hall, a black Jamaican who has spent most of his life researching and teaching in the UK, has argued wittily but tellingly that in one sense his 'immigrant' status does not make him marginal at all because it has dawned on him that we are all marginal; we all migrate. Speaking provocatively to a British audience he argued, 'What I've thought of as dispersed and fragmented comes, paradoxically, to be *the* representative modern experience! This is 'coming home' with a vengeance! Most of it I enjoy – welcome to migranthood' (Gray and McGuigan, 1997, p. 134, Hall's emphasis). Taken in these terms Winterbottom might be understood to be an exile.

Hall's witty discourse should not deceive us. Neither he nor I mean to be flippant. When Hall came to Britain from Jamaica in the 1950s he did so legally and without material hindrance, courtesy of a British passport and a place at Oxford University. Hall was and is, in Bauman's terms, a tourist. The vagabond Enayat died of suffocation in a container ship. There is migration and migration. The point I am making is somewhat different, concerning as it does the distinction between Winterbottom and accented filmmakers; a distinction that is not clear-cut. For example, Naficy rightly regards Atom Egoyan as a highly talented, accented filmmaker. He records Egoyan's emigration as follows:

Egoyan was born in Egypt in 1960 to two artists, who were descendants of Armenian refugees. His parents ran a successful furniture store until the rising tide of Nasserist nationalism and the parochialism of the local Armenian community encouraged their emigration in 1962 to Victoria, British Columbia. Egoyan was 3 years old at the time.

(Naficy, p. 3)

Naficy claims that ethnicity is at the centre of Egoyan's exilic experience. Michael Winterbottom was born in Blackburn, Lancashire, in the industrial north of England in 1961. His parents had lower middle class occupations; his mother was a teacher and his father was a draughtsman at the Phillips television factory. He studied English at Oxford University. After postgraduate work at film school, he began to make his way in the film and television industries. He formed his own film company, 'Revolution', with its distinct five-point red star logo with Andrew Eaton. Perhaps class – exile through class – is at the centre of Winterbottom's 'displaced' experience. Interestingly, the Berlin Film Festival main jury that awarded the Gold Bear prize to *In This World* in 2003 was chaired by Atom Egoyan. I would argue that Winterbottom's experience is much closer to that of Egoyan's than either of their experiences are to those of Jamal and Etayan.

Winterbottom is an outsider in filmmaking terms although his work receives modest mainstream release. He is certainly not a genre director and both the form and subject matter of each successive film is unpredictable. He is unafraid to work outside the conventional studio production regimes. *In This World* was shot on digital video, entirely on location, with an extremely small team of technicians and a larger team of researchers and translators; in short in what Naficy calls 'artisanal' fashion.

I argue that *In This World* can be understood as an accented film in many respects. If this is less clear by reference to Naficy's definition, I think it is much clearer if we look 'close-up', as Naficy's textual method requires, at the film itself. One of Naficy's most interesting chapters concerns accented films that involve, in one form or another, a journey or aspects of journeying including borders, entry and exit portals, lodging places, tunnels and vehicles. All of these features are present in *In This World* and they signify in a manner totally consistent with Naficy's discussion.

The most obvious reference to a journey is vehicles. As noted above, Jamal and Enayat travel by bus, lorry, pick-up truck and container ship and Jamal, the survivor, also rides the train. The further the cousins move away from their home, the more dangerous the journey becomes. The 'fixers' in whom the cousins have to place their trust become less and less accountable to Enayat's family. The increasing danger is represented by the fact that although in Pakistan they can travel openly once they get to Iran that becomes difficult. Whilst riding a comfortable bus they are challenged at a security check point and sent back to Pakistan from where they try to cross the border again, this time successfully. From there on they have to become more careful. They are passed on by their fixers from vehicle to vehicle and the need to be hidden becomes more and more apparent. They hide amongst sheep and behind walls made of boxes of fruit. Finally, together with other migrants, they are moved into a container lorry that is then locked and loaded onto a container ship. By the time the container is opened all the migrants except Jamal and a baby have died through suffocation.

Winterbottom uses two other devices to provide a sense of a journey's distance-related vulnerability: the telephone and language. In *In This World*, the telephone is crucial in more than one respect. First, it enables the cousins to contact their fixers. Sometimes, this is relatively easy but at other times it is more difficult; the phones are public ones located in cafés and streets. The film's tension is raised at those times when calls are not answered or there is an abrupt conversation. Secondly, the telephone is used by Jamal to phone home when he gets to London, as required by the family. It is by phone that he tells Enayat's father that Enayat is not with him, 'He's not in this world.' Rhetorically the phone has an ambivalent, bittersweet status in that at one and the same time it is both a means of connection and a means of signifying distance and separation.

Finally, language is a powerful signifier for accented film. Exiles arrive in the host society speaking their home language but they need to speak the new host language. Enayat cannot speak English so he needs a companion who can. Jamal not only speaks English but Pashtu and Farsi too. In Pakistan he speaks Pashtu but as he crosses the border into Iran he has to speak Farsi and English. When the cousins reach the Iranian/Turkish border, their driver cannot speak any of Jamal's languages and Jamal becomes anxious. The further they are from home the more they need to be able to communicate clearly with their fixers but the same distance makes this less likely to happen. There is no conversation with their fixers at all in Istanbul when they are locked in their containers. The cousin who survives is the one who is better equipped to do so, the multi-lingual Jamal. *In This World* is a British film, but it is subtitled throughout. In this way the English-speaking audience also experiences the feeling of linguistic alienation as it tries to come to terms with Jamal and Enayat's journey.

In This World is a film that shows the interrelationship between global forces, in this case US militarism, and local interests, here the economic instability of the refugees and the local economies of the fixers along the route. Winterbottom uses vehicles, telephones and language not only as material props for the characters' physical movement but also as signs of the personal, cultural and social border crossings that Jamal and Enayat, and millions like them, have to make.[21]

Jamal and Enayat's journey is not just the physical one between Shamshatoo and London but a journey from community to isolation. Writing about Palestine and Palestinian refugees, Julie Peteet (Delanty, 2003, p. 160) has argued that refugee camps provide conditions for a strong sense of community to emerge. This appears to be true, although it cannot be verified, of Shamshatoo at the beginning of the film. When Jamal and Enayat leave the relative safety of the camp they are not escaping from community in the way Bauman characterizes cosmopolitans, but they have to let it go for the sake of long-term security. Community can sustain life but it cannot guarantee it. Nothing can.

Conclusion

The question I posed at the beginning of this chapter was, 'How is mainstream cinema contributing to an understanding of the impact of globalization on the idea and practice of community?' In addressing this question, I chose films that exposed and explored diverse, even extreme accounts of the experience of globalization. They all have in common a focus on place and mobility, which was a key point of reference in the chapter's introduction (Massey, p. 234). Massey's argument was endorsed by Zygmunt Bauman, who suggested that in the global society social stratification could be measured in terms of 'access to global mobility' (1998, p. 87). However, mobility is not in principle the enemy of community.

Some people, individuals and groups, are better equipped than others to take advantage of the opportunities and challenges created by the economic, military and technological forces shaping our times. As Massey suggests, some are liberated by the new conditions of mobility whilst others, paradoxically, are imprisoned by them. Some communities, such as those surrounding the Verma and Rai families in Delhi, are enriched by the new conditions of mobility. The 'new' generation that could fly in from the States and from Australia and could just as easily fly out again, with or without a bride, crossed horizons barely visible to the elders of the families. Of course, the families' wealth was itself the product of a previous era of globalization set in train by British colonialism. This positive image of a vibrant communal life is in stark contrast to the experiences of Charlotte and Bob who also had an ease of mobility. Their boredom and confusion suggested that mobility in itself is not enough. The ennui of a certain form of cosmopolitanism exposed by *Lost in Translation* suggests the recognition only of an absence of community, at least in Calhoun's terms. A social network that can, at times, work as a means of providing mutual support and a resource for collective behaviour that Calhoun emphasizes and that the Verma and Rai families possess in abundance has no presence in Copolla's film.

Tanya, Artiom and Lilya's opportunities for mobility are structured around hope and betrayal. Locked in the collapsing social system of post-Soviet Russia, they are all promised new free lives but are delivered into prisons; the British refugee holding centre for Tanya and Artiom and the locked Swedish high-rise flat for Lilya. For such as Tanya, Artiom and Lilya mobility is at best conditional. Tanya and Artium are rescued by friendship but Lilya is destroyed by trade. Friendship provides the promise of community but trade, at least of this sort, denies its very possibility.

Jamal and Enyat begin in the transitional community of the refugee camp, which provides the opportunity and means for them to travel to join the new and hopefully permanent Afghan community forming in London 5000 road miles and five time zones away. The further they travel away from Shamshatoo and the closer they get to London, the less the young men's home community is able to support them and the more they become vulnerable to the callousness of trade.

Taken as a whole, my analysis in this chapter suggests that the cinema can offer the opportunity for audiences to reflect on the processes and products of globalization. The films I have focused on are diverse and thought provoking. My limited analysis of them tends to confirm that globalization need not necessarily eradicate community but it does challenge it in practice. The major challenge facing mainstream filmmakers is an old one. On the one hand, they have to find a way to address major issues such as access to mobility and so on without seeming to preach to audiences who, more often than not, see the cinema as a place of entertainment and not a religious or political site. There is some evidence that filmmakers are confronting this challenge.[22] On the other hand, they need to find a way to temper entertainment with an ethical edge that goes beyond catharsis and empathy to action. The major challenge facing national governments and international bodies such as the UN and UNICEF is much greater and more urgent. The transnational organizations must maximize the opportunities for people to experience the opportunities of the global society whilst not allowing a whole new generation of young people to be cast adrift by the disembedding forces of the sectarian interests of capital and, increasingly, fundamentalist religion.

8
Community, Structure and Anti-structure

Introduction

The main aims of *Cinema and Community* have been to provide an original and substantial analysis of largely mainstream and contemporary films that take either the idea and practice of community or its absence as a significant theme in the context of major social and cultural changes and, in addition, to explore the idea of community itself under these changing circumstances. Occasionally, for example, in discussing community in multicultural Britain, I have had to be relaxed about finding a guiding definition of community. However, in this chapter I wish to focus on the distinctive way of thinking about community that can be found in the work of Victor Turner. Specifically, I will explore how his ideas concerning community and its associated concepts such as communitas, liminality, structure and anti-structure are helpful in analysing three Scandinavian films about particular communities that exist on the margins of society. It is fitting that the films are from Scandinavian countries because these have provided the conditions for the self-conscious creation of many such marginal, frequently anti-establishment communities including the best known example, the Free City of Christiania, which was formed in Copenhagen in 1970.[1]

The films represent three distinct marginal communities at different stages of their formation and evolution. Lars von Trier's *The Idiots* (1998) does not show how the community, in this case a collective, has come together, but shows how it ends.[2] The community of Lone Scherfig's *Italian for Beginners* (2000) does not coalesce until the very end of the film. The central dynamic of Lukas Moodysson's *Together* (2001) is that the collective existing at the film's beginning is destructive, but by the film's end the possibility for the emergence of a more creative and mutually satisfying collective has become possible. *The Idiots* and *Italian for Beginners* are Dogme 95 films but *Together*, although sharing some formal characteristics with them, is not.

Culture, community and communitas

Victor Turner (1920–1983) was a British anthropologist who originally studied literature before turning to anthropology at Manchester and Oxford Universities after the Second World War. He rejected the dominant British anthropological tradition at this time, social structuralism,[3] in favour of an ethnographic approach in which he emphasized the importance of cultural expression. Roger D. Abrahams has suggested that Turner '[...] begs comparison with the great interpreters of cultural texts of his generation – figures like Kenneth Burke, Claude Levi-Strauss, Erving Goffman, and Clifford Geertz – though his sense of the dynamic details of cultural display was uniquely his own' (1995, p. vii). Turner's influence has extended beyond anthropology to literary and cultural studies.[4]

Turner's most significant contribution to anthropology is to be found in his monograph *The Ritual Process*, first published in 1969. Working with ideas originally articulated by Arnold van Gennep concerning the stages followed by rituals in African tribal societies, Turner presented his fieldwork research specifically on the rituals of the Ndembu (Zambia).[5] On the basis of these findings, he proceeded to build an account of what he regarded as general, universal qualities of life concerning social change and stasis and their cultural expression. His reference points ranged from the Ndembu through Franciscan monastic orders and the Sahajiya movement of Bengal to Hippies. In building his account Turner developed or redefined a new set of concepts including anti-structure, liminality and communitas.

Turner was particularly interested in the manner in which ritual subjects, such as neophytes, progress through rituals by entering into a liminal phase or space that occupies a 'betwixt and between' position (1990, p. 95). He argued that in this phase, the actions of the subjects are not determined either by the social structural forms, for example the clan structure, from where they come, or by the forms of the social order they are to join. Turner suggested that we can understand this phase as anti-structure.

It is worth quoting Turner at length:

> It is as though there are two major 'models' for human interrelatedness, juxtaposed and alternating. The first is of society as a

structured, differentiated, and often hierarchical system of political-legal-economic positions with many types of evaluation, separating men in terms of 'more' or 'less'. The second, which emerges recognizably in the liminal period, is of society as an unstructured or rudimentarily structured and relatively undifferentiated *comitatus*, community, or even communion of equal individuals who submit together to the general authority of the ritual elders.

(1990, p. 96)

Turner preferred to use the term 'communitas' rather than 'community' because he thought the latter, with its local territorial referent, was generally used in a structural way whereas Turner wanted to emphasize communitas's spontaneity and immediacy. He argued that communitas has an existential quality – it has potential and is generative – whereas community, typically, is restrictive. Drawing on evidence taken from his fieldwork, Turner concluded that communitas possesses a creative, even radical potential.[6] Turner argued,

Communitas breaks in through the interstices of structure, in liminality; at the edges of structure, in marginality; and from beneath structure, in inferiority. It is almost everywhere held to be sacred or 'holy', possibly because it transgresses or dissolves the norms that govern structured and institutionalized relationships and is accompanied by experiences of unprecedented potency.

(1990, p. 128)

Turner's fieldwork suggested that communitas's transgressive potential might be dangerous for a society unless it could be controlled. That, indeed, was the purpose of the ritual process; by creating the liminal isolation of communitas in the ritual process a society such as the Ndembu could conserve itself. However, Turner's conclusion was that communitas provided not just a safe, liminal moment in an act of conservative renewal but the source of energy for potential change.

It was this insight concerning the free radicality of communitas, rather than the structural conservatism of community, that led to Turner developing his ideas outside the particular study of ritual, and beyond the usual confines of the discipline of anthropology into the realm of cultural analysis and critique. In this context, Turner proposed that a society is composed of two forms of human interrelatedness; not only social structure, but also communitas, a form of anti-structure. Social structure, the agglomeration of roles and institutions found in classes, castes, gender groups and kinship systems and so on, is to be found in a multitude of different forms throughout the world, in the past, present and probable future. The roles and institutions are vitally important in their predict-ability and the certainty they offer, but they are not universal in their content nor are they necessarily natural. Turner went on to argue that structures that have been made can be repaired, remade or replaced because humans are not only rule followers but also rule makers who are creative, spontaneous and capable of turning over the tables and starting again. This is the place of communitas; that which '[...] emerges where social structure is not' (1990, p. 126).

Turner argued, however, that the freewheeling, betwixt and between liminal phase of human interrelatedness has a tendency to become firmly enstructured. Georg Simmel and Zygmunt Bauman had come to similar conclusions. In the early years of the twentieth century, Simmel had argued that the cultural process involves the constant act of creativity in producing sedimentary forms, or structures, such as art, religion and law.[7] In *Culture as Praxis*, Bauman, following Simmel, argues that these forms or structures constitute the stuff of everyday life in terms of ideas and practices, for example artistic standards or moral precepts. However, they also have a tendency to '[...] acquire a logic and lawfulness of their own [...]' (1999, p. xix). They enable us to think and act whilst at the same time inhibiting the range of thoughts and actions we can have or take. One might think, for example, of how, in art critic George Melly's (1989) terms, revolt – the avant-garde – turns into style. For Simmel this cultural process constituted the tragedy of culture but for Bauman it is culture's ambivalence.

In developing his general cultural model, Turner suggests that the pro-gression from structure through liminality – that is the condition of anti-structure – to structure involves three forms of communitas. The first is,

> *Existential* or *spontaneous* communitas – approximately what the hippies today would call "a happening," and William Blake might have called "the winged moment as it flies" or later, "mutual forgive-ness of each vice" [...].
>
> (1990, p. 132)

The second and third forms are sedimentations of the first.

> *Normative* communitas, where, under the influence of time, the need to mobilize and organize resources, and the necessity for social control

among the members of the group in pursuance of these goals, the existential communitas is organized into a perduring social system.

(ibid., p. 132)

Here emerging goals become codified. In the early phase of codification the set of goals is just one amongst other possibilities. However, in the third form of communitas, the set is given a value and becomes a rule.

and *Ideological* communitas, which is a label one can apply to a variety of utopian models of societies based on existential communitas.

(ibid., 1995, p. 132)

Turner is proposing, in terms Bauman and Simmel would have recognized, that '[...] the fate of all spontaneous communitas in history is to undergo what most people see as a "decline and fall" into structure and law' (ibid., p. 132).

This chapter takes up Turner's contribution to understanding cultural expression and process to analyse a number of films, each of which is concerned with groups of people who are betwixt and between structures. That is, they are located in the liminal time and space of existential or spontaneous communitas or are moving into either normative or ideological communitas. No attempt is made to force the films, or my analysis of them, to make a precise fit with Turner's work; his ideas do not constitute a set of laws in that manner. However, I contend that each film, made around the turn of the century, depicts, in quite different ways, the movement between structure – liminality/anti-structure – and structure, again.

Together

Despite having relatively small populations, Scandinavian countries have made a significant contribution to world cinema, most obviously through the work of directors such as Sweden's Ingmar Bergman and Denmark's Carl Theodore Dreyer. Tytti Soila et al. (1998) note, however, that despite their national and international reputations, Bergman and Dreyer's contributions to Swedish and Danish Cinema has been less substantial than those made by Swedish or Danish state support, either through direct financial aid for production or indirectly through film education. Such support encouraged the emergence of new filmmakers including Lukas Moodysson, although, ironically, he is not particularly impressed by the quality of some of the ensuing work.[8] *Show Me Love* (1998), his highly successful first feature film concerned two young girls' growing love for each other.[9] His second feature, *Together* (2001), is the first of the three films I want to discuss.

Largely shot on location, including interior scenes, Moodysson makes only limited use of hand-held camera techniques. As in *Lilya 4-Ever*, discussed in Chapter 7, he prefers using a tripod-mounted camera placed as far away from the actors as feasible to give them space to move in mid-shot (MacNab, 2001). The film is shot in full colour, bright in the commune but muted in other interior scenes. Much of the music soundtrack is diegetic with characters playing records and sometimes commenting on them. There is, for example, a particularly poignant scene in which Elizabeth (Lisa Lindgren) plays her favourite track, *Love Hurts*, to Anna (Jessica Liedberg). The major exception to the diegetic soundtrack is the Abba song, *S.O.S.*, that is heard early on, then used as a leitmotiv throughout and finally played in full during the euphoric concluding scene. Moodysson has remarked on the irony involved in playing this song on the grounds that members of the 1970s communes disliked Abba's music (MacNab, 2001, p. 33).

Generically the film might be described as a tragicomedy that presents itself as satirising the anti-bourgeois conventions of an eclectic group of communards. But it does so with a good deal of affection for some of them and a respect for the optimism of the new commune. The jokes are funny and the pathos hits home.

At its beginning, the relationships between the communards of *Together*, the film's eponymous commune, are in a state of flux bordering on implosion. First, Lasse (Ola Norrel) and feminist Anna, who have two children, Tet (Axel Zuber) – named after the Viet Cong's Tet offensive of the Vietnam War – and Måne (Emil Moodysson), have just divorced and display a good deal of hostility towards one another. Lasse enjoys mocking Eric's (Olle Sarri) naive Marxist/Leninist politics. Meanwhile Klas (Shanti Roney) makes no attempt to hide his desire for Lasse. Second, Göran (Gustaf Hammersten) and Lena (Anja Lundqvist) have an 'open relationship'. Lena, who seems more enthusiastic about this than Göran, beds Eric and achieves an orgasm, something, she tells Göran, she has not achieved with him. Göran, despite being an idealist who wants everyone to get on with each other, is clearly disturbed by this news. He nevertheless tells Lena that he is happy for her. Finally, Göran's brand of relaxed idealism annoys the intense hippy couple, Signe (Cecilia Frode) and Sigvard (Lars Frode). In sum, the communards appear to share little in common except a dislike of 'bourgeois values' or, in Lena's case, a fear of being like her Mum. This is expressed in various ways including vegetarianism, a rejection of materialist culture, including television, women shaving armpit hair and, in the case of Signe and Sigvard, a dislike of the Pippi Longstocking stories.

The film's narrative crisis is created by the arrival of Göran's sister Elizabeth and her children, Eva (Emma Samuelsson) and Stefan (Sam Kessel). Rolf (Mikael Nyqvist), Elizabeth's husband, drinks too much alcohol and, not for the first time, has struck her. She calls Göran and asks him to take her and the children into shelter at Together. Their arrival, of which some of the communards do not approve, coincides with an argument that began with a dispute regarding washing-up and had escalated to the pros and cons of Anna exposing her 'apparatus' in the kitchen as a means of getting rid of her fungal infection. The first that Elizabeth's children see of the commune is Lasse and Anna with their lower halves exposed.

Two other households are involved in the story. Together's neighbours, Margit (Therese Brunnander), Ragnar (Claes Hartellus) and their son Fredrik (Henrik Lundström) live an unhappy life. Ragnar spies on Together, finds the women exciting, and under the pretext of doing woodwork in his cellar workshop and with the aid of pornography, he masturbates. It transpires later that Margit knows about this. Friendless Fredrik is usually left much to his own devices but slowly forms a friendship with equally friendless Eva. The final household is Birger's (Sten Ljunggren). He lives a solitary existence in a flat following divorce from his wife. Rolf, who is a plumber, visits Birger's flat to repair a pipe and they form a friendship. Under Birger's influence, Rolf realizes the errors of his ways, dries out and cleans his flat. Birger, reflecting on his own experience, says, 'I think that loneliness is the most awful thing in the world. I'd rather eat porridge together than a pork cutlet alone.' He goes on to tell Rolf that he must do something to repair the damaged relationships with Elizabeth and the children.

As the film progresses, relationships between the characters begin to change. Anna, who has recently declared herself a lesbian, befriends Elizabeth. Lasse and Klas, at the latter's insistence and the former's curiosity, experiment with gay sex. Göran finally realizes that Lena is a manipulative person who is exploiting his good nature and throws her out. Eric sees that none of the others share his political zeal and departs, as do Signe and Sigvard despairing of the others' lack of seriousness regarding alternative lifestyles. By the end of the film Rolf is reconciled with Elizabeth and the children and is absorbed by the reconstituting commune, as are Birger, Margit and Fredrik.

Turner's study of the renewal rites used in some indigenous societies tended to centre on the importance of the ritual neophytes who were usually adolescents. It is appropriate, therefore, that Moodysson should also pay particular attention to the role of children in renewing *Together*. Although Moodysson had not been brought up in a commune, he was sensitive to the strengths and weaknesses that communes offer.

> A lot of children who lived in communes were hurt by it, as in the film. Some of the actresses I used grew up in communes in this period – some had a great time but I've also heard stories about bad experiences. It was quite strange for them in making the film to have to dress up and act like they remember their parents doing.
>
> (MacNab, 2001, pp. 33–4)

Tet befriends the slightly older Stefan and in return Stefan shows Tet his toys including some Lego, a cowboy set and a gun. Måne is too young to play with Eva but luckily Fredrik, the neighbour's son, is on hand to fill the void. These two outsiders, Eva and Fredrik, are drawn to each other and become firm friends. The children, frustrated by some of the rules of the house, set up a protest at the lack of meat on the menu and the absence of television. It is Göran and Anna's acquiescence to their requests that leads to Signe and Sigvard's departure. Just as significant as the expression of the children's non-ideological baggage is their determination to develop relationships with the adults. First, Eva and particularly Stefan do not want to lose contact with their father. Second, Fredrik exposes his father's sexual hypocrisy. This encourages his mother, Margit, to review her relationship with her husband. Third, Fredrik sees through Lena's predatory sexual overtures towards him, and confirms his affection for Eva. It is the children, in acting in a mature way, who expose the immaturity of some of the adults.

The structure of the old *Together*, which once must have seemed a safe liminal space, had become destructive.[10] The arrival of the lost and alienated outsiders, Elizabeth, Eva, Stefan and Fredrik can be understood in Turner's terms as creating the conditions for the formation of the antistructure necessary for renewal. Through no definite plan, but simply by arriving from the interstices, edges and underside of structure, they have forced the communards to look at what they were doing to themselves and to each other (Turner, 1990, p. 128). The turbulence of this betwixt and between liminal phase provided the conditions for a new existential or spontaneous communitas, in which there was 'mutual forgiveness of each vice'.[11] Although the film makes no promises for the future, the joy of being together is clearly expressed through an impromptu and ecstatic football match embracing all members of the new Together. The game in which the teams are selected at random and it is acceptable to cheer an opponent's goal is played in a new fall of snow, a ritual symbol, somewhat clichéd to be sure, of cleansing and renewal.

The Idiots

Moodysson's *Together* is a funny and even affectionate account of how, ultimately, it is possible for people to live together with mutual respect. It is also a critique of how 'progressive' collectives can become oppressive; how, in short, to use Turner's expression, existential communitas gives way to a 'perduring social system' (1990, p. 132). However, Moodysson's film, no matter how insightful and moving, is an isolated critique. To find a more sustained critique of how culture declines and falls into structure and law, it is necessary to cross from Sweden to Denmark, and the films of the Dogme 95 collective.

Chronicling the history of Danish cinema, Astrid Söderbergh Widding (Soila et al., 1998) has noted that while significant changes have taken place over the past 30 years, as one generation of filmmakers has given way to new ones, Danish cinema's success has relied on the work of individual directors such as Dreyer and Axel. A more significant moment arrived with the paradigm shift achieved by the filmmakers associated with the publication of 'The Dogme Manifesto' and 'Vow of Chastity' of Dogme 95. Taken together, the manifesto and vow represent a challenge not only to dominant national and international film production ideologies but also to Danish bourgeois values more generally.

Those seeking clarity concerning the genesis of Dogme 95 have interviewed leading figures of the movement. Some interviews are enlightening and thoughtful. Others, however, are playful and frequently elicit mock, self-effacing statements which, bordering on patronizing, are as unenlightening as they are tedious.[12]

Lars von Trier[13] and Thomas Vinterberg published 'The Dogme Manifesto' and 'Vow of Chastity' of Dogme 95 and were the original signatories to the latter. The two other members of the initial collective, known as the Brotherhood, were Søren Kragh-Jacobsen and Kristian Levring.[14] The manifesto specifically criticizes the predictability of bourgeois cinema; a cinema that creates 'An illusion of pathos and an illusion of love' (Stevenson, 2003, p. 22). It also critiques an even earlier critique of bourgeois cinema, namely the French New Wave, a movement from which von Trier and others drew inspiration. The manifesto claims that 'The auteur concept was bourgeois romanticism from the very start and thereby .... False!' (Stevenson, 2003, p. 21). In response to the decadence of bourgeois, individualist cinema von Trier and Vinterberg made their vow that had ten rules:

1. Shooting must be done on location.
2. The sound must never be produced apart from the images, or vice versa. (Music must not be used unless it occurs where the scene is being shot.)
3. The camera must be hand-held. Any movement or mobility attainable in the hand is permitted. (The film must not take place where the camera is standing; shooting must take place where the film takes place.)
4. The film must be in color. Special lighting is not acceptable. (If there is too little light for exposure the scene must be cut or a single lamp may be attached to the camera.)
5. Optical work and filters are forbidden.
6. The film must not contain superficial action. (Murders, weapons, etc., must not occur.)
7. Temporal and geographical alienation are forbidden. (That is to say that the film takes place here and now.)
8. Genre movies are not acceptable.
9. The film format must be Academy 35 mm.
10. The director must not be credited. (ibid., pp. 22–3.)

The emergence of Dogme 95 can be explained in Turner's terms. Dogme 95 was a collective response to the false, individualistic bourgeois and structurally ossifying, cinema of Denmark and elsewhere. It offered an anti-structural, liminal space within which a new, existential communitas could be formed and very quickly normalized. Dogme 95 invited the participation of those filmmakers from within and beyond Denmark who were prepared to work in the interstices and margins of the dominant film culture in order to transgress or dissolve, in Victor Turner's words, '[...] The norms that govern structured and insitutionalized relationships [...]' (1990, p. 128). Accordingly, it opened up film culture to an experience of an 'unprecedented potency' (1990, p. 128) which was evident in two films directed by Thomas Vinterberg and Lars von Trier: *Festen* (1998) and *The Idiots* (1998) respectively.

In these films, von Trier and Vinterberg stuck closely to the rules of Dogme 95. Von Trier argues that the rules constitute less of a decree than a provocation or corrective to the filmmaker who might be veering towards bourgeois romanticism. However, he is happy to acknowledge that '[...] the whole point behind the rules is that we, in setting limits to freedom, enhance freedom with circumscribed limits' (Bondebjerg, 2001, p. 220). Both *Festen* and *The Idiots* offer sharp and bitter critiques of bourgeois values. However, I wish to concentrate on *The Idiots* because it has something important to say about community and about communitas.

As I have noted, von Trier's *The Idiots* obeys almost all of the Dogme 95 manifesto rules. The only minor exceptions are, first, the occasional but brief use of a non-diegetic music soundtrack[15] and secondly some post-production light manipulation.[16] The effect of von Trier's particular way of adhering to the rules is that *The Idiots* looks and sounds very raw. This may be seen in a number of ways. *The Idiots* is shot solely using hand-held camera techniques with the result that the finished image is unsteady, even erratic.[17] Many scenes begin and end abruptly with little attention given to the dominant rhetoric of establishment shots. Sound is sporadically chaotic, making it difficult on occasions to get a sense of who is speaking and to what we should be listening. This gives an energy to the film that is enhanced by the fact that no back-stories concerning characters are provided except through direct or, as is more often the case, elliptical conversation.

The film's rawness and energy is evident in the script that von Trier claimed he wrote in 4 days. In fact the script evolved throughout the film's production with von Trier initially encouraging a good deal of actor improvisation (Stevenson, 2003, p. 97). However, according to Stevenson, such improvisation was undermined by von Trier's ultimate unwillingness to let go of directorial control and by the actors failure to find a base from which to improvise. The uncertainty engendered by the raw and energetic script is made more apparent by the device of having, at various points in the film, characters – or are they actors, speaking as themselves or in role? – comment on aspects of the plot and on other characters as if giving interviews to an observer or researcher.[18] The audience is left to reflect on the status of these interviews, but can hardly ignore them.

The basic plot of *The Idiots* centres on the activities of a collective of men and women who live in a large house on the outskirts of Copenhagen, Denmark, owned by the uncle of Stoffer (Jens Albinus), one of the inhabitants. The central activity of the collective, the history of which is never revealed, is 'spassing', that is acting like or as 'retards' both in public and in the house too.[19] After a while the collective breaks up and the inhabitants leave the house.

The narrative is constructed by following the entry of Karen (Bodil Jørgensen) into the collective right through to her departure and the collective's dissolution. Karen, who we first witness in a smart restaurant as at least upset and possibly depressed, does not initially participate in 'spassing' but slowly edges into it until, at the film's conclusion, she appears to be its most proficient exponent. Not only does Karen, and specifically the journey she makes, provide the keystone of the film's narrative structure, she also provides the audience with a cathartic presence without which the film might simply seem to be a formal exercise.

The counterpoint of Karen's role is provided by Stoffer. He is the dominant figure in the collective and for some unexplained reason seems to act as its de facto leader. It is Stoffer who always raises the 'spassing' stakes and acts as the critic of the others' performances and it is Stoffer who addresses Karen's scepticism and initial distaste for 'spassing'. Stoffer, however, does not seek to control Karen.

The purpose of 'spassing' is provocation, which seems to have two forms. The first is to force a response from the bourgeoisie and others in order to expose their hypocrisy. To this end members separately or together create scenes in a restaurant, at a factory, at the swimming baths, on their neighbours' doorsteps, at their own house when first the council and then prospective house purchasers come to call, and, oddly, at a working class bar. Some of the situations, particularly the latter, carry with them the potential for physical danger for the participants. In many of these situations, Stoffer pushes the extent of provocation or criticizes a member for not going far enough.

The second form of provocation is more complex. Stoffer explains to Karen that 'spassing' enables the collective's members to 'search for their inner idiot' and that 'idiots are the people of the future.' Karen asks how Stoffer can justify 'spassing' since there are 'real mentally handicapped people'. He responds in a matter-of-fact way that he cannot.

Although Stoffer provokes arguments with the others there is no self-evident reason why anyone should respond. When he is told that the collective is going to have a party for him, he tells them he wants it to take the form of a 'gang bang' and they agree. His final provocation is the ultimate challenge. He tells the collective, 'If you can go home to your families and jobs – and still be a "spasser", I'll believe you're serious.' They spin a bottle, leaving Karen out again, to determine who will go. The first choice, Axel (Knud Romer Jørgensen), refuses. The second, Henrik (Troels Lyby), accepts but chickens out later. It is left to Karen to take up the challenge. The reason why Karen does this and its significance requires some discussion.

Some of the most interesting, and for me, troubling moments in the film are those when it is not possible to distinguish between those in which characters act 'spass' or are behaving as people with psychological problems.[20] The character Jeppe (Nikolay Lie Kaas), who is accused by Stoffer at an early stage of 'copping out', is particularly difficult to read in this context. To a lesser extent this is also true of Josephine, who we learn may actually be on medication. This confusion or ambivalence is present with Stoffer, who provokes the audience to make sense of his mental condition, and later with Karen.

The confusion regarding Stoffer's 'spassing' is recognizable in the scene, and others immediately following, in which a representative of Søllerød Council, apparently under a misapprehension of the actual situation, visits the house in order to persuade the 'retards' carers to move the institution from Søllerød to Hvidovre. At first Stoffer appears to be pleased by the suggestion and eggs on the representative to make his case clear. However, soon the situation gets out of hand, and in an initially funny but then frightening scene Stoffer attacks the representative and his car and chases him on to the public highway. Stoffer strips off his clothes and acts 'hysterically', not even responding to the collective's support. He is restrained 'for his own good'. In one sense it does not matter whether Stoffer is acting mentally disturbed to provoke his colleagues or is actually disturbed, but the scene, shot in vérité documentary style is ambivalent, difficult to read and disturbing. It is after this scene, when Stoffer appears to have returned to normal, that he proposes the 'gang bang'.

Karen's case is very different from Stoffer's. Most 'spassing' scenes of provocation especially with Stoffer are discrete, constituting a type of temporary tableau. But the scenes in which Karen is active carry a strong narrative function. I have noted that Karen is initially sceptical over or even worried by what she has witnessed. Karen's first involvement with the collective's public activities is at the swimming baths where, in open access cubicles, she washes Stoffer who is clearly sexually aroused. Karen slowly begins to be comfortable with the collective and she tells Susanne (Ann Louise Hassing), the person with whom she most clearly strikes a bond, that she is happy. Immediately following this declaration Karen involves herself further with the group. Her next act still falls short of 'spassing', but she does assist other 'spassers' in selling 'spass-made' Christmas decorations to neighbours.

The scene in which the 'retards' visit the house appears to move Karen from being a 'spass-assistant' to a 'spasser'. The collective, except for Stoffer, seems to enjoy the visit but when the 'retards' leave, the characters, who comment to camera before and after the visit, seem disturbed. Nana (Trine Michelsen) tries to raise their spirits but fails. As she approaches

Karen, it is clear that Karen too is disturbed. She is making whimpering noises and staring out of the window. Nana calls Susanne to inform her that 'Karen's gone into spass.' The other characters enter the room smiling. The scene cuts to the swimming baths in open session, where Jeppe, acting 'spass', and Susanne help Karen into the water whilst the latter continues to whimper but also to grin. Von Trier provides an extreme close-up of Susanne, Jeppe and Karen who is now weeping. Whether Karen is or is not 'spassing' is a moot question. She was disturbed at the beginning of the film, and we learn that she is grieving for her son who died a fortnight previously. Karen felt unable to attend the funeral. Whimpering and crying are not only a sign of 'spassing' but also of the release of hitherto contained grief. The ambivalence is not resolved. It is difficult not to read Karen's entry into the water as a baptism into the collective. Indeed, her time in the collective bears the hallmarks of a ritual; a ritual in which the neophyte Karen is separated from her previous life, taken into a liminal space and thence into a new world.

Karen's final movement to full 'spassing' comes towards the end of the film. The collective is in terminal decline and it falls to Karen to symbolically declare it dead. Karen's valedictory speech in a crammed hallway praises the qualities of all her colleagues except Stoffer, who right to the end is provocative; 'Let them all go, Karen. It was all a lie.' Karen concludes her speech by saying that she accepts Stoffer's challenge to 'spass' with her own family and she asks Susanne to accompany her, noting that 'It may not be very pleasant.' And it isn't. Karen is received very coolly by her family including her husband, who strikes her as she begins to 'spass'. Her 'spassing', which takes the form of very messy eating, is different from anything the collective has done before because she isn't provoking strangers but a specific set of people, namely her family. It is impossible to know exactly why she is doing this, but it certainly gives the audience something to think about. Is it playful or political provocation? Is she proving that she can do something the others could not do? Is she grieving? Has she become mentally disturbed?

We do not know what the collective has done for other members, but we do know that it has provided Karen with a liminal space, betwixt and between her old life and a new one. Despite Stoffer's determination to provide a structure of provocation, a form of ideological communitas, for the group, it is Karen, and to a lesser extent other members, notably Susanne, Nana, Jeppe and Josephine (Louise Mieritz), who build an existential or spontaneous communitas. Karen wants to be in the collective. She tells her colleagues, 'I believe I love you all more than I have loved anybody. Maybe with one exception. But that was so long ago now.' For Karen, the collective has been the source of energy for potential change and, for some members of the collective, Karen's initiation has given them a new beginning.

There is a further point to make about *The Idiots*; about Stoffer, von Trier, 'spassing' and the rules of Dogme 95. I think it is possible to see a number of parallels between the control freak Stoffer and von Trier.[21] First, Stoffer is involved in a collective, albeit a very odd one, and von Trier makes claims to approve of collectivisation too. He tells Ib Bondebjerg that at his age he is comfortable with the 'collectivist spirit' that had fired his parents and that his ideas of collectivism are in line with those of 'the old collectivist ideal from the 1960s and 1970s' (2001, pp. 210–11). However, in making *The Idiots*, von Trier found it very difficult to let others, particularly the actors, take some control.

Second, Stoffer does not think his colleagues go far enough and neither does von Trier.Reiterating a point he had previously made to Kelly (2000, p. 139), von Trier tells Bondebjerg that 'Part of the problem with the Dogme concept has been that nobody has taken it completely seriously' (2001, p. 210). He makes a similar statement to.

Third, in the same way as Stoffer sees 'spassing' as a provocation to bourgeois values, von Trier sees the rules of the Dogme 95 Manifesto as a provocation to bourgeois cinema. Stoffer tells Karen of the virtue of searching for 'the inner idiot'. Ib Bondebjerg asked von Trier whether or not *The Idiots* was an effective use of living out an inner chaos. Von Trier asserted, 'Yes, I tried to use my left hand a bit there, the whole idea behind the rules is that we, in setting limits to freedom, enhance freedom within circumscribed limits' (Hjort, p. 220).[22] Finally, it could be argued that von Trier's occasionally patronising interview responses might themselves be understood as a form of 'spassing'. Indeed he tells Kelly that '[...] it's interesting that it is so great to spass [...] it's a wonderful thing, something that everyone should try' (Kelly, 2000, p. 139).

But if there are some similarities there is also one major difference. Stoffer only exists in a house in a film. Unlike Stoffer who fetishises 'spassing', von Trier is content to allow the rules to be broken, not least by himself. The rules function as a discipline, a corrective to bourgeois values. Perhaps von Trier's occasionally waspish or patronising responses to some interviews with critics and commentators reflects the possibility that he must have become bored, not to mention irritated, by those who mistook the rules as an end whereas for him they are, or were, a means.

I don't think it's necessarily crucial that the Dogma rules be followed. I think the issue of whether you can gain something from throwing away total freedom in exchange for a set of rules is worth discussing, and it's interesting to see whether some of these rules might be of use to others. I've created rules before, so I think I've demonstrated that rules can lead to something positive.

(Bondebjerg, 2001, p. 222)

Italian for Beginners

Lars von Trier noted in his interview with Ib Bondebjerg that the first three Danish Dogma films are profoundly different from each other and '[...] reflect their individual directors. It's amusing that this should be the case, but then why would talk of uniformity destroy individual qualities?' (2001, p. 221).

The extent of the difference within the Dogme project was made even more apparent by Lone Scherfig whose film *Italian for Beginners*, which she wrote and directed, was credited with being the fifth Danish, but twelfth overall, Dogme film. The difference does not lie in any failure on her part to adhere to the formal rules of the manifesto. For example, Scherfig scrupulously uses hand-held camera techniques and only uses available light. This is particularly effective in early scenes when the tone of the film is sombre. Nor does the difference lie in any neglect of the proposition, also set out in the manifesto, that it is necessary to 'force the truth from characters and settings'. Scherfig's writing allows the actors to present highly plausible and affecting performances of the sort one might find in a Loach or Leigh film. Finally, it is clear that Scherfig has paid strict attention to the way in which the 'characters' inner lives justify the plot. Hence the pathos and expression of love evident in the film is far from the illusion created by the 'bourgeois' cinema so reviled by von Trier and Vinterberg. (Stevenson, 2003, p. 22)

Similarly, in thematic terms *Italian for Beginners* shares with *Festen* and *The Idiots* an interest in people who have 'shadow sides', although in this case the shadow side 'is the possibility of becoming very happy' (Kelly, 2000, p. 126). It is by some distance the lightest of the five Danish films. Speaking in its pre-production stage, Scherfig expressed the hope that 'my film will be very light, bubbly, funny' (ibid., p. 127).

The plot centres on a number of characters, only some of whom are known to each other, that are variously lonely, unhappy, socially dysfunctional or socially marginal. They find happiness, somewhat by chance, but always through someone else taking an interest in their lives. As they move from being a cluster of separate individuals to a community, they realize their potential for happiness. Perhaps, here then, with happiness, is the main point of difference between *Italian for Beginners* and the earlier Dogme 95 films.

Discussing the plot before the script was put into production, Scherfig said, 'My film is about people deciding that they have the possibility of becoming very happy, and taking that chance. So it's the anatomy of a happy ending, you could say' (Kelly, 2000, pp. 126–7). Scherfig's critics were quick to point out that this does not seem very provocative. Jack Stevenson claimed that with *Italian for Beginners*, 'The Danish sense of coziness triumphs' (2003, p. 121). Reviewing the film for *Sight & Sound*, Kelly described it as '[...] a big ball of fluff, its plot hinged entirely upon happy coincidences' (2002, p. 47). Perhaps, as the plot of *The Idiots*, a film Kelly admires, relies on one extremely big coincidence, that is Karen meeting the 'spassers' in an expensive restaurant when she has virtually no money, the problem for Kelly is not so much the presence of coincidence but of happiness. However, there is nothing in the manifesto, including its rules, that denies happiness as the subject for a film.

Coincidences, of course, do abound in *Italian for Beginners*. Scherfig (Kelly, 2000, p. 126) makes no bones, for example, about the waitress, Giulia (Sara Indrio Jensen), and the hotel receptionist, Jørgen (Peter Gantzler), fancying each other but not realizing their reciprocal desires; nor about hardworking Karen (Ann Eleonora Jørgensen) and clumsy Olympia (Anette Støvelæk) not discovering they are sisters until after their mother dies; nor about Olympia being left money by her abusive father that enables her, in a *Babette's Feast*-like gesture, to take the whole Italian class to Venice.

In *Italian for Beginners*, as in *Together*, responsibility for the narrative is dispersed among the ensemble of characters and, consequently, much of the success of the film is owed to Scherfig's ability to ensure the audience can follow each of their journeys. She clearly defines the characters and reveals, as the manifesto requires, their 'inner lives' as they interact at a variety of locations. At the hairdressers', Karen cuts the hair of Jørgen, Andreas (Anders W. Berthelsen) and Halvfinn (Lars Kaalund), with whom she strikes up a romantic relationship. At numerous bars, including Halvfinn's stadium bar, characters 'naturally' find themselves in each other's company and reveal their lives to each other. Andreas' Church, the congregation of which has dwindled to a few due to the previous Pastor's flight from God, is another important communal site. It is here that Andreas meets the verger (Elsebeth Steentoft), who attends the Italian class. It is here, too, that he presides first over Olympia's father's funeral, then that of Marcello the initial teacher at the class, then the mother of Karen and also, we discover later, of Olympia. And it is at the Church that Andreas offers comfort and counsel to the sisters.

However as the film proceeds it is clear that the main site of the formation of the emerging community is the Italian class. At the beginning of the film, there appears to be only five class members; Halvfinn, Jørgen, Lise (Rikke Wölck) (the hospital nurse we see caring for Karen's mother), the verger (a former bank robber) and Kirsten (Karen-Lise Mynster, about whom we know very little). Marcello, the teacher, dies at one of the classes. After some delay Halvfinn takes over. Thereafter, the original members are joined, in chronological order, by Olympia, Andreas and Karen. Finally, Giulia, the Italian waitress, completes the group.

The fact that the subject taught at the class is Italian seems important and not simply because the film's credits thank Maeve Binchy, who had written a novel, *Evening Class* (1996), about staff and students on an Italian evening class who take a trip to Italy. More important is that Italy connotes romance. Italian is a romance language and Italy is, at least to northern European minds, a romantic country. The music hummed by characters and played by pianists in shot or on location is by Puccini, the most romantic of all Italian opera composers. And, finally, it is romance that motivates the attendance of some of the class members. We learn, for instance, that Halvfinn is studying Italian because he has romanticised about a visit made by the Italian Juventus team to the stadium where he works. We learn too, that Olympia thinks, mistakenly, her mother was an opera singer.

Although the film has a happy ending, there is also an underlying darkness, at the heart of which is the fear and fact of loneliness. As the film opens we can see that the main characters of the film, Andreas, Halvfinn, Jørgen, Karen and Olympia, are each in their own way alone. Halvfinn, for example, seems to have zero-tolerance for anyone else and appears to be perpetually angry. Olympia lives with her father but he is both abusive towards her and yet also entirely reliant upon her. They live in a Denmark in which the welfare system can not always help as much as its citizens need and in which fathers can be abusive and bosses are ruthless. But the film also shows that there is hope for some, and when the chance comes to make a better life then it is necessary to take it.

Andreas soliloquises about loneliness, love and about God too:

> It is in loneliness that God seems furthest away. But God is here in compassion, in friendship. Between us. Inside us. In love. In every movement. In the arm you slip around the waist of your beloved.

Andreas is a Pastor so it is to be expected that he talks about loneliness in religious terms. However, in his dealings with others, he makes no attempt to bring God into their discussions. It is through his hospitable actions and those of others that loneliness is confronted and banished, at least temporarily.

Perhaps it was the film's lightness that accounted for ensuring that *Italian for Beginners* was by far the most popular of the Dogme 95 films and one of the most popular Danish films of recent years both within and beyond Denmark. Despite or, possibly in a perverse way, because of its commercial success, there has been little critical discussion of either *Italian for Beginners* or its director. Hjort and Bondebjerg's otherwise comprehensive *The Danish Directors*, make no reference to it. Shohini Chaudhuri (2005) briefly acknowledges its market success. As I have commmented, Richard Kelly, who has written a book on Dogme 95, offers only grudging praise in his *Sight & Sound* review (2002). Stevenson notes the film's ambivalent status; it was a commercial success yet a Dogma film; it was conservative yet few critics had anything bad to say about it. Only Ib Bondebjerg in Hjort and MacKenzie's *Purity and Pro-vocation: Dogme 95* (2003) discusses the film at any length. He tellingly concludes his positive comments by noting that

> The strength of this Dogma film (*Italian for Beginners*) is that the banal wisdom of everyday life, social bonding and romance is given a new intense, poetic realism through the Dogma rules and the escape from the constraints of the cinema's over-reliance on the possibility of technologically manipulating the image.
>
> (2003, p. 79)

However, the relative silence of other critics is a shame because *Italian for Beginners*, as Bondebjerg suggests, does have something interesting to say. Rather like *Together*, *Italian for Beginners* shows that given the right conditions, lonely people can find ways to live a communal life; they gain individually from being together. Scherfig claims 'My film is about people deciding that they have the possibility of becoming very happy, and taking that chance' (Kelly, 2000, p. 126). The formation of community can be achieved not only by the intervention of a single outsider, as in Axel's *Babette's Feast*, but also through the mutual support of relative strangers for each other. This is the life that Karen made in *The Idiots* and it is also the life that Elizabeth and others found in *Together*. It is the communal life that, in Turner's terms, creates possibilities and it is the life that got short shrift, for example, in some of the films examined in Chapter 7.

The one rule that it might be possible to argue that Scherfig breaks is that concerning the avoidance of genre. One of the sins of bourgeois cinema, according to the Dogme Brotherhood, is predictability and genre cinema is predictable. Stevenson argued that Scherfig's work is marked by the narrative tricks she learned in her early melodrama writing. *Italian for Beginners* was '[. . .] clearly an example of what is called in trade parlance, a "women's picture" ' (2003, pp. 122–3). The use of this term is confusing here, since 'women's pictures' is often used as a term for 'romance' but it is also used as a term around which oppositional readings of such films can be constructed.[23] Stevenson, I suspect, means the former. Stevenson also acknowledged her skill, 'She knew how to make things work on a budget. It was pure story and pure acting, even if the story did reek of drugstore novel' (ibid., p. 123). The key difficulty, it seems for Stevenson as it was for Kelly, is that this women's picture has a happy ending. 'The film's message seems to be that the state of being single implies a perpetual pathetic quality, and that anyone can find happiness with whomever happens to be available if one just has the courage and gumption to engage them. Then everyone can be pathetic together' (ibid., p. 121). Such a story, neither tragic nor very comic, with its romance somewhat muted, had managed to '[. . .] seduce the critics too' (ibid., p. 123).

Stevenson and Kelly are right to note that the film is conservative with a small 'c' but it is still a Dogme 95 film, at least in formal terms. Indeed in one respect it is more Dogme than *The Idiots*. In addition to *Italian for Beginners* having the courage to break with the depressing tone found elsewhere – perhaps its lightness was a provocation in itself – the film also exposes Dogme's structural paradox. In her interview with Kelly, Scherfig stated, 'Also, the more I work with Dogme, the more it occurs to me that Dogme itself is a genre. And the more Dogme films that are made, the more you have to fight them, otherwise they become a system too' (Kelly, 2000, p. 126). This is a point acknowledged by the Dogme Secretariat in its 'closing down statement' issued in June 2002. 'The manifesto of Dogme 95 has almost grown into a genre formula, which was never the intention' (Stevenson, 2003, p. 291). This, for sure, is also the point made, in a different context, by Simmel, Bauman and Turner. The cultural process in which laws of freedom come to imprison creativity applies to radical or avant-garde cinema as much as to anything else.

There is one other aspect of *Italian for Beginners* that necessitates making a defence against Kelly and Stevenson. Unlike the social composition of the characters in *The Idiots* the main characters of *Italian for Beginners* are working class or lower middle class. The characters are shown doing jobs; largely boring, usually repetitive, low-paid jobs. Apart from the Pastor they are not highly educated. They are not living in an experimental space with the inclination, and apparently the money, to disrupt the smug complacency of the bourgeoisie. They do not have the luxury of taking time out from life to 'spass'. They have to make of their lives what, where and when they can. The closest the 'spassers' get to the working class is when they visit the factory, the bar and the public swimming baths, none of which seem to be symbols of bourgeois effetism.

Perhaps a latent social class dimension can be found in Kelly's review of *Italian for Beginners*, which is disdainful towards the evening class member's interest in things Italian. Their vision, his patrician argument claims, is a corny one, 'composed of pasta and vino, gondola rides and the language of lovers' (Kelly, 2002, p. 47). And so it is. But what vision of Italy does Kelly expect 'ordinary' people who are variously a hotel receptionist, a hairdresser, a patisserie shop assistant, a bar-manager and a Pastor to have? Dogme 95's vow of chastity requires that the director's '[. . .] supreme goal is to force the truth out of [her/his] characters and settings' (Stevenson, 2003, p. 23). The vow does not require the characters to be intellectuals.

Perhaps the occasional casual critical condescension towards *Italian for Beginners* compared with *The Idiots* and *Festen* has a further class aspect. In 2001, approximately one-third of all admissions to Danish cinemas was for *Italian for Beginners* (Hjort and MacKenzie, 2003, p. 4). The total admissions in Danish cinemas for *Italian for Beginners* and *The Idiots* that year were, respectively, 826 701 and 119 892.[24] Given that the population of Denmark is only 4.5 millions, this is a statistically significant difference. Unfortunately, there is no statistical breakdown of these figures that would show the social composition of the audience but it would be reasonable to argue that such a large audience figure implies that the working class was well represented. It is purely idle speculation to suggest that some of the bourgeois critics who lauded *The Idiots* and *Festen* are distancing themselves from the 'pathetic' behaviour of their working class brothers and sisters who, unlike them, have not yet seen past the superficial gloss of their 'corny' lives.[25]

Conclusion

Turner argued that the dynamics of social structure and social change constitute a continuous struggle between the inescapable human potential for creation on the one hand and the desire for order on the other. His major concepts of liminality, anti-structure and communitas were designed to make sense of this dynamic struggle. I have argued that each of the films can be understood, in different ways, in the light of Turner's work.

At the beginning of *Together*, the existential communitas of the commune had become normalized and was held up by some as a utopian model for its continued existence. However, it had also become destructive and its survival in any form was in doubt. The arrival of Elizabeth and, particularly, her children injected new energy into the commune. They did not take the existing rules for granted and the children, particularly, upset the way in which the communards were living. This created a liminal moment when the previous rules were thrown in the air and new arrangements were created. The film ended with an ecstatic rebirth of Together and neither the new communards nor the audience know what will happen next.

In *The Idiots*, the commune acts as the anti-structural other to a conservative bourgeois social structure whose values have been internally ritualized by its citizens. By 'spassing' the communards provocatively exposed the bourgeoisie's rituals and for a while at least, made them feel uncomfortable. The 'spassers' acted like the medieval court fool who is allowed to create mischief and mock the court. The angry, distinctly bourgeois Stoffer treated 'spassing', indeed commune life, like a game; one that only he fully understood. His ability to manipulate, cajole, bully and generally outface the communards created confusion and became destructive. The original anti-structural force of the commune had evolved, tragically if Simmel is to be believed, into a structure: Stoffer's game. Stoffer had succeeded in normalizing the existential communitas. Karen's arrival disrupted the game. Slowly, and without seeking to do so, she assumed a personal even moral authority that ultimately left Stoffer on one side. When Karen agreed to 'spass' with her family, she did something different from the others, including Stoffer. 'Spassing' for them was theoretical; any victim will do. When the 'spassers' disappear their bourgeois victims can go back to their lives. 'Spassing' for Karen was personal and when she 'spassed' with her family, the family would not easily recover.

The entire trajectory of *Italian for Beginners* is a death and rebirth cycle. The lonely and unhappy people are locked into a social structure in which they are dead, if not buried. Their work and domestic lives provide no pleasure, only responsibility. But the death of others, as Jean-Luc Nancy might argue, provides new opportunities for new relationships.[26] The characters first begin to see and then tentatively take their opportunities. They form a collective, not by following a set of rules, but by trial and error. The interesting point about Scherfig's characters is that moving from society's interstices, margins and depths to centre stage they are able to draw on their inner resources and, by offering mutual respect, create communitas. This is communitas as 'happening' with the characters recognizing William Blake's 'winged moment as it flies'. It has no rules, at least not yet, and may have no permanence.

One of the virtues of Turner's account of communitas is that he takes us straight past any need to think of community as a static condition, one that we can aspire to or be nostalgic over. As an unreconstructed humanist, he is also insistent that society and community, or communitas for him, are not strangers to each other. He writes,

> Society (societas) seems to be a process rather than a thing – a dialectical process with successive phases of structure and communitas. There would seem to be – if one can use such a controversial term – a human "need" to participate in both modalities.
>
> (1990, p. 203)

Each of the films in which the 'successive phases of structure and communitas' move from one modality to the other ends in uncertainty. Whether we view the uncertainty optimistically or pessimistically is another question.

9
Conclusion

In *Cinema and Community* I have sought to explore the idea and practice of community, as represented in the cinema, in the context of the impact of contemporary social and political forces at the turn of the twentieth century. Throughout, I have been conscious of a number of recurring issues that I might single out for comment in a conclusion, not necessarily for resolution but as a marker for further studies in the field. The first of these is of a general nature.

I was motivated to write the book, in part, by a concern with what I saw as the existence of a common composite intellectual failure within the field of study. One aspect of this failure concerns the clash between the empirical and rationalist traditions of enquiry that is endemic in the contemporary humanities and social sciences. It is present here too. I suggest in Chapter 1 that, in film and cinema studies, writers on community too often leave the word undefined. This omission is also repeated by even the most interesting and thoughtful scholars, such as Robert D. Putnam, who work from within the empirical social science tradition. Other writers, from a more philosophical or cultural critical position, such as Jean-Luc Nancy, focus almost exclusively on 'definitional' or conceptual matters without being overly concerned with applying their ideas to particular, substantial social situations.

I brought Putnam and Nancy's work together on to the same analytical ground in Chapter 3. Putnam's empirical work in assessing the present state of community in the USA is immensely valuable and provides interesting pointers for other societies. It has influenced academic and public debate in the USA and in Europe. However, he does not define community. Nancy, who does not discuss actual communities but defines the term, albeit in a complex fashion, offers a useful corrective to Putnam. Nancy's notion of the 'inoperative community' with its optimistic, open and energetic emphasis on the 'unleashing of passions', and a preference for understanding collectives in terms of 'in-commonness' rather than 'sameness' has an important contribution to make to the field of study. It provides a dynamic challenge to the traditional, rather self-contained and static understanding of community that is found in the work of communitarian political scientists, such as Amitai Etzioni (Chapter 4) and those, for example Bhikhu Parekh, who speak on behalf of frequently beleaguered citizens (Chapter 6). The emphasis on dynamism associated with the inoperative community, if not its precise philosophical discourse, is also found in the work of Zygmunt Bauman (inter alia), Alberto Melucci (Chapter 5), Hamid Naficy (Chapter 7) and Victor Turner (Chapter 8).

A second aspect of the composite intellectual failure of which I have been aware throughout this study involves the relationship between different disciplinary approaches to the study of cinema and community. Although I come from a background in sociology, I have been drawn not only to the field of culture but also to the disciplines frequently associated with the humanities that have addressed culture within their distinctive discourses. Of course, the temptations of the pleasures of interdisciplinary cross-dressing are commonly found in the history of cultural studies from Richard Hoggart (1958), the Professor of English who founded the Birmingham Centre for Contemporary Cultural Studies, the first centre of its kind anywhere, to Slavoj Žižek (2006), the Slovenian cultural theorist presently shaking up the critical establishment. Raymond Williams, about whom I wrote at length in Chapter 1, despite his academic title of Professor of Drama, built his career by challenging the boundaries of competing disciplines – literature, history, sociology and political theory. Williams' cultural materialism, on which I drew throughout the study, is an emphatic response to his frustration with narrowly defined disciplinary fields and an argument for interdisciplinary work. Nevertheless, despite the cross-dressing temptations, I tend to privilege the more sociological elements in my case study approach. The sub-text of my study has been to encourage film scholars to appreciate that community is an important idea and social practice, albeit a contested one. I hope that my study will encourage those film scholars who, whilst retaining an interest in the importance of community as a social practice, are better able than me to address its psychological and aesthetic aspects.

Other issues are more substantive. In Chapter 2, I address myself to the importance of the type of inclusionary and exclusionary practices that were clearly demonstrated in *Babette's Feast* and *The Magdalene Sisters* respectively. I suggest that the potential for exclusion and inclusion, not to mention peace and violence, is rarely far away in communities and representations of them. This potential is capable, of course, of being represented in quite distinct forms as I show in the cases of *My Son the Fanatic* (Chapter 6) and *The Idiots* (Chapter 8). Drawing on the work of Emmanuel Levinas and Zygmunt Bauman, I argue in Chapter 2 that these practices can be considered in ethical terms. There are examples of this throughout *Cinema and Community*. Thus, in Chapter 3, I argue that by the end of *American Beauty* and *Pleasantville*, many of the character's rights to take moral responsibility had been reasserted.

The ethical theme of inclusion and exclusion can also be found in Chapter 4 where I suggest that the narratives of *The Full Monty*, *Brassed Off* and *Billy Elliot* turn on the recognition by key characters of their moral responsibility for their children or family. However, I also argue that any ethical kudos gained by these significant male characters is achieved through a distinctly unethical marginalization of middle class women who are made to suffer double discrimination; first by virtue of their social class and secondly their gender. The middle class women of Sheffield, Grimley and Everington have the clear narrative function of forcing working class men to face up to the responsibility for caring for their children. However, they are represented as having no firm social base in middle class society and are marginal to the working class-community they have helped rebuild. *Calendar Girls* and *School for Seduction* (Chapter 5) demonstrate that, in the cinema at least, the patriarchal, communal exclusion or marginalization of women is by no means inevitable.

The second substantive issue, and possibly the central one of *Cinema and Community*, involves the complex relationship that Bauman identifies between community, security and freedom (Chapter 1). He argues, 'Missing community means missing security; gaining community, if it happens, would soon mean missing freedom' (2001, p. 4). Although this relationship is explored throughout the book, for example in Chapters 3, 7 and 8 where I discuss *Pleasantville*, *Last Resort* and *Italian for Beginners*, its clearest and most pertinent expression is in Chapter 6 where I examine the place of Muslim fathers in contemporary multicultural Britain. I argue that the films' narratives centre on the relationship between first-generation Pakistani Muslim fathers and their children. The fathers believe that some of the aspirations and behaviour of their children will inevitably endanger *izzath*, family honour, in the eyes of the Muslim community. The turns in the aspirations and behaviour in question take two contrasting directions. On the one hand, in *East is East* and *Ae Fond Kiss*, the fathers fear their children are becoming secularised and are in danger of turning away from Islam. On the other hand, in *My Son the Fanatic* and *Yasmin*, the fathers are appalled that some of their children are turning towards a different Islam; a fundamental, militant Islam. In each case the fathers fear the Muslim community, that has given them security through the difficult time of settlement, will interpret the children's action as an expression of a freedom from parental control, a result of failed Muslim parenting. The fathers fear that their families will no longer be respected. The psychological effect of shame is serious indeed, and the material effect of this, for example, by the withdrawal of marriage opportunities for the families involved is devastating.

The shifting dynamics of Muslim family and community life constitute a stark example of the general case concerning the changing conditions in which people are trying to find ways of living together in the face of major social and political changes, from capital financing of new nano-industries in Taiwan through the development of the fundamentalist Christian right in the USA to the national and post-national political movements of the Russian Federation. These developments and more are shifting the balance between social security and personal freedom. The appeal to community is a part of the response to these changes and, as I have shown, the cinema is well placed to represent it implicitly and explicitly. But as academics review the changes, their implications for community and their representation in the cinema, it will be as well that they give some thought to just what they mean when, like Starla O'Grady in *Slap Her . . . She's French*, they appeal to the value of community.

Notes

1 Reading community in the cinema

1. When I refer to a film for the first time in a chapter, I name the film's director and year of first exhibition. Subsequently I only name the film. A full list of films discussed or mentioned is provided at pp. 215–218.
2. Home Office poster witnessed by the author in December 2004.
3. Witnessed by the author on 20 August 2003 in Leeds, UK.
4. See K. Christensen and D. Levinson (eds) (2003).
5. For an overview of the sociology of community, see Delanty (2003). I found Delanty's book an invaluable resource in my attempt to try and hold the concept of community still long enough for me to say something about it.
6. Lee Tamahori's *Once Were Warriors* (1994) presents an altogether darker picture of Maori society. It shows a family struggling to cope with economic failure and cultural marginalization.
7. The films, discovered in the basement of an empty shop, were restored and archived by the British Film Institute (BFI) and shown for the first time in nearly a century in 2004. For an extended discussion of Mitchell and Kenyon's work see V. Toulmin et al. (eds) (2004).
8. See D. Morley's interesting contribution, 'Bounded realms: household, family, community, and nation' in H. Naficy and T. H. Gabriel (eds) (1989, pp. 151–68).
9. A further although less developed example can be found in Philip Gillett's fascinating *The British Working Class in Postwar Film* (2003). In 'People don't lock their doors: the working class community', Gillett briefly discusses the difference between 'community' and 'communality'.
10. Studies of contemporary French cinema explicitly address the idea of community only occasionally. Elizabeth Ezra's discussion of *Chacun Cherche Son Chat* (dir. Cédric Klapisch, 1996) is an important exception. Here Ezra (1999) notes that Klapisch seems to be suggesting, rather like Caro in *Whale Rider*, that communities need to accept change if they are to survive. Other studies, it might be argued, in discussing films such as *La Haine* (dir. Mathieu Kassowitz, 1996) and *Bye, Bye* (dir. Karim Dridi, 1995) that depict the *banlieues*, youth, ethnicity and the post-colonial city, actually address the idea of community implicitly. See, for example, Will Higbee (2005).
11. See, for example, how J. Nelmes (ed.) (2003, p. xxii) introduces Searle Kochberg's contribution.
12. See A. Milner (2002) and T. Eagleton (ed.) (1989) for more about Williams' work.
13. See Williams (1979, pp. 156–65) for a discussion between him and representatives of *New Left Review* on the strengths and weakness of the term. See M. Pickering (1997) Chapter 2, for a comprehensive account of the development of the concept and an incisive critical review.

14. See the work of R. Hoggart, first director of the Centre for Contemporary Cultural Studies at Birmingham University. In his landmark book, *The Uses of Literacy* (1957), Hoggart analysed the demise of the working class community of Hunslet, Leeds. Mike Leigh's film *Vera Drake* (2004) captures very well something of the working class-community culture described by Hoggart.
15. This point finds a powerful reiteration in M. Joseph's *Against the Romance of Community* (2002).
16. Williams uses this and similar terms as near-synonyms for community.
17. The lecture was delivered on July 13, 1977, published in *Radical Wales*, 18, Summer, 1988 and reprinted in Raymond Williams (1988). Plaid Cymru is the largest Welsh nationalist political party.
18. Davies' work has attracted much critical discussion see, for example, Geoff Eley (1995).
19. For an extraordinarily insightful discussion of pub and club singing in 1940s and 1950s Britain, see Hoggart (1958, Chapter 5c).
20. On the subject of taste, Pierre Bourdieu famously argued, 'Taste classifies and it classifies the classifier' (1984, p. 6).
21. Much of Bauman's writings return to the ideas of order and waste, most obviously in *Wasted Lives: Modernity and its Outcasts* (2004). The US Government's Guantanamo Bay is a contemporary use of rational calculation for sweeping up the 'waste product' of the 'war on terror'.
22. For a terrifying description of how assimilated Jews fell victim to Nazi violence, see Bauman (1989, Chapter 4).
23. The success of Roberto Benigni's Oscar winning film, *Life is Beautiful* (1997), exposed the ambivalence frequently experienced in making and watching representations of the Holocaust in mainstream cinema. Benigni's film went against the generic expectations that such films should eschew comedy. See Carlo Celli (2000) and Slavoj Žižek (2000).
24. Interestingly when looked at in international terms, films that were considered to be 'popular' in the country of production are sometimes regarded as 'art-house' when exhibited abroad. For a discussion of this relating to French cinema, see L. Mazdon (ed.) (2000).

2   Representing the ambivalence of community

1. Isak Dinesen's 'Babette's Feast' was first published in 1957 and reprinted in her collection *Anecdotes of Destiny* (1986). Isak Dinesen is the nom de plume of Karen Blixen.
2. In this regard the film bears comparison with Roberto Rossellini's banquet scene in *The Rise to Power of Louis 14th* (1966).
3. The Magdalene laundries formed part of a larger chain of rescue missions in Great Britain and Ireland. Only in Ireland, however, did the missions take on such horrific forms for so long. Not all laundries were as severe in their attitudes as that depicted in the film.
4. The scandal of the brutal laundries was not unique in Ireland. Amongst other scandals exposed at around this time were those concerning the care

of children in orphanages and 'industrial schools'. See M. Tanner (2003, pp. 408–9).

5. Michael S. Rose, 'The scandal of the Magdalene Laundries' in Cruxnews.com. See http://cruxnews.org/arts-magdalene.html for Rose's extensive overview of the critical response to *The Magdalene Sisters*. Site visited on 11 April 2007.

6. Stephen D. Greydanus, 'The Magdalene controversy' in *Decent Film Guides: Film Appreciation, Information and Criticism Informed by Christian Faith*. See http://www:///decentfilmguides.com/sections/article/2551. Site visited on 11 April 2007.

7. Crispin Jackson, 'Why no mercy for the sisters?' *The Tablet*. See http://www.thetablet.co.uk/pages/magdalenesisters. Site visited on 11 April 2007.

8. According to Erving Goffman's typology, the Magdalene laundry is a particularly pernicious form of 'total institution' on a par with concentration camps. See S. Clegg et al. (2006) for a discussion of Magdalene laundries in the light of Goffman's work.

9. Sr Bridget is a devotee of the cinema. As a Christmas treat she arranges for the inmates to be shown *The Bells of Saint Mary* (dir. Leo McCarey, 1945). This very sentimental film tells of the alliance between Sr Benedict (Ingrid Bergman) and Fr Chuck O'Malley (Bing Crosby) to gain new school premises and of their developing personal closeness.

10. The film's version of the song is an abridgement. Fuller versions strongly imply incest with the maiden's uncle, brother and father. The song is probably based on the story of Jesus and the woman from Samaria related in St. John, Chapter IV. Many Irish cinemagoers would know the song and the Gospel. See http://www.mudcat.org@/displaysong.cfm?SongID=7138. Site visited on 12 April 2007.

11. Tourism Ireland is a body set up by the British and Irish governments under the Belfast Agreement (1988) to encourage tourism. It publishes *Your Very Own Ireland: Holiday Planner 2007*.

12. A film that represents both aspects of community is Stephen Spielberg's *The Color Purple* (1982), which is based on Alice Walker's novel of the same title. Walker co-scripted the film. Through the visual representation of contrasting circles, Spielberg captures both the power of community to embrace its kind and to exclude or imprison its unwanted or undesired others.

3 Realizing community in suburban America

1. For a critical discussion of Robert Putnam's work, see G. Delanty (2003).
2. See A. Kenyon (2004, Chapter 2, passim).
3. These blanket statistics hide a complex story that Putnam discusses at some length (2000, pp. 204–15).
4. For a brief discussion of gated communities, see R. Putnam (2000, p. 210) and Z. Bauman (2001, p. 54).
5. A. Kenyon (2004, pp. 20–1) notes the importance of the car in the development of the suburbs in the 1920s.
6. See R. Putnam (2000, Chapter 13).

7. Putnam argues that the larger the suburb, the less civic engagement is likely to be found (2000, figure 59, p. 206).
8. Note that in representations of suburbia in mainstream cinema, the differences between 'small town' and 'suburban' America are elided. This is not surprising given the way in which the latter was designed to 'mimic' certain aspects of the former.
9. P. Cook (1985, p. 169) notes that in *Mr. Deeds Goes to Town* (1936) , for example, Capra contrasts the city with the country and sophisticated smart talking with common sense. By the film's close, all the characters, except the lawyers, are speaking the same language.
10. British Prime Minister Mr Edward Heath coined the phrase to describe Mr Tiny Rowland's approach to business in 1973.
11. R. Fallows (1997) notes that Potter, who is old at the outset, does not age throughout the length of the film.
12. For an extended discussion of Capra's skills in *It's a Wonderful Life*, see Sam B. Girgus (1998).
13. There are two black characters in *It's a Wonderful Life*. Annie is Peter and Ma Bailey's stereotypically wisecracking and loveable servant. The other is one of the hundred or so unnamed Bedfordians who lend money to support George and Mary in their hour of need.
14. The Levitt brothers had been active in up-market house building before the Second World War. After the war they turned to building suburbs for working Americans. See Kenyon (2004, pp. 30–2).
15. For a useful discussion of the place of self-help guides in US culture, see Michael Bugeja (2005, Chapter 2).
16. See George Cotkin (2003) for an extended discussion of the significance of existential philosophy in American culture including a brief discussion of *American Beauty*.
17. U. Beck (1992) has given Mills' discussion an interesting twist in his work on risk society, noting that individuals are frequently asked to seek biographical solutions to systemic contradictions.
18. In what follows *Pleasantville* designates the title of the film, 'Pleasantville' the title of the TV programme and Pleasantville the name of the fictional town.
19. See L. Spigel (1992). Donna Reed, who played the part of Mary Bailey in *It's a Wonderful Life*, took the lead in the highly popular television suburban sitcom, *The Donna Reed Show* (1958–1966). Deborah Chambers (2001, pp. 60–91) provides an interesting account of family life on screen and in the home.
20. Mary Sue is the name given in writing circles, particularly fan-fiction, to an impossibly idealized character that is often a projection of the author.
21. Is it a coincidence that Mrs Carter's first name is Betty?
22. I have made reference throughout this chapter to the absence of black characters not only from the three films discussed, but also from suburb films more generally. It might be argued that *Pleasantville*'s focus on the absence of colour from the streets of Pleasantville might be read metaphorically to refer to the absence of 'coloured' people in representations of blacks in US popular culture. Even if this was the case it does not excuse the neglect of the representation of racial segregation in films concerned with suburbia in American cinema. See A. Kenyon (2004, pp. 74–8).

23. The outsider status of some young Americans has been explored to great comic effect in *Napoleon Dynamite* (dir. Jared Hess, 2004). Michael Moore's *Bowling for Columbine* (2002) offers a tragic reminder of where such a status can end up.

24. For a critical discussion of Nancy's philosophy, see Oleg Domanov (2006).

25. In *Pleasantville*, our knowing heroes, particularly David/Bud, are able to articulate the boundaries and constitution of Pleasantville and do not even have to have it explained to them. Pleasantville is perhaps another total institution not unlike the Magdalene laundry discussed in Chapter 2.

26. E. Levinas makes a similar point with regard to ethics. See Chapter 2.

27. G. Delanty (2003) discusses this briefly in his introduction to Nancy's work. Constitutionally Diana's correct title was Diana, Princess of Wales and not Princess Diana.

4   Class, gender and communitarianism

1. For a discussion of fatherhood and masculinity with reference to *The Full Monty*, see E. Tinknell and D. Chambers (2002).

2. See Chapter 1 for a discussion of structure of feeling.

3. Tony Blair's instrumentalist, communitarian approach to community is precisely the idea of community that J.-L. Nancy criticizes. See Chapter 3.

4. 'The power of community can change the world' www.ppionline.org/ ppi_ci.cfm?knlgAreaID.

5. See C. Gledhill (ed.) (1987) for a wide-ranging discussion of what she calls the 'melodramatic field'.

6. See A. Spicer (2003) for an extremely interesting account of shifts in the representation of masculinity in popular British cinema from 1940s to 1990s.

7. See G. Watson's tour de force *The Cinema of Mike Leigh* (2004) and M. O'Hagan Hardy (2007).

8. J. Hill provides an excellent discussion of Margaret Thatcher's administrations' political, social and economic policies. He also draws attention to the tensions between her family values rhetoric and her policies towards the family. See J. Hill (ed.) (1999, pp. 11–12).

9. G. Eley (1995, p. 25) argues that '[. . .] the Thatcherite emphasis on "family values" and individual over class or other mass-based politics has reconfirmed the "working class" as a phenomenon of culture as opposed to politics.'

10. Newspaper editorials of the centre and centre-left expressed a touch of 'Schadenfreude' at the demise of Thatcherism.

11. See T. Blair, *The Times*, 17 July 1995. Tony Blair's position was amply endorsed and elaborated by his fellow ideologues, P. Mandelson and R. Liddle (1996), and commented on more critically by S. Driver and L. Martel (1998).

12. Writing in her published biography, *The Downing Street Years*, Mrs Thatcher (1993) acknowledges that she had neglected social policy concerning the family but was working on appropriate policy at the time that she was forced out of office.

13. Quoted in P. Riddle (1993, p. 171).

14. Paradoxically perhaps Thatcher's endorsement of 'Victorian values' in the 1980s and John Major's appeal to go 'back to basics' in 1995 can be read as symptomatic of the decline in family values over which they presided. See J. Young (1999, pp. 25, 113, 155) for an interesting discussion of this issue.
15. T. Blair, 'New Labour, New Britain' from a speech given to the Labour party Conference, Blackpool, 4 October 1994 reprinted in T. Blair (1996, pp. 29–30).
16. See R. Levitas (1998).
17. Note Blair's moral philosophy is 'contract' based, unlike E. Levinas's which is unconditional.
18. *The Full Monty* was the biggest box office success of these films. With a budget of $3.5 millions it grossed $205 millions worldwide, grossing approximately $70 millions in the UK alone. See *BFI Film and Television Handbook: 1999* (London: BFI, 1999, Tab. 26, p. 41).
19. The film does not specify the date but as Billy was performing in Matthew Bourne's all-male version of Swan Lake, which had its first performance in 1995, it must have been after then.
20. See J. Hill (ed.) (1999, p. 136) for an interesting discussion of nonstraight realism.
21. It is tempting to read the films as melodramas, albeit masculine ones. Indeed, they do exhibit elements of the melodrama genre: much of the action of each film takes place in the home, each presents characters as victims, each presents serious conflict between men and women and each tell moral tales. However, it might be more appropriate to argue that the films are shaped by what C. Gledhill (2000) calls the melodramatic modality but do not conform to the strict rules of the melodrama genre. For a compelling discussion of the latter see T. Elsaesser (1972).
22. During the period covered by the films, the number of collieries in the UK fell from 231 in 1985 to 50 in 1993. The number of people employed in the coal industry fell from 154 600 to 44 000 over the same period. See C. Cook and J. Stevenson (1996).
23. Of the three films under scrutiny, it is *Brassed Off* that provides the most interesting representation of working class women. The film presents a range of characters from those such as Sandra, desperately trying to protect her children, to those shown actively supporting the miners' action on the picket line.
24. For a discussion of traditional narrative as 'problem solving', see S. Chatman (1980).
25. Gran repeats the phrase 'Mind they said I could have been a professional' or variations on it.
26. Note that men gather together in a range of social spaces, for example working men's clubs and band halls, in which women are not present. There are no similar spaces available for women. Mandy, in *The Full Monty*, is in one respect a partial exception to this.
27. 'Homosocial' is a term coined by E. K. Sedgwick (1985) to describe how men, straight or gay enjoy social bonds that desire the attention of men and not women.
28. British cinema is rarely short of troublesome middle class women in working class situations. For recent examples, see *Kinky Boots* (dir. Julian Jarrold, 2005) and *Grow Your Own* (dir. Richard Laxton, 2007).

5   Leaving the margins: women and community

1. See BFI Film Handbook, 2005.
2. For a comprehensive discussion of the history of feminism, see S. Gamble (1998).
3. See N. Wolf (1991) for an interesting and much-debated account of this development.
4. See also J. Hollows and R. Moseley, *Feminism in Popular Culture* (2006).
5. For an extremely valuable discussion of everyday life and feminism, see R. Felski (1999).
6. A good example of the development of women's action groups that led to public mobilizations involved the large number of support groups that grew around the miners' strike of 1984/1985. Although this began spontaneously as a series of specifically local activities, it quickly became a national movement with its own infrastructure. National conferences, such as Women Against Pit Closures were organized. Following the defeat of the miners' strike, the support groups continued and new activities ensued. See T. Holden (2005) for an inspiring, detailed history of the movement through which women were able to transform their lives.
7. 'The Women's Institute exists to educate women to enable them to provide an effective role in the community, to expand their horizons and to develop and pass on important skills.' See www.womens.institute.co.uk visited on 2nd October 2006. In her history of the Women's Institute Movement, established in 1915, M. Andrews (1997, p. 14) argues, 'Thus it is my contention that the W.I. Movement was a significant and certainly the largest, feminist organization in the post-suffrage era.'
8. See www.paloaltoonline.com/movies/moviescreener.php?id=001888+type= long. Site visited on 20 February 2007.
9. There is, however, a contradictory aspect in the choice of calendar images in that the activities shown do not represent women tending towards social action.
10. J. Hollows and R. Moseley (2006, pp. 13–15) and their contributors have much to say of the 'generational politics of feminism' but little about women of middle and advanced age.
11. See G. Orwell (2000) for the sharpest discussion of McGill's work.
12. A second caption reads, 'A real man understands this, unless he is a complete twat.'
13. Ann Summers is a High street chain of sex aid and lingerie shops. It also organizes home sales parties that have proven to be every bit as popular in the UK as Tupperware parties ever were.
14. In the light of the discussion in Chapter 4 concerning the marginalization of middle class women, it is interesting to note that no barrier is erected between middle and working class women in *School for Seduction*.
15. See R. Felski (1999) for a discussion of time, space and modality in the culture of everyday life.
16. M. Castells' work on collective identities distinguishes between resistance and project identities. Some social movements based on principles at odds with the dominant ideology, enable people to survive or resist it. A project identity goes beyond resistance to opposition. 'This is the case for instance,

when feminism moves out of the trenches of resistance of women's identity and women's rights, to challenge patriarchalism, and thus the entire structure of production, reproduction, sexuality, and personality on which societies have been historically based' See Castells (1997, pp. 6–12).

17. *Volver* (dir. Pedro Almodóvar, 2006) provides a brilliant example of this capacity.

6   Honour and community in multicultural Britain

1. South Asian citizens are those whose families originate from Bangladesh, India, Pakistan and Sri Lanka. For an excellent account of South Asian migration to Britain, see www.movinghere.org.uk.
2. Asante was given the Carl Foreman award as Most Promising Newcomer. For a brief discussion of the film see www.blackworld.bfi.org/nuvisions/theinsiders/ammaasante.html. www.screenonline.org.uk/film/id, which provides an excellent overview of British Black film.
3. See www.cilt.org.uk/commlangs/index.htm. Site visited on 27 June 2007.
4. R. Hansen (2000, p. 3).
5. The *Empire Windrush* docked at Tilbury, London, on 22 June 1948.When 492 passengers disembarked the first major migration from the Caribbean to the UK began.
6. Pakistan, at this time, was physically divided into West Pakistan and East Pakistan by the land mass of India. Pakistan eventually split into two states with East Pakistan adopting the name of Bangladesh.
7. 'New Commonwealth' is a term that specifically refers to ex-African, Caribbean and Asian colonies whose citizens were largely non-white.
8. White groups attacked Caribbean citizens.
9. Peter Griffith, the successful local candidate, used the slogan, 'If you want a nigger for a neighbour, vote Liberal or Labour.' See Hansen (2000, pp. 131–5).
10. Ibid., pp. 182–90.
11. Ibid., pp. 154–76.
12. See B. Parekh (1989, pp. 29–33). The 'affair' was revived in June 2007 when the Queen awarded Rushdie a knighthood.
13. Sir W. Macpherson's *Stephen Lawrence Inquiry* (1999) severely criticized the police investigation.
14. D. Bell, the Chief Inspector of Schools, noted in a lecture to the Hansard Society that in 2004 there were around 300 independent faith schools of which 100 were Muslim. Mr Bell's lecture caused some controversy amongst Muslim groups because, according to them, he singled them out when criticizing schools for paying insufficient attention to citizenship. See http://www.hansard-society.org.uk and *The Muslim News*, Issue 190, Friday 25 February 2005–16 Muharram 1426.
15. See T. Modood et al. (1994).
16. 'Britocide!' (www.bnp.org.uk/news_feb/news-feb14.htm). Site visited on 14 February 2003.
17. See P. Bagguley and Y. Hussain (2006).
18. The most celebrated film produced in the independent sector at this time was Black Audio Film Collective's, *Handsworth Songs* (dir. John Akomfrah,

1986). It sought to represent the contradictory experiences of ethnic minority British citizens in Handsworth, a suburb of Birmingham. For a closely argued discussion of *Handsworth Songs*, see A. Butler (1988). For a sharp critique of the film, see S. Rushdie (1987).

19. Sally Hibbin, *Yasmin's* producer, told *The Guardian* that despite interest abroad they found it difficult to get a film distributor interested. The company worked with Verve Pictures who '[...] couldn't find an opening at cinemas for a long while. And that wasn't good enough for us, because the film is clearly very topical and any delay would weaken its impact. So we went to Channel 4. I think there is a nervousness about how this kind of film will play at the British box office' (See http://www.guardian.co.uk/g2/story/0,1389092,00.html).

20. See M. Gillespie (1995, 2000).

21. See B. Korte and C. Sternberg (2004) for a comprehensive discussion of British Black and Asian film in the cinema and on television since the 1990s. *Bhaji on the Beach*, in particular, has been much discussed. See, for example, J. Roscoe (2000).

22. See J. Hill (1999) and S. Malik (1996) for discussions of *My Beautiful Laundrette*. It is interesting to note that *My Beautiful Laundrette* addresses issues of class, 'race', gender, sexuality and politics but not religion. Film and academic criticism at that time payed no attention to the absence either.

23. See T. Abbas (2005, passim).

24. Conservative M. P. Norman Tebbit, a very close associate of the then Prime Minister Margaret Thatcher, proposed the use of a cricket test (sic) as a means of judging whether members of the 'Asian community' were 'integrated or just living here'. If the Asian community cheered on England in a cricket test match then they passed the nationalism test! (Reported in *The Times*, 22 April 1990).

25. For methodological details, see T. Modood (1997, pp. 1–17) and T. Modood (1994, pp. 9–15).

26. P. Bagguley and Y. Hussain (2005) recorded 34 interviews and one focus group with 19 men and 21 women (16 to 60+) in June 2002 in Bradford.

27. See C. Peach 'Muslims in the UK' in T. Abbas (2005, p. 24).

28. See, Saied R Ameli et al.'s report for the Islamic Human Rights Commission, *The British Media and Muslim Representation: The Ideology of Demonisation* (2006, p. 45), for a highly critical review of *East is East*.

29. I. Julien and K. Mercer (1988) define the burden thus: 'If only one voice is given the "right to speak", that voice will be heard, by the majority culture, as "speaking for" the many who are excluded or marginalized from access to the means of representation' (p. 4).

30. Honour is an important feature of Islam but 'honour killings' are not. At the time of writing, the British press has been reporting the murder of Banz Mahmod by her Muslim Kurdish father and uncle. The murder has been described as an 'honour killing.' Diana Sammi, director of the Iranian and Kurdish Women's Rights Organisation, puts the blame for the killings firmly on the shoulders of patriarchal Islamic fundamentalists. See 'Dishonourable acts' in *The Guardian*, G2, 13 June 2007, pp. 17–18.

31. For a discussion of K. Loach's approach to direction, see G. McKnight (1995).

32. Loach's interview is a Warner Home Video/DVD special feature.

33. Most Catholic children at a Catholic school would support Celtic. In areas in which an Islamic faith school is not available, it is not uncommon for Muslims to send their children to a Christian faith school.
34. Hindus and Sikhs, likewise, had to move from Muslim-dominated Pakistan.
35. The Census 2001 recorded the Pakistani-origin population of Bradford as 67 994. This represented 14.5 percent of Bradford's total, and that is ten times higher than the British national Pakistani average. See www.cre.gov.uk/diversity/map/yorkshiteandthehumber/bradford.html. Site visited on 26 June 2007.
36. Miranda Husain, 'Post-9/11 – the diverse Muslim experience', *Daily Times*: A New Voice for a New Pakistan, 10 June 2005 at www.dailytimes.co.pk. pp. 3–5.
37. Khalid is demonstrating 'the low sense of security within the country' that P. Bagguley and Y. Hussain (2005, p. 417) demonstrate is typical of first-generation Bradford Pakistanis. Through research carried out after the 2001 Bradford riots, Bagguley and Hussain argue that whilst second-generation Bradford Pakistanis regard themselves as ' [. . .] British citizens with the same "rights" as any other British citizen', first-generation Bradford Pakistanis regard themselves as having 'the status of being a denizen' (p. 418). Khalid, like George (*East is East*) and Tariq Khan (*Ae Fond Kiss*) may also be considered to be denizens.
38. See S. Huntington (1996) for a substantial development of his hypothesis. For a brief but telling critique, see P. Hirst and G. Thompson (1996, p. 210).

7 Globalization, mobility and community

1. See George Modelski (1972) for an early but still authoritative overview of the pre-history of globalization.
2. See M. Castells (1997, Chapters 2 and 5 passim).
3. See M. Bugeja (2005) for a deeply pessimistic discussion of this point.
4. 'Mira Nair Peels Back Layers of Punjabi Society', Interview with Mira Nair by Joan Dupont, *International Herald Tribune*, 21 September 2001. See http://mirabaifilms.com/wordpress/?page_id=32. Site visited on 28 October 2006.
5. There is no shortage of films dealing with economic migrancy, see, for example, Stephen Frear's *Dirty, Pretty Things* (2002) and Ken Loach's *Bread and Roses* (2000).
6. See Chapter 8 for a discussion of *Together*.
7. *Stolen Smiles: A Summary Report on the Physical and Psychological Health Consequences of Women and Adolescents Trafficked in Europe* is available at http://lshtm.ac.uk/hpu/docs/StolenSmiles.pdf.90% The women interviewed reported that they had been 'physically forced or intimidated into sex or doing something sexual' (p. 12).
8. See www.undoc.org/pdf/trafficking in persons_report_2006ver2.pdf. The term 'very high' is the UN's highest one. See www.eaves4women.co.uk and the United Nations Interregional Crime and Justice Research Institute (www.UNICRI/index.php) for further information regarding human trafficking, particularly for sexual exploitation.

9. For an interesting discussion of the representation of sex-trafficking in television documentaries and dramas, see Jane Arthurs (2006).
10. See www.unhcr.org/basics. Site visited on 24 October, 2006.
11. Jawed Wasel's *FireDancer* (2002) received limited exhibition opportunities at festivals in the USA.
12. See S. Chaudhuri (2005, pp. 71–92) for a detailed and incisive account of recent Iranian cinema.
13. I will use 'refugee' as the generic term for displaced people who are 'of concern' to organizations such as UNHCR. Where appropriate, I will specify other terms.
14. See www.hrw.org/reports/2002/Pakistan. On 1 January 2006, the UNHCR estimated that there were 20.8 million refugees, asylum seekers, returnees, internally displaced, returned IDPS and others of which 8.4 were refugees and 773 500 were asylum seekers. See www.UNHCR.org/basics Site visited 24 October 2006.
15. The Silk Route is not a single route but a rationalisation of a number of diverse paths from China, crossing Asia and ending in Venice. In the film it ends in London.
16. See www.who.int/countries/afg/en. Site visited on 24 October 2006.
17. Michel Agiers (2002, pp. 55–6) quoted in Zygmunt Bauman (2004, p. 76).
18. See www.unhcr.org/statistics/STATISTICS/4641be4ell.pdf. Site visited on 16 August 2007.
19. See www.news.bbc.co.uk/1/hi/uk.politics/2003399.stm. Site visited on 28 October 2006.
20. Naficy suggests that accented style is an emergent structure of feeling that is '[. . .] not yet fully recognized or formalized [. . .] it is rooted in the filmmaker's profound experiences of deterritorialization, which oscillate between dysphoria and euphoria, celibacy and celebration' (2001, pp. 26–7).
21. The conditions of relatively low-budget filmmaking of this sort involving crossing national borders and through culturally diverse worlds means that Winterbottom is also in the hands of fixers and translators.
22. For example, the episodic narrative of Alejandro González Iñárritu's *Babel* (2006) describes the way in which an act of appreciation – a grateful Japanese hunter makes a present of his gun to his reliable Moroccan guide – impacts on people's lives across three continents. The film depicts the unforeseen consequences of the ease of mobility made possible for some in the new global society. Through the adaptation of John le Carré's *The Constant Gardener* (dir. Fernando Meirelles, 2005), cinema audiences were introduced to the intimate relations between national governments and the pharmaceutical industries as they impact on developing countries.

8   Community, structure and anti-structure

1. At its peak, somewhere between 800 and 1 000 people lived in the 'alternative' consensus-based, ecology-conscious, self-managed, city-within-a-city that was run separately in most respects from the rest of Copenhagen. Christiania's official website is www.christiania.org/folderus.

2. I am conscious that although *The Idiots* did receive commercial release in some countries, I am stretching the definition of my rule concerning prioritizing mainstream cinema to its limits. In mitigation, as von Trier might argue, rules are there to be broken.

3. British social structural anthropology focused on identifying the key social systems, particularly political, economic and religious systems, found in indigenous societies.

4. See K. M. Ashley (1990). In particular, comparisons with Mikhail Bakhtin's account of the carnivalesque are frequently made. See M. Bakhtin (1965) and C. Flanigan in Ashley (1990).

5. Arnold van Gennep's *The Rites of Passage* was first published in 1909.

6. There are clear similarities between Turner's work and that of J.-L. Nancy whose work I discussed briefly in Chapter 3.

7. Georg Simmel was an early twentieth-century German sociologist. See Simmel in 'On the concept and the tragedy of culture', in D. Frisby and M. Featherstone (eds) (1997).

8. See G. MacNab (2001).

9. Referring specifically to *Show Me Love*, released in Sweden as *Fucking Åmål*, Ingmar Bergman described Moodysson as a 'genius film narrator'. See S. Björkman (2001, p. 15).

10. Moodysson commenting on the 1970s' style communes, says, 'The bad thing for me was the fundamentalism – the dogmatic rules that could be very hurtful and in the end destroyed the movement's potential to change society' (G. MacNab, 2001, p. 33).

11. Turner is quoting William Blake's Prologue to *The Gates of Paradise*.

12. See, for example, Richard Kelly's interview with Lars von Trier in R. Kelly (2000).

13. Von Trier had achieved major international success with *Europa* (1991) and particularly with *Breaking the Waves* (1996). He was also an experienced hand at publishing manifestos having produced a succession of them in 1981, 1984 and 1990.

14. In the interview with Kelly, von Trier describes the Brotherhood as a 'forced' one (R. Kelly, 2000, p. 136).

15. A harmonica rendition of 'The dying swan', from Saint-Saëns, *Carnival of the Animals*.

16. See M. Hjort and I. Bondebjerg *The Danish Directors: Dialogues on a Contemporary National Cinema* (Intellect: Bristol, 2001, p. 222).

17. Commentators such as S. Chaudhuri (2005) and G. MacNab (2001) have noted similarities between Moodysson and Dogme 95. For example, both *The Idiots* and *Together* are shot on location with available light. However Moodysson, unlike von Trier and Vinterberg, is happy to change the lighting in post-production.

18. Jesper Jargil recorded a documentary, *The Humiliated* (1998), on the making of *The Idiot*.

19. The term 'spassing' is taken from the film. Inverted commas are used in the secondary literature when discussing the activity; a practice I support. I employ inverted commas to signal other offensive, at least to me, terms such as 'retards' deployed in the film. Where such words are direct quotes from character's speeches I do not use inverted commas.

20. See M. Smith in M. Hjort and S. MacKenzie (eds) (2003).
21. Stoffer might better be described as a bully.
22. Von Trier uses the term 'left hand' to refer to a more unstructured, less academic style of filmmaking.
23. The complexities associated with this term have been brilliantly discussed by Annette Kuhn (1982).
24. Figures supplied by the Danish Film Institute at www.dfi.dk. Site visited on 6 September 2006.
25. For an interesting discussion of this phenomenon, see T. J. Clark (1973a,b) who wrote about the critical response to Gustav Courbet's historical painting.
26. See Chapter 3 for a discussion of J.-L. Nancy's work (1991).

Bibliography

Abbas, T. (ed.) *Muslim Britain: Communities Under Pressure* (London: Zed, 2005).

Abrahams, R. D. 'Foreword' in Turner, V. (1995) pp. v–xii.

Agiers, M. *Aux bords du monde, les réfugiés* (Paris: Flammarion, 2002) pp. 55–6 quoted in Bauman, Z. (2004) p. 76.

Ameli, S. R., Marandai, S., Ahmed, S. T., Kara, S. and Merali, A. *The British Media and Muslim Representation: The Ideology of Demonisation* (London: Islamic Human Rights Commission, 2007).

Anderson, B. *Imagined Communities: Reflections on the Origin and Spread of Nationalism* (London: Verso, 1983).

Andrews, M. *The Women's Institute as a Social Movement* (London: Lawrence and Wishart, 1997).

Arthurs, J. 'Sex workers incorporated', in Hollows, J. and Moseley, R. (eds) (2006) pp. 119–39.

Ashley, K. M. (ed.) *Victor Turner and the Construction of Cultural Criticism* (Bloomington & Indianapolis: Indiana University Press, 1990).

Bagguley, P. and Hussain, Y. 'Citizenship, ethnicity and identity: British Pakistanis after the 2001 "Riots"'. *Sociology*, 39 (3) (2005) 407–25.

Bagguley, P. and Hussain, Y. 'Conflict and cohesion: official constructions of "Community" around the 2001 "Riots" in Britain' in Herbrechter, S. and Higgins, M. (eds) (2006) pp. 347–66.

Bakhtin, M. *Rabelais and His World*, Trans. Iswolsky, H. (Bloomington & Indianapolis: Indiana University Press, 1965).

Barr, C. *Ealing Studios* 3rd ed. (London: British Film Institute, 1998).

Bauman, Z. *Modernity and the Holocaust* (Cambridge: Polity Press, 1989).

Bauman, Z. *Modernity and Ambivalence* (Cambridge: Polity Press, 1993a).

Bauman, Z. *Postmodern Ethics* (Oxford: Blackwell, 1993b).

Bauman, Z. *Globalization: The Human Consequences* (Cambridge: Polity, 1998).

Bauman, Z. *Culture as Praxis* (London: Sage, 1999).

Bauman, Z. *Community: Seeking Safety in an Insecure World* (Cambridge: Polity Press, 2001).

Bauman, Z. *Wasted Lives: Modernity and its Outcasts* (Cambridge: Polity Press, 2004).

Baumgartner, M. P. *The Moral Order of a Suburb* (New York: Oxford University Press, 1988).

Beck, U. *Risk Society – Towards a New Modernity* (London: Sage, 1992).

Beuka, R. ' "Just one word ... plastics": suburban malaise, masculinity, and Oedipal drive in *The Graduate*'. *Journal of Popular Film and Television*, 28 Spring (2000) 12–21.

Binchy, M. *Evening Class* (London: Orion, 1996).

Björkman, S. 'Pure knowledge'. *Sight and Sound* (9) (2001) 14–15.

Blair, T. *New Britain: My Vision of a Young Country* (London: Fourth Estate, 1996).

Bondebjerg, I. 'Lars von Trier' in Hjort, M. and Bondebjerg, I. (2001) pp. 208–28.

Bondebjerg, I. 'Dogma 95 and the new Danish cinema' in Hjort, M. and MacKenzie, S. (eds) (2003) pp. 70–88.

Bourdieu, P. *Distinction: A Social Critique of the Judgement of Taste* (London: Routledge, 1984).

Brunsdon, C. *Screen Tastes* (London: Routledge, 1997).

Bugeja, M. *Interpersonal Divide: The Search for Community in a Technological Age* (Oxford: Oxford University Press, 2005).

Butler, A. '*Handsworth Songs*: An Occasion for Hope in Britain's Third Cinema'. *International Documentary*, Winter/Spring (1988) 19–22.

Butler, A. *Women's Cinema: The Contested Screen* (London: Wallflower Press, 2002).

Butler, J. *Gender Trouble: Feminism and the Subversion of Identity* (New York: Routledge, 1990).

Butler, M. *Film and Community in Britain and France: 'From La Règle du Jeu' to 'Room at the Top'* (London: I. B. Taurus, 2004).

Calhoun, C. 'Populist politics, communications media and large scale social integration'. *Sociological Theory*, 6 (2) (1988) 219–41.

Cashmore, E. *Dictionary of Race and Ethnic Relations*, 3rd ed. (London: Routledge, 1994).

Castells, M. *The Information Age: Economy, Society and Culture: Vol. I, The Rise of the Network Society* (Oxford: Blackwell, 1996).

Castells, M. *The Information Age: Economy, Society and Culture: Vol. II, The Power of Identity* (Oxford: Blackwell, 1997).

Castells, M. *The Information Age: Economy, Society and Culture: Vol. III, The End of the Millenium* (Oxford: Blackwell, 1998).

Celli, C. 'The representation of evil in Roberto Benigni's *Life is Beautiful*'. *Journal of Popular Film and Television*, 28 (2) (2000) 74–9.

Chadha, G. *I'm British But...* (dir. Gurinder Chadha 1989).

Chambers, D. *Representing the Family* (London: Sage, 2001).

Chatman, S. *Story and Discourse* (Cornell: Cornell University Press, 1980).

Chaudhuri, S. *Contemporary World Cinema: Europe/Middle East/Asia/South Asia* (Edinburgh: Edinburgh University Press, 2005).

Christensen, K. and Levinson, D. (eds) *Encylopedia of Community*, Vols 1–4 (London: Sage, 2003).

Clark, T. J. *The Absolute Bourgeois: Artists and Politics in France, 1848–1851* (London: Thames and Hudson, 1973a).

Clark, T. J. *The Image of the People* (London: Thames and Hudson, 1973b).

Clegg, S., Courpasson, D. and Phillips, N. *Power and Organizations* (London: Sage, 2006).

Cohen, R. *Global Diasporas: An Introduction* (London: UCL Press, 1997).

Cook, C. and Stevenson, J. *Britain Since 1945* (London: Longman, 1996).

Cook, P. (ed.) *The Cinema Book*, 9th ed. (London: British Film Institute, 1985).

Cotkin, G. *Existential America* (Baltimore: Johns Hopkins University Press, 2003).

Cottle, S. (ed.) *Ethnic Minorities and the Media: Changing Cultural Boundaries* (Buckingham: Open University Press, 2000).

Crane, R. J. (ed.) *Shifting Continents/Colliding Cultures: Diaspora Writings of the Indian Subcontinent* (Amsterdam: Rodopi, 2000).

Delanty, G. *Community* (London: Routledge, 2003).

Dinesen, I. 'Babette's feast' in *Anecdotes of Destiny* (Harmondsworth: Penguin, 1986) pp. 23–68.

Dollimore, J. and Sinfield, A. (eds) *Political Shakespeare: Essays in Cultural Materi-alism*, 2nd (ed.) (Manchester: Manchester University Press, 1994).
Domanov, O. 'Jean-Luc Nancy: An attempt to reduce community to ontology' in Herbrechter, S. and Higgins, M. (eds) (2006) pp. 111–26.
Dostoyevsky, F. *The Brothers Karamazov*, Vol. 1, trans. Magarshack, D. (Harmond sworth: Penguin, 1958).
Douglas, M. *Purity and Danger* (Harmondsworth: Penguin, 1966).
Driver, S. and Martell, L. *New Labour: Politics After Thatcherism* (Oxford: Polity, 1998).
Eagleton, T. (ed.) *Raymond Williams: Critical Perspectives* (Oxford: Polity, 1989).
Eley, G. '*Distant Voices, Still Lives*: The family is a dangerous place: memory, gender and the image of the working class' (1995) in Rosenstone, R. A. (ed.) (1995) pp. 17–43.
Elsaesser, T. 'Tales of sound and fury: observations on the family melodrama'. *Monogram* (4) (1972) 2–15 reprinted in Gledhill, C. (ed.) (1987) pp. 43–69.
Elsaesser, T. 'The pathos of failure: American films in the 70s'. *Monogram*, (6) (1975) 14.
Ezra, E. 'Cats in the 'Hood: The unspeakable truth about *Chacun Cherche Son Chat*' in Powrie, P. (ed.) (1999) pp. 211–22.
Fallows, R. 'George Bailey in the Vital Center: postwar liberal politics and *It's a Wonderful Life*'. *Journal of Popular Film and Television*, 25 (2) (1997) 50–6.
Faludi, S. *Backlash: The Undeclared War Against Women* (London: Vintage, 1992).
Felski, R. 'The invention of everyday life'. *New Formations* (39) (1999) 15–31.
Ferriter, D. *The Transformation of Ireland, 1900–2000* (London: Profile Books, 2005).
Flanigan, C. C. 'Liminality, carnival and social structure' in Ashley, K. M. (ed.) (1990) pp. 42–63.
Friedan, B. *The Feminine Mystique* (Harmondsworth: Penguin, 1965).
Friedman, L. (ed.) *British Cinema and Thatcherism* (London: University College of London Press, 1993).
Frisby, D. and Featherstone, M. (eds) *Simmel on Culture: Selected Essays* (London: Sage, 1997).
Fryer, P. *Staying Power* (London: Pluto, 1984).
Gamble, S. (ed.) *The Routledge Companion to Feminism and Postfeminism* (London: Routledge, 1998).
Giddens, A. *The Consequences of Modernity* (Cambridge: Polity, 1990).
Gillespie, M. *Television, Ethnicity and Cultural Change* (London: Routledge, 1995).
Gillespie, M. 'Transnational communications and diaspora communities' in Cottle, S. (ed.) (2000) pp. 164–78.
Gillett, P. *The British Working Class in Postwar Film* (Manchester: Manchester University Press, 2003).
Gilroy, P. *There Ain't no Black in the Union Jack* (London: Hutchinson, 1987).
Gilroy, P. *The Black Atlantic: Modernity and Double Consciousness* (London: Verso, 1993).
Girgus, S. B. *Hollywood Renaissance: The Cinema of Democracy in the Era of Ford, Capra and Kazan* (Cambridge: Cambridge University Press, 1998).
Gledhill, C. (ed.) *Home is Where the Heart is: Studies in Melodrama and the Woman's Film* (London: British Film Institute, 1987).
Gledhill, C. 'Rethinking genre' in Gledhill, C. and Williams, L. (eds) (2000) pp. 221–43.

Gledhill, C. and Williams, L. (eds) *Reinventing Film Studies* (London: Arnold, 2000).

Glenny, M. *The Rebirth of History: Eastern Europe in the Age of Democracy*, 2nd ed. (Harmondsworth: Penguin, 1992).

Goffman, E. *Asylums: Essays in the Social Situations of Mental Patients and Other Inmates* (New York: Doubleday, 1961).

Goodhart, P. 'Too diverse? Is Britain becoming too diverse to sustain the mutual obligations behind the good society and the welfare state?' *Prospect* (95) (2004) 30–7.

Gopalan, L. 'Indian cinema' in Nelmes, J. (ed.) (2003) pp. 359–88.

Graffy, J. 'Trading places'. *Sight and Sound* (4) (2003) 22–3.

Gray, A. *Video Playtime* (London: Routledge, 1992).

Gray, A. and McGuigan, J. (eds) *Studying Culture*, 2nd ed. (London: Arnold, 1997).

Guidry, J., Kennedy, M. and Zald, M. (eds) *Globalization and Social Movements: Culture, Power, and the Transnational Public Sphere* (Ann Arbor, MI: The University of Michigan Press, 2000).

Hall, L. *Billy Elliot* (London: Faber and Faber, 2000).

Hall, S. 'Minimal selves', in *Identity – The Real Me – Postmodernism and the Question of Identity*, London, ICA Documents 6 (1987) reprinted in Gray, A. and McGuigan, J. (eds) (1997) pp. 122–33.

Halloran, J. D., Elliot, P. and Murdock, G. *Demonstrations and Communication: A Case Study* (Harmondsworth: Pelican, 1971).

Hand, S. (ed.) *The Levinas Reader* (Oxford: Blackwell, 1989).

Hansen, R. *Citizenship and Immigration in Post-war Britain* (London and New York: Oxford University Press, 2000).

Haeri, S. F. *The Elements of Islam* (Shaftsbury: Element, 1993).

Held, D. and McGrew, A. (eds) *The Global Transformations Reader: An Introduction to the Globalization Debate* (Cambridge: Polity, 2000).

Herbrechter, S. and Higgins, M. (eds) *Returning (to) Community: Theory, Culture and Political Practice of the Communal* (Amsterdam: Rodopi, 2006).

Higbee, W. 'The return of the political, or designer visions of exclusion? The case for Mathieu Kassowitz's *fracture sociale* trilogy'. *Studies in French Cinema*, 5 (2) (2005) 123–35.

Higson, A. *Waving the Flag: Constructing a National Cinema in Britain* (Oxford: Oxford University Press, 1995).

Higson, A. (ed.) *Dissolving Views: Key Writings in British Cinema* (London: Cassell, 1996).

Hill, J. *Sex, Class and Realism: British Cinema 1956–1963* (London: BFI, 1986).

Hill, J. (ed.) *British Cinema in the 1980s* (Oxford: Clarendon Press, 1999).

Hill, J. 'Failure and utopianism: representations of the working class in British cinema of the 1990s' in Murphy, R. (ed.) (2000) pp. 178–87.

Hirst, P. and Thompson, G. *Globalization in Question* (Cambridge: Polity, 1996).

Hjort, M. and Bondebjerg, I. *The Danish Directors: Dialogues on a Contemporary National Cinema* (Intellect: Bristol, 2001).

Hjort, M. and MacKenzie, S. (eds) *Purity and Provocation: Dogme 95* (London: British Film Institute, 2003).

Hobson, D. *Crossroads* (London: Methuen, 1982).

Hoggart, R. *The Uses of Literacy* (Harmondsworth: Penguin, 1958).

Holden, T. *Queen Coal: Women of the Miners' Strike* (Stroud: Sutton Publishinig, 2005).

Hollows, J. *Feminism, Femininity and Popular Culture* (Manchester: MUP, 2000).

Hollows, J. and Moseley, R. (eds) *Feminism in Popular Culture* (Oxford: Berg, 2006).

Huntington, S. T. 'The clash of civilizations?', *Foreign Affairs*, Vol. 72 (3) (1993) pp. 22–49.

Huntington, S. T. *The Clash of Civilizations and the Remaking of World Order* (New York: Simon and Schuster, 1996).

Institute of Advanced Study 'The cultural globalization project' *Insight*, Spring in Culture (2000) 3–5 in Bauman, Z. (2001) p. 55.

Islamic Human Rights Commission *The British Media and Muslim Representation: the Ideology of Demonisation* (London: IRHC, 2007).

Jaafar, A. 'School for Seduction'. *Sight and Sound*, 2 (2005) 68–9.

Jancovich, M., Faire, L. and Stubbings, S. *The Place of the Audience: Cultural Geographies of Film Consumption* (London: British Film Institute, 2003).

Johnson, H. and Klandermans, B. (eds) *Social Movements and Culture* (London: UCL, 1995).

Joseph, M. *Against the Romance of Community* (Minneapolis: Minnesota University Press, 2002).

Julien, I. and Mercer, K. 'De margin and de centre'. *Screen*, 29 (4) (1988) 2–10.

Kelly, R. *The Name of This Book is Dogme 95* (London: Faber and Faber, 2000).

Kelly, R. 'Italian for Beginners'. *Sight and Sound* (4) (2002) 47.

Kenyon, A. M. *Dreaming Suburbia: Detroit and the Production of Postwar Space and Culture* (Detroit: Wayne State University Press, 2004).

Korte, B. and Sternberg, C. *Bidding for the Mainstream: Black and Asian British Film since the 1990s* (Amsterdam: Rodopi, 2004).

Kuhn, A. *Women's Pictures* (London: Routledge and Kegan Paul, 1982).

Kuhn, A. *An Everyday Magic: Cinema and Cultural Memory* (London: I. B. Taurus, 2002).

Levinas, E. *Ethics as First Philosophy* (1989) reprinted in Hand, S. (ed.) (1989) pp. 76–87.

Levitas, R. *The Inclusive Society? Social Exclusion and New Labour* (London: Macmillan, 1998).

Luckett, M. 'Image and nation in 1990s British cinema' in Murphy, R. (ed.) (2000) pp. 88–99.

MacArthur, B. (ed.) *The Penguin Book of Twentieth Century Speeches* (London: Penguin, 1999).

MacNab, G. 'House rules'. *Sight and Sound*, (6) (2001) 32–4.

MacPherson, W. *The Stephen Lawrence Enquiry: Report of an Inquiry by Sir William Macpherson of Cluny* (London: HMSO, Cmnd 4262–1, 1999).

Malik, S. 'Beyond "the cinema of duty?" The pleasures of hybridity: Black British film of the 1980s and 1990s' in Higson, A. (ed.) (1996) pp. 202–15.

Mandelson, P. and Liddle, R. *The Blair Revolution: Can Labour Deliver?* (London: Faber and Faber, 1996).

Marx, K. and Engels, F. *The Communist Manifesto* (Moscow: Progress Publishers, 1952).

Massey, D. 'A global sense of place', *Marxism Today*, June, 1991, reprinted in Gray, A. and McGuigan, J. (eds) (1997) pp. 232–40.

Mazdon, L. (ed.) *France on Film: Reflections on Popular French Cinema* (London: Wallflower, 2000).

McKnight, G. *Agent of Challenge and Defiance: The Films of Ken Loach* (London: Flick Books, 1995).

McLuhan, M. *The Gutenberg Galaxy: The Making of Typographic Man* (Toronto: Toronto University Press, 1962).

Melly, G. *Revolt into Style* (London: Oxford University Press, 1989).

Melucci, A. 'The process of collective identity' (1995) in Johnson, H. and Klandermans, B. (eds) (1995) pp. 41–63.

Melucci, A. *Challenging Codes: Collective Action in the Information Age* (Cambridge: CUP, 1996).

Mills, C. W. *The Sociological Imagination* (Harmondsworth: Penguin, 1959).

Milner, A. *Re-imagining Cultural Studies: The Promise of Cultural Materialism* (London: Sage, 2002).

Modelski, G. *Principles of World Politics* (New York: The Free Press, 1972).

Modood, T., Beishon, S. and Virdes, S. *Changing Ethnic Identities* (London: Policy Studies Institute, 1994).

Modood, T., Lakey, J., Nazroo, J., Smith, P., Virdes, S. and Beishon, S. *Ethnic Minorities in Britain* (London: Policy Studies Institute, 1997).

Morley, D. 'Bounded realms: household, family, community, and nation' in Naficy, H. and Gabriel, T. H. (eds) (1989) pp. 151–68.

Mulhern, F. 'Towards 2000, or news from you-know-where' in Eagleton, T. (ed.) (1989) pp. 67–94.

Mulvey, L. *Visual and Other Pleasures* (London: Macmillan, 1989).

Murphy, R. (ed.) *British Cinema of the 90s* (London: BFI, 2000).

Murtuja, B. 'The bubble of diaspora' in Herbrechter, S. and Higgins, M. (eds) (2006) pp. 293–311.

Naficy, H. *An Accented Cinema: Exilic and Diasporic Filmmaking* (Princeton: Princeton University Press, 2001).

Naficy, H. and Gabriel, T. H. (eds) *Home, Exile, Homeland: Film, Media and the Politics of Place* (New York: Routledge, 1989).

Nancy, J.-L. *The Inoperative Community* (Minneapolis: University of Minnesota Press, 1991).

Nelmes, J. (ed.) *An Introduction to Film Studies*, 3rd ed. (London: Routledge, 2003).

Nicholson, L. J. *Feminism/Postfeminism* (London: Routledge, 1990).

O'Hagen Hardy, M. 'Gendered trauma in Mike Leigh's Vera Drake (2004)'. *Studies in European Cinema*, 3 (3) (2007) pp. 211–21.

Orwell, G. 'The art of Donald McGill' in *Essays* (London: Penguin Classics, 2000) pp. 193–202.

Parekh, B. 'Between holy text and moral void', *New Statesman and Society*, 24 March (1989) pp. 29–33

Parekh, B. *The Future of Multi-Ethnic Britain* (London: Runnymede Trust, 2000a).

Parekh, B. *Rethinking Multiculturalism* (London: MacMillan, 2000b).

Peteet, J. 'Refugees, resistance, and identity' in Guidry, J., Kennedy, M. and Zald, M. (eds) (2000) pp. 200–3.

Pickering, M. *History, Experience and Cultural Studies* (London: Macmillan, 1997).

Powrie, P. (ed.) *French Cinema in the 1990s: Continuity and Difference* (Oxford: Oxford University Press, 1999).

Putnam, R. D. *Bowling Alone; The Collapse and Revival of American Community* (New York: Simon and Schuster, 2000).

Quart, L. and Auster, A. *American Film and Society Since 1945*, 3rd ed. (Westport: Praeger, 2002).

Riddle, P. *The Thatcher Era and its Legacy* (Oxford: Blackwell, 1993).

Roscoe, J. 'From Bombay to Blackpool: the construction of Indian femininity in *Bhaji on the Beach*' in Crane, R. J. (ed.) (2000) pp. 197–216.

Rosenstone, R. A. (ed.) *Revisioning History: The Construction of a New Past* (Princeton: Princeton University Press, 1995).

Rushdie, S. 'Songs don't know the score', *The Guardian* (January 12, 1987) p. 10.

Said, E. *Orientalism* (Harmondsworth: Penguin, 1985).

Sconce, J. 'Smart cinema' in Williams, L. R. and Hammond, M. (eds) (2006) pp. 426–39.

Sedgwick, E. K. *Between Men: English Literature and Male Homosocial Desire* (New York: Columbia University Press, 1985).

Singh, D. *Our Shared Future* (Wetherby: Commission on Integration and Cohesion, 2007).

Skeggs, B. *Formations of Class and Gender* (London: Sage, 1997).

Smith, M. 'Lars von Trier: Sentimental surrealist' in Hjort, M. and MacKenzie, S. (eds) (2003) pp. 111–21.

Soila, T., Söderbergh, A. and Iversen, G. (eds) *Nordic National Cinemas* (London: Routledge, 1998).

Spencer, L. 'Hello Mr Chips'. *Sight and Sound* (11) (1999) 36–7.

Spicer, A. *Typical Men: The Representation of Masculinity in Popular British Cinema*, 2nd ed. (London: I. B. Taurus, 2003).

Spigel, L. *Make Room for TV: Television and the Family Ideal in Postwar America* (Chicago: University of Chicago Press, 1992).

Stevenson, J. *Dogme Uncut: Lars von Trier, Thomas Vinterberg and the Gang That Took on Hollywood* (Santa Monica: Santa Monica Press, 2003).

Tanner, M. *Ireland's Holy War* (New Haven: Yale University Press, 2003).

Thatcher, M. *The Downing Street Years* (London: Harper Collins, 1993).

Thompson, E. P. *The Making of the English Working Class* (Harmondsworth: Penguin, 1968).

Tincknell, E. and Chambers, D. 'Performing the crisis: fathering, gender and representation in two 1990s films', *Journal of Popular Film & Television*, 29 (4) (2002) 146–155.

Tönnies, M. and Viol, C. *British Political Speeches: From Churchill to Blair* (Stuttgart: Reclam, 2001).

Toulmin, V., Popple, S. and Russell, P. (eds) *The Lost World of Mitchell and Kenyon* (London: BFI, 2004).

Turner, F. 'Hyperion to a Satyr' in Ashley, K. M. (ed.) (1990) pp. 147–62.

Turner, V. *The Ritual Process* (New York: Aldine de Gruyter, 1969).

Van Gennep, A. *The Rites of Passage* (London: Routledge and Kegan Paul, 1967).

Wallerstein, I. *Historical Capitalism* (London: Verso, 1984).

Walters, S. *Material Girls* (Berkeley and Los Angeles: University of California Press, 1995).

Watson, G. *The Cinema of Mike Leigh: A Sense of the Real* (London: Wallflower, 2004).

Williams, L. R. and Hammond, M. (eds) *Contemporary American Cinema* (Maidenhead: Open University Press, 2006).

Williams, R. *Culture and Society: 1780–1950* (Harmondsworth: Penguin, 1959).

Williams, R. *The Long Revolution* (Harmondsworth: Penguin, 1961).

Williams, R. *The Country and the City* (Oxford: Oxford University Press, 1973).

Williams, R. *Marxism and Literature* (Oxford: Oxford University Press, 1977).

Williams, R. *Politics and Letters: Interviews with New Left Review* (London: Verso, 1979).

Williams, R. *Problems in Materialism and Culture* (London: New Left Books, 1980).

Williams, R. *Resources of Hope* (London: Verso, 1988).

Williams, R. and Orrom, M. *Preface to Film* (London: Film Drama, 1954).

Williams, T. 'The masochistic fix: gender oppression in the films of Terence Davies' in Friedman, L. (ed.) (1993) pp. 237–254.

Wolf, N. *The Beauty Myth* (London: Vintage, 1991).

Young, I. M. 'The ideal of community and the politics of difference' (1990) in Nicholson, L. J. (ed.) (1990) pp. 300–23.

Young, J. *The Exclusive Society* (London: Sage, 1999).

Žižek, S. 'Camp comedy', *Sight and Sound*, (4) (2000) 26–9.

Žižek, S. *The Parallax View* (Cambridge M.A.: M.I.T., 2006).

Filmography

About Schmidt (dir. Alexander Payne, 2002)
Ae Fond Kiss (dir. Ken Loach, 2004)
American Beauty (dir. Sam Mendes, 1999)
At Five in the Afternoon (dir. Samira Makhmalbaf, 2003)
Babel (dir. Alejandro González Iñárritu, 2006)
Babette's Feast (dir. Gabriel Axel, 1987)
Babymother (dir. Julien Henriques, 1998)
The Bells of Saint Mary (dir. Leo McCarey, 1945)
Bhaji on the Beach (dir. Gurinder Chadha, 1993)
Billy Elliot (dir. Stephen Daldry, 2000)
Blue Velvet (dir. David Lynch, 1986)
Bowling for Columbine (dir. Michael Moore, 2002)
Brassed Off (dir. Mark Herman, 1996)
Bread and Roses (dir. Ken Loach, 2000)
Breaking the Waves (dir. Lars von Trier, 1996)
Bridget Jones: The Edge of Reason (dir. Beeban Kidron, 2004)
Bullet Boy (dir. Saul Dibb, 2004)
Calendar Girls (dir. Nigel Cole, 2003)
Cinema Paradiso (dir. Giuseppe Tornatore, 1988)
Clueless (dir. Amy Heckerling, 1995)
The Color Purple (dir. Stephen Spielberg, 1982)
The Constant Gardener (dir. Fernando Meirelles, 2005)
Dirty, Pretty Things (dir. Stephen Frears, 2002)
Distant Voices, Still Lives (dir. Terence Davies, 1988)
Donnie Darko (dir. Richard Kelly, 2001)
East is East (dir. Daniel O'Donnell, 1999)
Election (dir. Alexander Payne, 1999)
Europa (dir. Lars von Trier, 1991)
Far from Heaven (dir. Todd Haynes, 2002)
Festen (dir. Thomas Vinterberg, 1998)
FireDancer (dir. Jawed Wasel, 2002)
The Full Monty (dir. Peter Cataneo, 1997)
Garden State (dir. Zach Braff, 2006)
Ghost World (dir. Terry Zwigoff, 2001)
Glengarry Glen Ross (dir. James Foley, 1992)
The Graduate (dir. Mike Nichols, 1967)
Grow Your Own (dir. Richard Laxton, 2007)
Hamburg Cell (dir. Antonio Bird, 2004)
Handsworth Songs (dir. John Akomfrah, 1986)
Happiness (dir. Todd Solondz, 1997)

Heat and Dust (dir. James Ivory, 1983)
The Humiliated (dir. Jesper Jargil, 1998)
The Ice Storm (dir. Ang Lee, 1997)
The Idiots (dir. Lars von Trier, 1998)
An Inconvenient Truth (dir. David Guggenheim, 2006)
In This World (dir. Michael Winterbottom, 2003)
Italian for Beginners (dir. Lone Scherfig, 2000)
It's a Wonderful Life (dir. Frank Capra, 1946)
Kandahar (dir. Mohsen Makhmalbaf, 2001)
Kinky Boots (dir. Julian Jarrold, 2005)
Last Resort (dir. Pawel Pawlikowski, 2000)
Life is Beautiful (dir. Roberto Benigni, 1997)
Lilya 4-Ever (dir. Lukas Moodysson, 2002)
Little Voice (dir. Mark Herman, 1998)
Local Hero (dir. Bill Forsyth, 1982)
The Long Day Closes (dir. Terence Davies, 1992)
Lost in Translation (dir. Sofia Coppola, 2003)
The Magdalene Sisters (dir. Peter Mullan, 2002)
The Man Who Went Up a Hill, But Came Down a Mountain (dir. Christopher
    Monger, 1995)
Monsoon Wedding (dir. Mira Nair, 2001)
My Beautiful Laundrette (dir. Stephen Frears, 1986)
My Name is Joe (dir. Ken Loach, 1998)
My Son the Fanatic (dir. Udayan Prasad, 1997)
Napoleon Dynamite (dir. Jared Hess, 2004)
Once Were Warriors (dir. Lee Tamahori, 1994)
A Passage to India (dir. David Lean, 1984)
Pleasantville (dir. Gary Ross, 1998)
Plein Soleil (dir. René Clément, 1960)
Pressure (dir. Horace Ové, 1975)
Rebecca (dir. Alfred Hitchcock, 1940)
The Rise to Power of Louis 14th (dir. Roberto Rossellini, 1966)
Salaam Bombay! (dir. Mira Nair, 1988)
School for Seduction (dir. Sue Heel, 2004)
Secrets and Lies (dir. Mike Leigh, 1996)
Sex in a Cold Climate (dir. Steve Humphries, 1998)
Shall We Dance? (dir. Peter Chelsom, 2004)
Shall We Dance? (dir. Masayuki Suo, 1996)
Show Me Love (dir. Lukas Moodysson, 1998)
Slap Her . . . She's French (dir. Melanie Mayron, 2002)
The Stepford Wives (dir. Bryan Forbes, 1974)
SubUrbia (dir. Richard Linklater, 1996)
The Sweet Hereafter (dir. Atom Egoyan, 1997)
The Talented Mr Ripley (dir. Anthony Minghella, 1999)
This is England (dir. Shane Meadow, 2007)
Together (dir. Lukas Moodysson, 2001)
The Truman Show (dir. Peter Weir, 1998)
United 93 (dir. Peter Greengrass, 2006)
Up 'n' Under (dir. John Godber, 1998)

Vera Drake (dir. Mike Leigh, 2004)
The Virgin Suicides (dir. Sofia Coppola, 1999)
Volver (dir. Pedro Almodóvar, 2006)
A Way of Life (dir. Amma Asante, 2004)
Whale Rider (dir. Niki Caro, 2002)
Yasmin (dir. Kevin Glenaan, 2004)
Young Soul Rebels (Isaac Juliens, 1983)

Index

Bridget Jones: the Edge of Reason, 86
British Coal (ex-National Coal Board),
 71
British Film Institute (BFI), 194, 200
British National Party (BNP), 71, 113
The Brothers Karamazov, 33
Brunsdon, Charlotte, 87–8, 90, 93, 106
Bugeja, Michael, 197, 203
Bullet Boy, 108
burden of representation, 124, 202
Burke, Kenneth, 168
Bush, George W., 54, 68, 117, 125, 139
Butler, Alison, 161, 201
Butler, Judith, 88, 100
Butler, Margaret, 7
Bye, Bye, 194

Calendar Girls, 22, 85–6, 91–7, 102,
 105–6, 197
Calhoun, Craig, 142, 150, 153, 156
Capra, Frank, 22, 40, 43, 197
Caro, Niki, 4, 194
Castells, Manuel, 141, 200–1, 203
Cataneo, Peter, 21, 63
Celli, Carlo, 195
Chacun Cherche Son Chat, 194
Chadha, Gurinder, 115, 116
Chambers, Deborah, 65, 82, 197, 198
Chatman, Seymour, 199
Chaudhuri, Shahini, 160, 185, 204
Chavez, Hugo, 112
Chelsom, Peter, 147
Christensen, Karen, 194
Christiania, 167, 204
cinema
 accented cinema, 9, 147–8, 161–4
 bourgeois cinema, 175–7, 181–2,
  186
 and community, 4–9
 ethical cinema, 62
 and film, 8–9
 independent cinema, 115
 mainstream cinema, 21, 114–17
 smart cinema, 52–4, 62
 women's pictures, 186
 world cinema, 160–1
Cinema Paradiso, 5
citizens, 120, 136, 203
Clark, Timothy. J., 206

Clash of civilizations?, 138–9
class
 and individuals, 70–5
 middle-class, 73, 74, 79–84, 192
 working-class, 68–84
 respectability, 99–100, 101
classification, 16–18
Clegg, Stuart, 196
Clément, René, 144
Clinton, President Bill, 54
Clocking Off, 98
Clueless, 1
Cohen, Robin, 161
Cole, Nigel, 22, 93
collective action, 85–6, 89–106
collective identity, 6, 85, 86, 89–106
collective memory, 6
The Color Purple, 196
Commission on Integration and
  Community (ex-Commission for
  Racial Equality (CRE)) 113, 139
communes (and collectives), 171–82,
 185, 187–9
 Christiania, Free city of, 167, 204
communitarianism, 10, 22, 63–84, 191
 communitarianism defined, 67–8
 and the family, 66–8
 and morality, 63–84
 and regenerating moral community,
  63–79
  responsibility of individuals in
   moral community, 69–79
  structural ambivalence of women
   in moral community, 79–84
communitas, 20, 23, 167, 174, 185,
 187–9
 anti-structure, 23, 167, 168, 169,
  174, 187–9
 communitas defined, 167–71
 existential communitas, 170, 175,
  180, 188
 ideological communitas, 171, 180
 liminality, 164, 168, 169, 170, 171,
  180, 187–9
 Normative communitas, 170–1

community
  action defining community, 90–106
  ambivalence and community, 2,
    3–4, 18–21, 24
  boundaries, 10, 16–19, 24–35
  communication, 12–13, 89–98
  'community of communities',
    110–112, 119
  community, security and freedom,
    18–20, 58–62, 136–9, 192–3
  community defined, 3, 7, 23, 37,
    64–5, 114, 189, 190–1
  and difference, 13–16
  gated community, 39, 145
  and gender, 14–16, 85–106
  imagined community, 6, 143
  and inclusion/exclusion, 10, 16–17,
    24–35, 77–94, 191–2
  and individuals, 69–71
  inoperative community, 20, 58–62,
    190, 191
  marginalization of women, 22,
    77–84, 85
  regenerating moral community, *see*
    communitarianism
  and rhetoric, 2–3
  sociology of community, 194
  too much/too little community,
    46–53, 54–8
  working-class community, 12–13,
    14–16, 71–5, 195
The Constant Gardener, 204
Cook, Chris, 199
Cook, Pam, 197
Coppola, Sofia, 21, 23, 144, 145–7
Coronation Street, 98
cosmopolitanism, 23, 144–50, 164,
  165
  tourists, 140, 150, 157, 162
  vagabonds, 140, 150, 157, 162
Cotkin, George, 197
cultural diversity, 112–14, 128, 138
cultural dreaming, 41–2
cultural materialism, 9–16, 191
  structure of feeling, 11–12, 53, 63–4,
    84, 96, 115, 137
culture, 9–19, 168–71
  and ambivalence, 16–18, 170
  and structure, 16–18

as tragedy, 17, 170
as waste, 17–18, 151, 157, 195

Daldry, Stephen, 22, 63
Danish Film Institute, 206
Davies, Terence, 5, 14–16, 65, 195
Day, Kikai, 146
Delanty, Gerard, 194, 195, 196, 198
denizens, 120, 138, 203
diaspora, 115, 147, 161
Dibb, Saul, 108
Dinesen, Isak, 24, 26, 28, 195
Dirty, Pretty Things, 203
Distant Voices, Still Lives, 14–16, 17
Dogma 95, 21, 149, 168, 175–7, 181,
    182, 183, 185
  the Brotherhood, 175, 186, 205
  and genre, 186
  manifesto, 175, 181, 183
  vow, 175, 176, 177, 181, 183
Dollimore, Jonathan, 9, 10
Domanov, Oleg, 198
Donnie Darko, 52
Dostoyevsky, Fyodor, 33
Douglas, Mary, 17
Dreyer, Carl Theodore, 171, 175
Dridi, Karim, 194
Driver, Stephen, 198
Duany, Andres, 40, 53

Eagleton, Terry, 194
Ealing Studios, 5–6
East is East, 23, 115, 120–4, 128, 131,
    132, 134, 137–8, 192, 202, 203
Egoyan, Atom, 52, 162
Election, 52
Eley, Geoff, 65, 195, 198
Elsaesser, Thomas, 75
Empire Windrush, 108, 201
Engels, Friedrich, 140
ethics
  first philosophy, 27–8, 34
  right to be ethical, 33–4, 192
  strangers, 28, 60, 61, 152, 153, 180,
    185